797,885 Books

are available to read at

www.ForgottenBooks.com

Forgotten Books' App
Available for mobile, tablet & eReader

ISBN 978-1-330-02052-4
PIBN 10005817

This book is a reproduction of an important historical work. Forgotten Books uses state-of-the-art technology to digitally reconstruct the work, preserving the original format whilst repairing imperfections present in the aged copy. In rare cases, an imperfection in the original, such as a blemish or missing page, may be replicated in our edition. We do, however, repair the vast majority of imperfections successfully; any imperfections that remain are intentionally left to preserve the state of such historical works.

Forgotten Books is a registered trademark of FB &c Ltd.
Copyright © 2015 FB &c Ltd.
FB &c Ltd, Dalton House, 60 Windsor Avenue, London, SW19 2RR.
Company number 08720141. Registered in England and Wales.

For support please visit www.forgottenbooks.com

1 MONTH OF FREE READING

at

www.ForgottenBooks.com

By purchasing this book you are eligible for one month membership to ForgottenBooks.com, giving you unlimited access to our entire collection of over 700,000 titles via our web site and mobile apps.

To claim your free month visit:

www.forgottenbooks.com/free5817

* Offer is valid for 45 days from date of purchase. Terms and conditions apply.

Similar Books Are Available from
www.forgottenbooks.com

Things Mother Used to Make
by Lydia Maria Gurney

Neighborhood Club Cook Book
Containing Two Hundred and Eighty Recipes, by Neighborhood Club

Low-Cost Meals for High-Cost Times
by Unknown Author

365 Breakfast Dishes
by George W. C. Jacobs

Rice for Breakfast, Dinner, Supper
by Bessie R. Murphy

Mrs. Allen's Book of Meat Substitutes
by Ida C. Bailey Allen

Science in the Kitchen
by E. E. Kellogg

The Art of German Cooking and Baking
by Lina Wachtelborn Meier

One Thousand Salads
by Olive Green

The Chinese Cook Book
by Shiu Wong Chan

Just for Two
A Collection of Recipes, Designed for Two Persons, by Amelie Langdon

Bread Making and Bread Baking
by Minnie E. Brothers

One Thousand Favorite Recipes
by Sigismund Aronsou

What to Serve at Parties
by Lilian Miranda Gunn

Vegetarian Cook Book
Substitutes for Flesh Foods, by E. G. Fulton

The Myrtle Reed Cookbook
by Myrtle Reed

The International Jewish Cook Book
A Modern Kosher Cook Book, by Florence Kreisler Greenbaum

Canning, Preserving, Pickling and Fruit Desserts
by Jeanette C. Slade

A Book of Practical Recipes for the Housewife
by Chicago Evening American

Dehydrating Foods, Fruits, Vegetables, Fish and Meats
by A. Louise Andrea

BREAKFAST TABLE LAID FOR TWO

COOKING FOR TWO

A HANDBOOK
FOR YOUNG HOUSEKEEPERS

By
JANET MACKENZIE HILL
Author of "Salads, Sandwiches, and Chafing Dish Dainties,"
"The Up-to-Date Waitress," etc.

ILLUSTRATED

LITTLE, BROWN, AND COMPANY
1909

Copyright, 1909,
BY JANET MACKENZIE HILL.

All rights reserved

Published, May, 1909.

Electrotyped and Printed at
THE COLONIAL PRESS:
C. H. Simonds & Co., Boston, U.S.A.

Foreword

"The best things are nearest. . . . Then do not grasp at the stars, but do life's plain, common work as it comes, certain that daily duties and daily bread are the sweetest things of life."

Contents

CHAPTER		PAGE
I.	A Talk on Food	1
II.	The Gas Range, Tables of Measures, Utensils, Supplies, etc.	14
III.	Water, Making of Tea, Coffee, etc. . .	27
IV.	Cooking of True Proteids, Tissue Builders, Milk and Cheese	39
V.	Cooking of True Proteids Continued: Eggs	56
VI.	Cooking of True Proteids Continued: Fish .	73
VII.	Cooking of True Proteids Continued: Meat	93
VIII.	Left-Overs of Meat, Fish, etc.	122
IX.	Gelatinous Soups and Jellies. Proteid Sparers . . . . . , . . .	131
X.	Introducing the Cooking of Carbohydrates, the True Heat and Work Foods	141
XI.	Carbohydrates (Work Foods) Continued .	154
XII.	Introducing The Great Fuel Foods: Fats (Cream, Butter, Olive Oil and Salads) .	186
XIII.	Foods Supplying Mineral Salts and Organic Acids, More Particularly Fruit	212
XIV.	Sugar: a Great Source of Heat and Energy	229
XV.	Preservation of Fruit and Vegetables by Canning, etc.	252
XVI.	Flour Mixtures: Quick Breads . .	272
XVII.	Flour Mixtures Continued: Bread and Other Yeast Mixtures	287

Contents

CHAPTER		PAGE
XVIII.	FLOUR MIXTURES CONTINUED: PASTRY AND PIES	309
XIX.	FLOUR MIXTURES CONTINUED: CAKE	322
XX.	OTHER SWEET DISHES	342
	A SERMONET	373
	MENUS FOR EACH MONTH IN THE YEAR	379
	INDEX	397

List of Illustrations

Breakfast Table Laid for Two }	*Frontispiece*
Dinner Table Laid for Two }	FACING PAGE
Useful Utensils in Housekeeping for Two	8
Improvised and Real Double Boilers	8
Utensils for Measuring	8
Removing Ice Cream from Mold	9
Pastry Bag with Tubes . .	9
Sieve Frame with Adjustable Plates of Different Mesh	9
Frying Croquettes	26
Zinc Covered Table on Casters. Unharmed by Hot Dishes	26
Making Tea with Tea Ball	27
Why is a Coffee Pot made with the Nozzle near the Top and a Teapot with the Nozzle near the Bottom? . .	27
Hot Toasted Wafers with Cream Cheese and Slice of Stuffed Olive	44
Cheese Toast with Bacon	44
Cheese Ramequins	44
Creamed Macaroni au Gratin	45
Macaroni Croquettes	45
Macaroni Baked with Milk and Cheese	45
Poaching Eggs	62
Poached Eggs with Tomatoes and Bacon	62
Omelet Pans	62
Fillets of Black Bass with Bread Dressing. Cucumber Salad	80
Fresh Codfish, Broiled	80
Fresh Fish en Casserole	80
Halibut Steak	81
Rolled Fillets of Black Bass	81
Truffled Fish Mousse	81
Lamb Chops, Mashed Potatoes	98

List of Illustrations

	FACING PAGE
Lamb Chops, Planked	98
Sirloin Steak en Casserole, Rathskeller Style	98
Two Sets of Sweetbreads	99
Boiled Lamb for Two, Turnip and Carrot	99
Scrag End and Breast of Lamb cut for Small Family	99
Chicken Breast, Cooked for Two	116
Roast Chicken, Garnish of Cranberry Branches	116
Chicken Pie for Two	116
Chicken in Potato Patty Cases	134
Boston Baked Beans on Toast. Bacon Rolls	134
Rizzoletti, "Left-Over" Dish	134
Ham-and-Macaroni Timbales, for Two	135
Cottage Pie	135
Veal Pot Pie, Baked Dumplings	135
Chopped Chicken Molded with Aspic	152
Strainer, Cloth and Colander, Ready to Strain Liquid Aspic or Consommé	152
Hard Cooked Eggs Molded in Aspic	152
One Service of Cream of Corn Soup	153
Utensils needed to make Purées for Cream Soup	153
Flaky Pastry Croutons for Soup	153
Cold Baked Bean Sandwich, Club Style	170
Corn Fritters with Creamed Chicken	170
Mashed Potato	170
Lima Beans Baked with Salt Pork	171
Frying Saratoga Potatoes	171
Baked Potatoes	171
German Apple Cup	188
Beets Stuffed with Cabbage-and-Nut Salad	188
How to Beat Cream	188
Potato Salad, French Style	189
Egg Salad for Two	189
Astoria Salad	206
Celery-and-Apple Salad	206
Asparagus Salad	206
Baked Bananas, Sultana Sauce	224
Macedoine of Midwinter Fruit	224
Grapefruit	224
Grapefruit Jelly	225

List of Illustrations

FACING PAGE

Apple, Pralinée	225
Sliced Figs in Sherry Wine Jelly	225
Choice Caramels Wrapped in Paper	242
Chocolate Bon Bons	242
Divinity Fudge or Spanish Nougat	242
Dipping Oysterettes, Nuts, etc., in "Dot" Chocolate	243
Fruit Fudge	243
Making Impressions in Starch to Mold Fondant	243
Fruit Cooked in the Jars	260
Apple and Raspberry Jelly	260
Canned String Beans	260
Pop-Overs	261
Baking Powder Biscuit	261
Fruit-and-Nut Rolls	261
Olive Sandwiches	278
Shaping Parker House Rolls	278
Making Noisette Sandwiches	278
Bread and Coffee Cake made with One Yeast Cake	279
Shaping Lady Finger Rolls	279
Ready to Make Bread	279
One Loaf of Bread and of Rolls made with One Yeast Cake	296
Graham Bread made without Kneading	296
One Loaf of Bread and Parker House Rolls, Baked	296
Bread Sticks, tied with Yellow Ribbon	297
Lady Finger Rolls	297
Preparing the Sponge for Kaiser Rolls	297
Peach Tarts	314
Apple Tarts	314
Apple Pie with Meringue	314
Pineapple Tarts	315
Custard Pie	315
Strawberry Tarts, St. Honore Style	315
Loaf of Biscuit d'Épernay. Tea Pretzels	332
Roxbury Cakes, Biscuits d'Épernay, Strawberry Preserves Between	332
White Cake, cut in Diamonds	332
Plain Ginger Cakes	333
Tiny Cream Cakes	333

List of Illustrations

	FACING PAGE
Shaping Tea Pretzels	333
Steamed Custard	350
Charlotte Russe for Two	350
Chocolate Custard with Whipped Cream	350
Custard Renversée with Almonds	351
Orange Marmalade Bavariose	351
Canned Pear Meringues	351
Vanilla and Strawberry Ice Cream in One Glass	368
Ginger Bavarian Cream	368
Peach Ice Cream for Two	368
Strawberry-and-Marshmallow Dessert	369
Golden Parfait with Fruit	369
Banana Parfait	369

Cooking for Two

CHAPTER I

A TALK ON FOOD

IN the morning you work about the house, putting it in order, or you work in the garden with your flowers, or you go to market. Your husband attends to his work out-of-doors or in the office, and when mid-day is reached neither of you feel willing to do any more work, until you have eaten your mid-day meal. Your energy and motive power are gone. The movements you have made, not only those you have made of your own accord in working about the house, but also those made involuntarily by your heart in beating, your lungs in breathing, and your brain in thinking, have wasted your stock of energy and worn away tissues of flesh, blood and bones. This waste must be renewed at once, or you will remain faint and inactive; or, if the renewal be deferred for days, you will cease to live. More than this, if you have not attained your full normal growth, there must be a constant supply of material for this purpose. The material to renew energy and tissues and supply new growth comes from the food that is eaten. Not all the articles that we use as food contain elements for growth and repair of tissues; from this fact you can see that, if those whom you send from your tables each day have not been supplied with the proper articles of food, you can not expect them to retain health or have the energy and courage to do their work in the world. An old saying expresses this in concise form, which you can easily remember; it is: " The stomach is the seat of courage."

EXPERIENCE THE FIRST TEACHER REGARDING FOOD

We use for food substances that are found in the world around us. How the earliest men and women learned what substances would best satisfy hunger and build strong bodies we have no means of knowing. Experience is a dear teacher, but, doubtless, outside of natural instinct, she was the first teacher in the primitive world. Poisonous berries, though bright and attractive in color, are avoided by birds and four-footed animals by instinct. The instincts of early man, as far as everything that pertained to the preservation of life was concerned, must have been very acute. At the present time the discovery of a really new article of food is of such rare occurrence that we are justified in saying there are none such to be discovered. Of course there may be foods new to us, but some one else has already known and used them.

WATER, AIR, CARBON AND COMBUSTION

Water and air are vital necessities to us, but they are not accounted as food, as they cannot stay hunger, build tissues or supply heat or energy; still food is of no value to us without them, and, in composition with other compounds, they enter into all food. Carbon is another compound that occurs in food and in almost all matter in the world around us. When a crust of bread is toasted until it is charred throughout, we know it as carbon. So also is the smoke left upon the lamp chimney, when the wick of a lamp is turned too high. The charred remains of all substances are carbon.

Air is composed of two invisible gases, oxygen and nitrogen; when carbon is ignited, the oxygen from the air unites with it rapidly, giving off light and heat, and we have what is called combustion, burning or a fire.

CARBON DIOXIDE A PRODUCT OF COMBUSTION BOTH OUTSIDE OF THE BODY AND IN IT

Pour a little lime-water into a glass jar, shake the jar and note there is no change in the appearance of the lime-water. Pour out the lime-water, rinse the jar, dry it and set into it a lighted candle, cover the top of the jar with a pane of glass and note what happens. The candle burns for a few moments, then, when there is no more oxygen to unite with the carbon of the candle, combustion ceases. Remove the candle, pour in a little lime-water and shake the jar — the lime-water becomes cloudy. Now put a glass tube into a bottle containing lime-water, letting one opening come below the water, put the other end of the tube into the mouth and exhale from the lungs, letting the air pass into the tube; now shake the jar and note that the lime-water becomes cloudy.

When lime-water takes on a cloudy appearance, we know that it contains carbon dioxide. Carbon dioxide is a product of combustion. The carbon dioxide exhaled from the lungs was formed in the body. Oxygen taken in through the lungs unites with the carbon in the food, thus producing carbon dioxide and, incidentally, heat to warm the body. The process of combustion in this case is, probably, almost synonymous with the process of digestion. Thus the process of digestion, or we might say of living, is largely dependent upon our breathing in a full supply of air, pregnant with oxygen.

NITROGEN, ITS ABUNDANCE IN THE BODY AND SOURCE OF SUPPLY

Nitrogen is the other element of which air is composed. Every active tissue in plant and animal contains nitrogen. Brain, muscle, bone, even the digestive juices and other bodily secretions are all largely made up of nitrogen. If nitrogen be withheld from the body, the body dies, though for a time the vital organs will draw upon the nitrogen stored in the various tissues of the system and the body will carry on its work by feeding upon itself. But it is impossible for the body to take its supply of nitrogen, first hand, as it were, from the air, and though air is four-fifths nitrogen, all of this element is returned to the air, when the oxygen in composition has been taken in by the lungs. Nitrogen must be supplied in composition with other elements in food. The articles we use as food are complex in their composition.

ELEMENTS FOUND IN OUR FOOD

Our food, then, must contain the elements that make up the body; it must contain carbon, oxygen, nitrogen, hydrogen, iron, sulphur, and all the minor elements that go to make up the body; these exist in articles of food not as simple elements but as compounds, to which, partly on account of their repetition in this and that article of food, we give the name of proximate food compounds or principles.

PROXIMATE OR FOOD PRINCIPLES

The chief of these proximate principles are classified as water, mineral matter, proteids, fats and carbohydrates. The body of a man of average weight is said to contain 108 pounds of water, 11 pounds of mineral matter, 29.75 pounds of proteid, 5 pounds of fat and .25 of a pound of carbohydrates. From this we can judge *somewhat* of the quantity of the different principles to be supplied in the food; but, as we shall see later on, the proportion of the different principles needed depends on still other conditions than the quantity in the body.

The most important of these principles are the proteids, because they are the only ones that can supply the nitrogen so needful in tissue building and repairing; proteid *may* also furnish heat and energy, but proteid is represented chiefly in our most expensive foods; and, as fats and carbohydrates are less expensive and even better than proteid as a source of heat and energy, it were the part of wisdom to reserve proteid food to build tissue and choose fats and carbohydrates to supply the body with its heat and energy. Indeed, foods abounding in these two latter principles are often called proteid sparers and, also, fuel foods. Thus, if the carbohydrates are to act as fuel foods, furnishing us with heat and energy, we can see that we must supply them in the food in greater proportion than would be indicated by the quantity present in the body as shown above.

Now we wish to look more closely at these proximate principles. Let us begin with the most important and the most expensive, the proteids.

PROTEIDS

There are five important substances and quite a number of less important ones that we group under the term proteids. These substances are thus grouped, because each and every one of them has a similar chemical composition and thus performs the same function in the body. They contain *nitrogen*, an element found in no other food principle, carbon, hydrogen, oxygen, sulphur, and are tissue builders. These five proteids have marked *physical* characteristics which we can note in our kitchens, if we do not have a laboratory in which to study their chemical composition. Carefully try the following experiments and you will, in the future, have a fairly good understanding of what is meant by the term proteid.

PHYSICAL PROPERTIES OF PROTEIDS

Gradually stir two tablespoonfuls of water into half a cup of flour, to form a dough; knead the dough until it becomes smooth and elastic, then work it (in the hands or on a sieve) under a faucet of running water until the water, running off from the dough, loses its milky appearance. The gray substance left in your hands you will find tenacious and elastic; you can stretch and fold it as you would molasses candy or rubber bands. This elastic mass is *gluten,* one of the five representative proteids.

Add one or two tablespoonfuls of vinegar to half a cup of milk and let the whole become slightly warm; drain off the whey and wash the curd remaining; this curd is elastic and tenacious; it is casein, a second representative proteid. The white of an egg, which is largely *albumin,* another proteid, is also elastic and tenacious. The pulp of lean meat, scraped from the white connective tissues, represents the chief proteid in meat, by name *myosin.* The fifth of the group is *legumin,* the proteid found in the pulse family (peas, beans, lentils, etc.) When you come to have experience in cooking these five substances, you will learn that all are toughened by a high degree of heat. All of them when dried may be reduced to a similar, fine, powdery state.

GELATINOIDS

When we first spoke of proteids, we referred to a number that were of less importance than the five true proteids, which we have now referred to under the names gluten, casein, albumin, myosin and legumin; these others are set in a class by themselves, for, though they contain nitrogen, they can not alone supply the nitrogen needed by the body — they lack something present in the true proteids, though they may replace a part of the proteid in the diet. The best known of these substances is *gelatine;* others are *ossein* of which bone is largely composed, *heratin*, present in the hair and in the horns and hoofs of animals, and *collagen,* which forms the greater part of the connective tissue of meat. All of these are not toughened by boiling, but are changed into gelatine. These are the gelatinoids.

EXTRACTIVES

In meat there are nitrogenous substances that give it flavor; we notice these prominently in beef-tea and clear soup; these are called extractives; they are not true foods, inasmuch as they do not build tissue or supply heat, but they influence digestion.

USEFUL UTENSILS IN HOUSEKEEPIN

Removing Ice Cream from Mold — *Page 364*

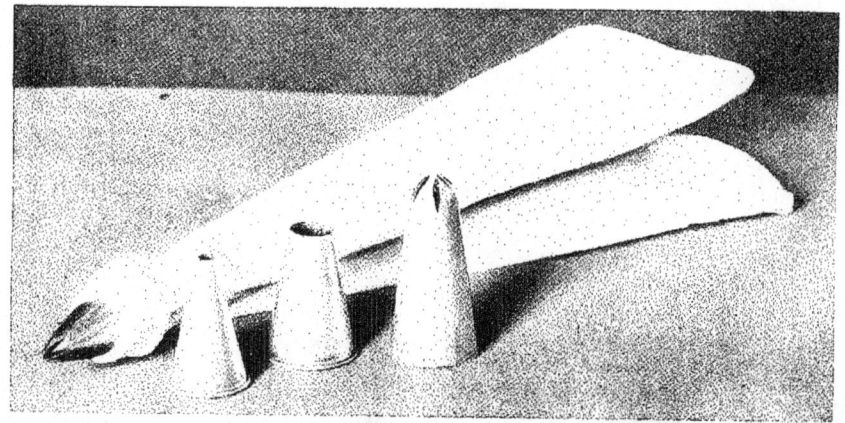

Pastry Bag with Tubes — *Page 227*

Sieve Frame with Adjustable Plates of Different Mesh for Sifting Sugar, Purées and Bread Crumbs — *Page 22.*

PROTEIN

The proteids, gelatinoids and extractives are classed together under the name protein.

CARBOHYDRATES

A carbohydrate is composed of the elements, carbon, hydrogen and oxygen, the last two in the proportion in which they are found in water. The principal carbohydrates may be arranged in three groups as below. The letters C H O stand for the three elements of which this principle is composed; the figures indicate the number of atoms of the different elements that enter in combination, in each group.

Starch Group	Cane Sugar Group	Grape Sugar Group
$C_6 H_{10} O_5$	$C_{12} H_{22} O_{11}$	$C_6 H_{12} O_6$
Starch	Cane Sugar	Grape Sugar
Dextrin	Malt Sugar	Fruit Sugar
Cellulose	Milk Sugar	
Gums		
Glycogen		

STARCH

You are already familiar with starch, having washed it away from the gluten in the dough you made of flour and water. Starch is found only in the vegetable kingdom. It is produced by all green plants and stored, in varying proportions, as microscopic grains, throughout the plant structure.

In the laboratory, iodine is the test for starch; pour a few drops of iodine, diluted with water, into half a cup of laundry starch, cooked and cooled for use, and the starch will assume a deep blue color. Or you may grind a vegetable substance in a mortar with a little warm water, add a drop of iodine solution, and note the effect. What is true in these cases is true of all starch mixtures and is thus tested. But in your kitchen you will recognize starch by its thickening when cooked. When you come to cook rice, tapioca, the breakfast cereals, etc., in liquid, you will note the thickening of the liquid and come to know that it shows the presence of starch.

DEXTRIN, CELLULOSE, GLYCOGEN, ETC.

Starch ultimately becomes sugar. In an intermediate state it is in the form of dextrin. The composition of dextrin and starch is the same, as can be seen by looking at the starch group, but that dextrin is not starch can be determined by the use of iodine. In cookery starch becomes dextrin on being subjected to high heat, as in the crust of bread. This change is also brought about by the digestive ferments.

The framework of plants and vegetables, or the cellular structure that enfolds the starch grains, is cellulose. From a nutritive point of view cellulose cannot be considered valuable; much, however, depends upon the tenderness to which it can be reduced by cooking; but it gives bulk, a necessary item in food. Gums are largely found in the juices of plants. Not all the carbohydrate principle, taken as food, enters at once into the circulation; a part is stored in the liver, as glycogen, and may be drawn upon as needed.

Use of Starch. Starch when digested furnishes energy, which is expended as work or as heat, or it is stored between the tissues as fat. As it builds no tissue, it cannot be used alone as food, but needs be combined with proteid.

SUGAR

The difference between starch and sugar is merely a difference in the proportions of the same elements, these being repeated indefinitely in composition. In the cane and grape sugar groups we refer to five varieties of sugar; these are made up of the same kind of atoms and, in the case of grape and fruit sugar, of the same number of atoms, but the atoms in each case are grouped differently. This difference in the grouping of the atoms results in sugars of different properties, which, when partaken of as food, differ in digestibility.

Sources of Sugar. Sugar is found in a large number of vegetable juices; it is in the stems and roots of all the grasses and in many of the vegetables served on our tables, as the carrot, parsnip, turnip, beet and sweet potato. It is found in the sap of the sugar maple, in most of the sweet fruits, as bananas, dates and figs, in the nectar of flowers, which is stored by bees as honey, and in the milk of certain animals. The sugar of commerce is usually obtained from sugar cane or beets and is a manufactured product. When we consider how much vegetable matter must be taken to obtain half a cup of granulated sugar, we understand that this sugar contains certain elements in a very concentrated form. If it is best to take food compounds as they occur in nature — diluted with other natural elements — ought we not to consider rather carefully the quantity of commercial sugar used at our tables? Of course, when we eat milk and sweet fruits, we are eating sugar in its natural condition. The beet properly cooked affords sugar in a wholesome and natural form. In chewing sugar-cane, though the fibres be not swallowed, we get the sweet product in a comparatively dilute form. But these foods are not available to all and the manufacture of sugar, at a price that puts it within the reach of every one, must be considered as one of the blessings of the age. The proper use of sugar will be taken up more fully in lessons where its use is indicated.

Fats. Fat comes from both the animal and the vegetable kingdom; like the carbohydrate it is composed of carbon, hydrogen and oxygen. There is, however, in fat, a much larger proportion of carbon and less of oxygen than in starch and sugar, and on this account it burns very freely and gives intense heat. For heating purposes in the body fat is more valuable than carbohydrate and thus its use as food in cold weather is indicated. Olive oil, butter, bacon, cream and the fat of meat are the principal sources from which this compound is obtained.

Water and Mineral Matter. In discussing the value of a food we commonly consider only the proteid, carbohydrate and fat it contains. Water is a necessity, but, as all food contains this compound in generous measure, we need not pay particular attention to it now. As regards mineral matter, except in the case of growing children, enough will be present in our food, unless our diet be extremely restricted.

Nutrient Ratio. When we speak of the food value of any article of food we refer to the quantity of proteid, carbohydrate and fat present in the article, and the ratio that exists between the proteid, on one side, and the carbohydrate and fat, on the other. One part of fat (on account of the heat it liberates) is estimated as equal to two and one-fourth parts of starch. Thus corn meal, having a composition of 9 per cent. protein, 75.4 per cent. carbohydrate and 1.9 per cent. fat would have a nutrient ratio of about 1 to 9. 75.4 starch + 4.3 (fat in equivalent starch) — 79.7; i. e., 9 per cent. protein to 79.7 per cent. starch or about 1 to 9. There are many things to influence a decision as to the nutrient ratio desirable in the food to be supplied daily by the young housekeeper, as bodily weight, degree and kind of activity, climate, health, etc., but, in general, the ratio to be sought for in the diet of an adult is about 1 part protein to five and three-tenths parts carbohydrate and fat; while in the diet of a child the proportions are as 1 : 4.3.

CHAPTER II

THE GAS RANGE, TABLES OF MEASURES, ETC.

PRIMITIVE man ate his food untouched by other heat than that of the sun. Using artificial heat, as a means of better fitting crude food substances to the purposes of nutrition, is a result of human culture, and, the higher the culture of a people, the greater its progress in the science of food preparation or cooking. Different processes in cooking call for widely differing degrees of heat; the food compounds must be retained, not dissipated and lost, during the changes that take place while cooking is going on. Thus appliances that will quickly respond to regulation, and give the nice gradations of heat called for, without undue expense and labor, are demanded. When gas is available, the gas range will be found well adapted to the needs of the young housekeeper.

The parts of an ordinary gas range are: —

1. Two single top burners.
2. Two double top burners (one with "simmerer," one with medium burner).
3. Two oven burners (these heat both ovens).
4. A baking oven with movable grates.
5. A broiling oven with movable grate and pan.

6. Gas cocks, one for each burner and for the "pilot light."
7. A "pilot light" for lighting the oven burners.
8. A movable iron sheet under the top burners.
9. A pipe connecting with the chimney.

The oven burners are in the lower or broiling oven. In this oven cooking is by direct heat. This oven is used for broiling fish, chops and steak, for toasting bread and quick browning of food. The baking oven is heated by indirect heat, currents of hot air passing around the oven.

To manage a gas range: 1. Learn which pipe and gas cock supplies fuel to each burner.

2. Learn to turn the gas cocks to the left for a supply of gas and to the right to shut off the supply.

3. Do not turn on the gas until the match is lighted.

4. Open the doors of both ovens wide before lighting the oven burners or the "pilot light."

5. To shut off gas from the range, when it is not in use, do not depend entirely upon the gas cock of the main supply pipe, but keep all gas cocks of the top and oven turned hard to the right.

6. Keep all parts of the range perfectly clean. Wash the floor of the ovens and the movable sheet under the top burners with soap and water often.

7. Turn off the flow of gas the instant you are done cooking.

8. Air is admitted to the burners through openings in an enlarged portion (air-chamber) of the pipe near the stop-cocks, (this air causes the gas to burn

with a blue and exceedingly hot flame). Sometimes in lighting a burner the gas will "burn back" in this air chamber, making a roaring noise. When this happens, turn the gas cock to the right, to shut off the gas. After a few moments the gas will pass from the air chamber, then turn on and relight.

To light a gas range: To light a top burner, turn the gas cock supplying the burner to the left, and apply a lighted match. To light a double burner, light one burner as above; turn the gas cock admitting gas to the other burner and the gas will light from the first burner. *To light the oven burners,* open both oven doors; turn the cock of the "pilot light" to the left and light the pilot light at the opening made for the purpose, outside the oven; then turn the cock of one of the oven burners to the left and the gas will ignite from the pilot light; turn the cock of the other oven burner to the left and the gas will ignite as before from the pilot light. When the gas in both burners flows well throughout the whole length of the burners, turn out the pilot light.

To use gas economically. 1. As soon as the contents of a sauce-pan boil, turn the gas as low as possible without stopping the boiling. 2. Use the simmering burner, whenever cooking at a gentle simmer is all that is desired. 3. When the oven has been made hot, turn down both burners. 4. Turn off the gas the instant the cooking is completed. 5. The oven burners use a large quantity of gas and, when these are to be lighted, plan to cook several things at the same time. 6. If you are roasting meat, have baked rather than boiled potatoes, and a dessert cooked in the oven rather than on top of the range. 7. Dishes may be kept hot in the oven after the gas is turned off. 8. If the oven has not been used, food may be kept hot in a steam kettle set over the simmering burner. 9. A whole meal may also be cooked in a steam kettle over one burner. 10. A small portable oven that may be set over a single burner will prove an economical investment.

The gas range in use: For broiling, toasting, browning dishes covered with buttered crumbs, etc., have the oven burners lighted and the doors closed five or six minutes before using the oven. Set the oven pan and rack holding the article to be cooked close under the burners and watch it carefully. A roast may be cooked in the broiling oven, while baking is being done in the upper oven; turn the roast frequently.

For baking, light the oven burners and close the door ten or twelve minutes before putting in the food. When the lower oven is not in use and food is being cooked in the baking oven, it is well to leave the door of the lower oven open.

To read the gas meter: Dial of a gas meter (x) at the beginning of a month; (y) after gas has been used a month.

Read (x) from left to right, the arrows show the way the hands are going, and add two ciphers and you have the reading when gas began to be used

(57,600 ft.). Read (y) in the same way and you have the reading at the end of the month (63,800 ft.); the difference (6,200 ft.) is the quantity of gas used in the month. As the "two ciphers" may be perplexing to some, we can get at this in another way. Always read the figures last passed by the hand; on dial "a" 50,000 ft. are indicated, on "b" 7000, and on "c" 600, which equal 57,600 ft.

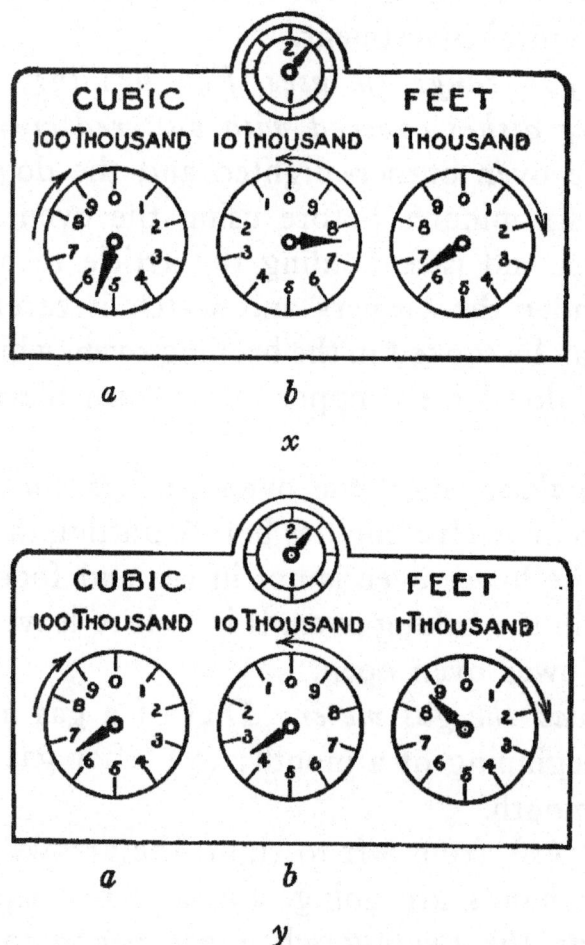

MEASUREMENTS

Measurements by weight are the most accurate, but, as a pair of scales is not included in the kitchen outfit of all young housekeepers, measurements by cup, table or teaspoon are usually designated. Measuring cups hold half a pint and divisions into quarters and thirds are indicated on the side. A cup of liquid is more than can be carried across the room without spilling.

To measure half a cup of butter or chopped meat, press the article into the cup solidly and on a line with the ridge indicating half a cup. To measure a cup of these articles pack solidly to the top, making level with a knife. To measure flour fill the cup with a spoon and level the top with a knife. Measure a tablespoonful or a teaspoonful of flour or butter in the same way as the cup is measured. For half a spoonful, level the material with a knife, then divide lengthwise of the spoon; divide a half spoonful crosswise, for a quarter spoonful.

TABLE OF MEASURES

3 teaspoonfuls make 1 tablespoonful.
2 cups make 1 pint
4 cups or 2 pints make 1 quart.

TABLE OF COMPARISONS OF WEIGHTS AND MEASURES

2 tablespoonfuls of butter make 1 ounce.
4 tablespoonfuls of flour make one ounce.
1 cup of flour is equal to ¼ pound.

4 cups of flour are equal to 1 pound.
1 cup of milk or water is equal to ½ pound.
½ cup of butter (solidly packed) is equal to ¼ pound.
1 cup of butter (solidly packed) is equal to ½ pound.
1 cup of granulated sugar is equal to ½ pound.
1 cup of chopped meat (solidly packed) is equal to ½ pound.
5 eggs without shells are equal to ½ pound.
4 eggs with shells are equal to ½ pound.

PRINCIPAL METHODS OF COOKING

1. Cooking by direct application of heat,
    Broiling.
    Roasting.
2. Cooking by means of heated air
    Baking.
3. Cooking by direct application of hot water,
    Boiling.
    Stewing.
4. Cooking by direct contact with steam,
    Steaming.
5. Cooking by indirect contact with boiling water.
    Double Boiler.
6. Heat applied by means of hot fat,
    Frying.
    Sautéing.
7. Heat applied by means of a heated metal,
    Pan Broiling.
8. A combination of stewing and baking results in,
    Braising.
9. A combination of frying and stewing results in,
    Fricasseeing.

LIST OF INDISPENSABLE UTENSILS FOR KITCHEN AND PANTRY

The following list is given as indispensable, but even from this list, if necessary, some things might

Cooking for Two

be omitted. Let us remember, however, that good work calls for good tools. And when the nerve racking effects of trying to get along with utensils ill adapted to the purpose for which they are used are considered, who shall say that a pantry well-stocked with useful utensils is not a prime requisite to the cheerful happy home.

GLASS AND EARTHEN WARE

6 Fruit Jars, pint size, for storing supplies
6 Fruit Jars, quart size, for storing supplies
Lemon Squeezer
1 Bowl for mixing bread, 4 quart
Plate or cover for the same
1 Bowl for mixing cake, muffins, etc, 2 quart
2 Pint Bowls
2 Half-pint Bowls
6 Kitchen Saucers or small plates to cover food

1 Quart Baking Dish (round or oval)
1 Pint Baking Dish (round or oval)
1 Quart Au Gratin Dish
1 Teapot
1 Casserole or Earthen Dish with Cover
1 Molasses Jug (2 quart)
1 Jar with Cover for storing bread (2 gallon)
1 Jar with Cover for storing butter (1 gallon, low and wide)

AGATE WARE

1 Coffee Pot
1 Double Boiler (quart)
1 Kettle with Cover (4 quart)
2 Kettles with Covers (2 quart)
2 Saucepans (pint)
2 Saucepans (half-pint)
1 Hand Basin

1 Colander
1 Roasting Pan for Meat (10 to 12 inches long)
1 Roasting Pan for Fish (10 to 12 inches long)
1 Omelet Pan (about 7 ins. in diameter)

ALUMINUM WARE

1 Tea Kettle
1 Saucepan for boiling rice and macaroni (2 quart)

Cooking for Two

IRON AND STEEL

Scales
1 Cast Iron Frying Pan (double lipped) to fit range
1 Cast Iron Muffin Pan
1 Cast Iron Scotch Bowl, for frying, to fit range
3 Common Case Knives (steel)
3 Common Four Tined Forks (steel)
1 Large Knife (for mixing Dough)
1 Palette Knife
1 Chopping Knife

1 Small French Knife
1 Bread Knife
1 Can Opener
3 Tablespoons (plated)
3 Teaspoons (plated)
1 Griddle Cake Turner
1 Meat Rack to fit Meat Pan
1 Fish Sheet to fit Fish Pan
1 Cork Screw
1 Egg Beater (Hill or Dover)
1 Ice Pick
Scissors
Chain Dish Cloth

TIN AND WIRE WARE

1 Biscuit Pan
2 Bread Pans (brick-loaf)
2 Measuring Cups (half-pint)
Potato Ricer
Gravy Strainer
Skimmer
Dredger for Flour (half pint)
Dredger for Sugar (half pint)
Dredger for Salt (quarter pint)
Wire Rack for Cooling Bread, etc.
Flour Sieve (Hunter's)
2 Milk Pans (3 quart)
1 Lemon Grater

1 Apple Corer
1 Small Tunnel
2 Biscuit Cutters (different sizes)
1 Wire Broiler for Steak Chops, etc.
1 Wire Broiler for Fish
1 Small Wire Strainer
1 Dish Pan
1 Draining Basket
1 Cannister for Tea
1 Cannister for Coffee
Garbage Can

WOODEN WARE

1 Rolling Pin
1 Bread Board
1 Meat Board (hard wood)
1 Chopping Bowl (small)
1 Perforated Wooden Spoon

1 Brush, small, for pastry, etc.
1 Brush for Cleaning Vegetables (05)
1 Scrubbing Pail
1 Broom (Corn)

Cooking for Two 23

- 1 Broom (Bristles)
- 1 Deck Mop
- 2 Brush Brooms (small) (stove and floor)
- 1 Bristle Brush (floor)
- 1 Bristle Brush (stove)
- 1 Scrub Brush
- 1 Bucket for Sugar (10 lbs.)
- 1 High Stool
- 1 Rocking Chair
- 1 Common Chair
- 1 Step Ladder and Seat combined
- Pole with Hook to open windows
- Pole with Brush to wash windows (outside)
- Small Zinc Covered Table on Casters
- Refrigerator

LINEN, COTTON AND MISCELLANEOUS

- 6 Fine Linen Towels (dish)
- 6 Coarse Linen Towels (dish)
- 6 Dish Cloths
- 6 Hand Towels
- 6 Holders
- 3 Sink Cloths (new, not old and linty)
- 3 Floor Cloths (new, not old and linty)
- 3 Lamp Cloths
- 6 Dusting Cloths (new, not old and linty)
- 5 yards of Cheese Cloth
- Fine Linen Strainers (table linen not too much worn)
- Napkins of Old Linen Tablecloths for use under augratin and other hot dishes
- 1 Heavy Canvas Bag (for pounding ice)
- Fine Twine
- Coarse Twine
- Straight Brass Hooks, 1 dozen
- Curved Brass Hooks, 1 dozen
- Tissue Paper
- Waxed Paper
- Thin Brown Paper (lining cake pans, etc.)

LIST OF INDISPENSABLE UTENSILS AND FURNISHINGS IN DINING ROOM

- Dining Table
- Dining Chairs
- Sideboard or Serving Table (or both)
- 3 Linen Covers for above
- 1 Heavy Cover for table, 1½ yds long (silence cloth)
- 1 Heavy Cover for table, 2 yds. long
- 3 Tablecloths, 2 yards long
- 1 Tablecloth, 2½ yards long
- 1 Dozen Dinner Napkins to match longest cloth
- 1 Dozen Smaller Napkins
- 1 Dozen Fringed Napkins
- 3 Platter Cloths
- 3 Tray Cloths

GLASS

1 Dozen Tumblers
1 Caraffe or Water Pitcher
2 Pepper Shakers
2 Salt Shakers
1 Bottle for Oil
1 Bottle for Vinegar
1 Bowl for Canned Fruit, etc.
Two "Rests" for Carving Knife and Fork.

SILVER

1 Dozen Medium Knives
1 Dozen Medium Forks
1 Dozen Dessert Forks
1 Dozen Dessert or Soup Spoons
4 Tablespoons
1 Dozen Teaspoons
1 Butter Knife
Sugar Tongs
Sugar Scoop
Small Tray for Spoons
Carving Knife and Fork

CHINA FROM STOCK PATTERN

Soup Plates, 1 Dozen
Dinner Plates, 1 Dozen
Breakfast Plates, 1 Dozen
Tea Plates, 1 Dozen
Saucers, Coffee, 1 Dozen
Saucers, Tea, 1 Dozen
Sauce Dishes, 1 Dozen
Coffee Cups, 1 Dozen
Tea Cups, 1 Dozen
Sugar Bowl
Cream Pitcher
Milk Pitcher
Bread Plates, Two
Platters, Three
Vegetable Dishes, Two
Tile or Stand for Coffee and Tea Pot

LIST OF SUPPLIES NEEDED IN COOKING — APART FROM THOSE BOUGHT FROM DAY TO DAY

Cocoa, ½ lb.
Coffee, 1 lb.
Tea, 1 lb.
Granulated Sugar, 5 lbs.
Loaf Sugar, 2 lbs.
Powdered Sugar, 2 lbs.
Molasses, ½ gallon
Rolled Oats, 1 package
Wheat Cereal, 1 package
Tapioca, 1 package
Rice, 1 lb.
Macaroni, 1 package
Butter, 2 lbs.
Lard or Cottolene, 1 2-lb. pail
Bread Flour, 1 sack
Pastry Flour, 1 sack
Entire-Wheat Flour, 5 lbs.
Rye Meal, 3 lbs.

Cooking for Two

Corn Meal, 3 lbs.
Salt, 1 small bag
Black Pepper, ¼ lb. box
Mustard, ¼ lb. box
Mace, ¼ lb. box
Vanilla, 1 2 oz. bottle
Edam Cheese, 1 small
Sultana Raisins, 1 lb., or
Cleaned Currants, 1 lb.
Baking Powder, ½ lb. box
Cream-of-Tartar, ¼ lb.
Baking Soda, 1 package

Vinegar, 1 quart
Lemons, ½ doz.
Gelatine, 2 packages
Chocolate, 1 lb.
Cornstarch, 1 package
Pea Beans, 2 lbs.
Dried Lima Beans, 2 lbs.
Prunes, 2 lbs.
Potatoes, 1 peck
Apples, 1 peck (if seasonable)
Bacon or Salt Pork, 1 lb.

NOTE: By a careful reading of these first two chapters the answers to the following questions are easily worked out, and it is recommended that all beginners in cookery endeavor to answer these satisfactorily to themselves as preliminary to their work.

1. Why is an abundant supply of air essential to life?

2. If the protein is not supplied in the food — as when one is sick and does not eat — from what source is protein obtained for life's processes?

3. Why do we call proteids the most important of the proximate principles?

4. Give a list of twelve articles of food that are classed as rich in the proteid principle.

5. How much time did it take to wash the starch from the gluten in the ball of dough?

6. Name three physical characteristics of the proteids. What is the meaning of the word proteid?

7. In what way do extractives influence digestion?

8. Does heat affect proteids and gelatinoids in the same way?

9. Which is the broader term, protein or proteid?

10. Name ten articles of food that are largely carbohydrate.

11. Name five articles of food that contain both proteid and carbohydrate.

12. Is there any difference in the digestibility of the crumb and the crust of bread?

13. Give reasons for your opinion on the preceding question.

14. Can a loaf of bread be baked to insure the highest digestibility of both the proteid and carbohydrate principles which are present in it? If so, how? If not which principle will you sacrifice, and why?

15. Read your gas meter before and after cooking your dinner and estimate the cost of the gas used in getting the meal. If you use coal or wood, note the quantity used in cooking for the day and estimate the cost.

16. Why open the oven doors of a gas range before lighting the pilot light and oven burners?

17. Can you bake on the floor of the oven of your gas range; or is it necessary to bake on a grate raised an inch or more from the floor?

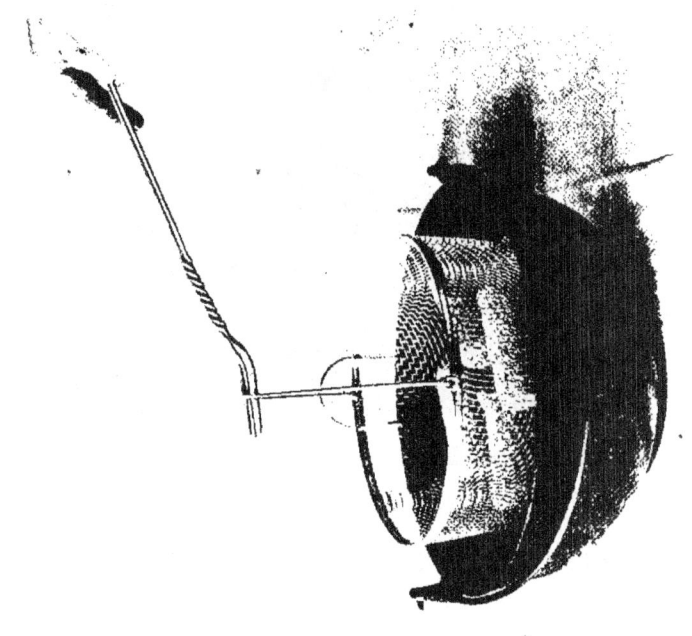

FRYING CROQUETTES. — Page

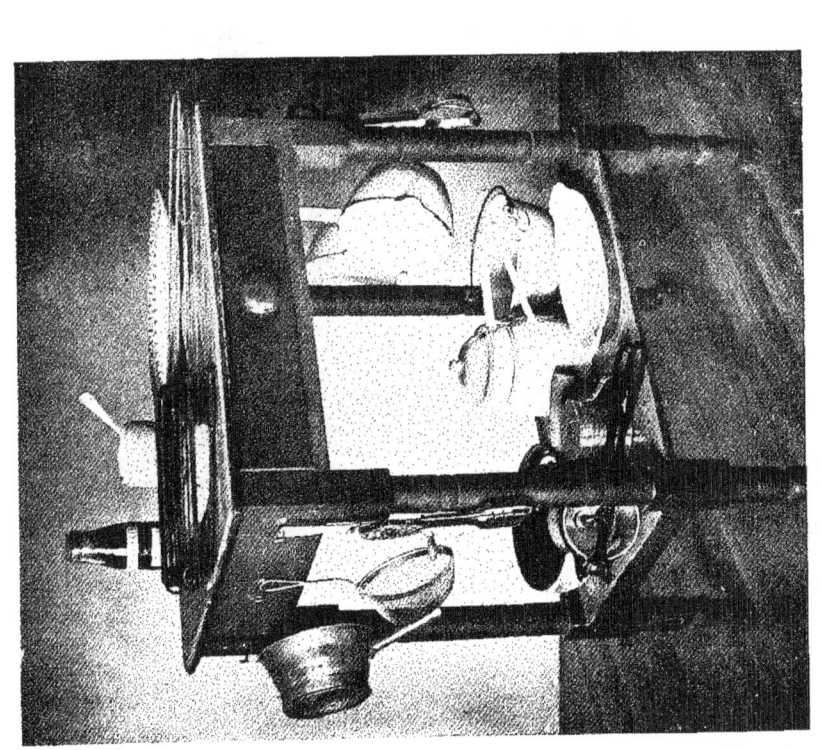

ZINC-COVERED TABLE ON CASTERS UNHARMED BY HOT DISHES.
Page 23

Making Tea with Tea Ball — *Page 31.*

Why is a Coffee Pot made with the nozzle near the top and a Teapot with the nozzle near the bottom? — *Page 38*

CHAPTER III

WATER, MAKING OF TEA, COFFEE, ETC.

Water is boiled in the kitchen for two distinct purposes: First, for the cooking of itself; second, for the cooking of other things.
  Mattieu Williams.

WATER is a very important item in cookery. It is often made the vehicle of conveying heat to the article to be cooked, and the character of the cook is shown by her skill in regulating the degree of heat thus conveyed.

If you put a spoonful of salt or sugar into a glass of cold water and stir the water, the sugar or salt seems lost. You can not see it, but a taste of the water proves to you that it is there. If you use hot water instead of cold, the substance will disappear even more quickly. We say of these substances that they are soluble in water.

If a pound of steak, in one piece or in several small pieces, be covered with cold water, the water will soon be colored by the juices of the meat. More of the juices will be drawn out into the water, in a given time, if the meat be cut into small pieces than if it be left in one large piece, just as granulated sugar will dissolve more quickly than a cube of loaf sugar.

Water is nature's great solvent; all substances are in some degree soluble in water.

Water is hard or soft; hard water contains salts of lime and is less solvent than soft water. Hard water is distinguished by the fact that in it soap will not lather freely. This solvent property of water is made much use of in cookery, and both in cookery and in nature it may be of great benefit to us or quite the reverse; for, on account of its solvent property, water may become contaminated with the germs of disease or with lead from the pipe in which it stands. If water be boiled in a teakettle, day after day, and the kettle be left unwashed, lime and other salts that settle upon the bottom of the kettle will become dissolved in the water, thus making it even more hard than when it is first drawn from its source. Water in a stationary boiler often holds in solution rust and other deposits from lead, copper and brass. None of this water is fit for drinking or cooking.

SAFE DRINKING WATER

If the presence of disease germs be suspected in water, boiling is the only remedy. Let the water boil vigorously half an hour, then pour it from a height into a vessel, (fruit jars are convenient), that has been washed in boiled water, then filled with the same and let stand in a hot place half an hour. Cover the vessel closely and store in a cool place. Such water tastes flat and dead, because some of the gases in combination have been driven off in boiling. By pouring the water into the receptacle from a height, gases are absorbed during the passage through the air, which give the water a more natural taste.

Joints are made in lead pipe more easily than in iron or steel pipe, and so the former is generally used in plumbing, after the pipe enters the walls of the house, or above the cellar. To obviate any danger of lead poisoning, before using the water, let it run two or three minutes, thus discarding the water that has been standing in the pipe. Never take water from the hot-water pipe for drinking or cooking purposes.

TEMPERATURE OF WATER FOR COOKING

We have said that heat hardens proteid substances, and that high heat changes starch to soluble compounds; thus it is evident, at once, that proteid substances and starch should not be subjected to water at the same temperature. Then, first of all, the young cook needs to acquaint herself with the nature of water at different temperatures. An ordinary thermometer, if handled carefully, will be of assistance in learning to secure accurate temperatures. In using the thermometer avoid subjecting it too suddenly to extremes of heat and cold.

BOILING AND SIMMERING WATER

Nine women out of ten will say that " a teakettle boils," some time before it has reached that state.

Water holds gases and when heated — even by standing in a warm room, — these gases expand and appear as tiny bubbles on the bottom of the vessel; as the heat is increased these bubbles rise and break at or near the surface of the water. By the time most of the air has been driven off from the water, the heat causes larger bubbles to collect at the bottom of the pan; these bubbles are of an invisible gas known as steam. The first break before they reach the surface, because they are not strong enough to withstand the pressure above them. At this point a thermometer set in the water would register about 185° F. If the water were in a teakettle, a steady stream of very fine mist would slowly pass from the spout of the kettle. Such water is said to simmer. By and by, as the water becomes hotter, the bubbles become stronger and will not break until they reach the surface of the water; the thermometer (at sea level) now indicates 212° F. and we say the water boils. From a teakettle of boiling water the steam comes in forcible jets through the spout. Above sea level, the pressure being decreased, water boils at several degrees lower than 212° F. By increasing the heat water may be made to boil furiously, but it will not grow hotter.

TO HEAT WATER QUICKLY

When boiling water is needed at short notice, set the water over the fire in a saucepan that presents considerable surface to the fire, and cover the dish to retain heat.

COMPOSITION OF TEA

A cup of tea, outside of the cream and sugar often taken with it, possesses no nutritive qualities. It is a stimulant and has a mildly exhilarating effect. The desirable elements in tea are the stimulating principle theine, and the essential oil, which gives fragrance. An undesirable element in tea is tannin, a bitter astringent substance. Tannin in the stomach interferes with digestion by hardening the proteid substances in the food; it also toughens and hardens the lining of the stomach. The problem is to make tea so as to secure the desirable qualities and avoid the tannin. This is really a very simple thing to do. The essential oil and theine are readily and quickly dissolved from the tea leaves upon the application of boiling water. Simmering water makes a weak, insipid infusion of tea. After the water has stood on the leaves five minutes, the presence of the astringent tannin is apparent, and if the water with the leaves be boiled rather than steeped, tannin is extracted in quantity. Tea, made by pouring water over the " spent " tea leaves that have been left standing in a teapot from a previous meal, is a slow but sure poison.

THE TEAPOT AND TEA BALL

The pot in which tea is steeped deserves consideration, for tannin combines with the elements in some metals, as tin, producing most unwholesome compounds. China, earthen ware and silver, all are satisfactory wares in a teapot. It doubtless is needless to add that both the tea and coffee-pot should be emptied at once after use, then cleansed and dried with care, and again scalded and dried before use. Perhaps, for two, a silver tea ball is quite as desirable for tea making as a teapot.

STEEPING THE TEA

Let the cups and tea-ball be made hot in the warming oven, or by immersing in hot water and then drying. Put a generous teaspoonful of tea into the ball; have fresh-drawn water boiling on the range or over the alcohol lamp. Pour the water into the cups and lift the ball up and down, first in one cup and then in the other, until the color shows that the right strength of tea is secured. Do not let the ball remain in the cups more than five minutes. If a stronger cup be desired, use the tea leaves in the ball for one cup, remove the spent leaves and take a fresh portion of leaves for the second cup. When tea is made in the teapot, let the pot stand in a warm place four or five minutes after the boiling water has been poured over the leaves, then pour off the liquid at once. As there has been no motion in a pot of tea that has not been boiled, it is quite evident that the strongest tea will be at the bottom of the pot.

COFFEE AND COFFEE MAKING

When the paper-like covering and the soft pulp are removed from the fruit of the coffee tree, two seeds remain; these are the coffee beans of commerce. By roasting these beans moisture is driven off and fragrance is developed. By grinding or otherwise pulverizing the beans a larger extent of surface is presented to the solvent action of water, and, if the water be heated to the boiling point, a fragrant, mildly stimulating beverage is produced. Tannin is present in coffee, but in less quantity than in tea, and it is not dissolved from the coffee bean so readily as from the more fragile tea leaf. Breakfast coffee may be made by boiling the ground coffee in the water, or by filtering water at the boiling point through the pulverized product. A silver or white enameled pot is the proper receptacle for coffee that is to be boiled; two level tablespoonfuls of ground coffee, to each cup of water, is the accepted proportion for the beverage. This proportion holds good also, if the coffee is to be made in a filter. For after-dinner coffee, double the measure of coffee is the rule.

In our talk on proteid, we said that heat hardened proteid substances. We make use of this fact to secure clear, boiled coffee. By mixing a little white of egg (which contains a large proportion of proteid substance) with the ground coffee, the egg will harden about the grains of coffee, when the liquid boils, and the mass thus held together will settle to the bottom of the pot, leaving the liquid clear and sparkling. The white that adheres to the shells of two eggs (broken for some other purpose) will be sufficient to clear two cups of coffee. If too much egg be used, such a firm coating will be formed around the coffee that the water can not act upon it and the decoction will be weak.

TWO CUPS OF BOILED COFFEE

Five level tablespoonfuls of ground coffee.
The crushed shells of two eggs or a little white of egg.
Four tablespoonfuls of cold water.
Two cups and one-half of boiling water.
Three tablespoonfuls of cold water.

Mix together thoroughly the coffee, the crushed shells and the four tablespoonfuls of cold water; let stand five or six minutes, then pour on the boiling water, cover closely, and let boil three or four minutes after boiling begins. Remove the pot to a cooler part of the range, pour the three tablespoonfuls of water down the spout and let stand for about eight minutes, then carefully pour off two cups of the liquid. Keep the inside of the coffee-pot immaculate, as coffee absorbs odors and flavors most readily. Always scald the pot before using.

FILTERED COFFEE

A large variety of pots, in which filtered coffee may be made, are to be seen in kitchen furnishing stores. Full directions for making the coffee come with the pots. The items most essential to note are, that the water used be *at the boiling point,* and the liquid be hot when it is served. A pound of coffee will serve two people, once a day, nearly two weeks.

COCOA AND CHOCOLATE

Average composition of cocoa and chocolate as purchased. — Atwater.

	Water Per cent.	Protein Per cent.	Fat Per cent.
Cocoa	. 4 6	21.6	28 9
Chocolate	. 5 9	12 9	48 7

	Carbohydrates Per cent.	Ash Per cent	Food Value Per lb
Cocoa	37.3	7.2	2 320 Cal.
Chocolate	30 3	2.2	2.860 Cal.

In tea and coffee, properties of the leaf and bean, respectively, soluble in water, are all that are used in the beverage, but in cocoa and chocolate, both of which are made from cocoa seeds or beans, the beans themselves, fine-powdered, form an integral part of the beverage. Then cocoa and chocolate become food as well as drink. Theobromine, the stimulating principle in cocoa beans, is much less pronounced in its effects than the corresponding principle in tea or coffee. The high percentage of fat present in the bean (see composition), though some of this is removed in the process of manufacture, together with the other food principles, renders the beverage too rich for use in conjunction with hearty food. As a rule, in making cocoa, follow the directions presented with the package, keeping in mind that, in general, boiling the mixture will improve it. In the manufacture of chocolate, starch is added, and thus beverages made from chocolate call for cooking.

TWO CUPS OF CHOCOLATE

One ounce of chocolate.
Two tablespoonfuls of sugar.
One-half cup of boiling water.
One cup and one-half of hot milk (or part milk and part water).

Melt the chocolate in a small saucepan set over the teakettle; add the sugar and half-cup of water, and cook and stir directly over the fire until smooth and glossy; continue cooking, stirring occasionally, about six minutes, then stir into the milk, scalded over hot water; beat with an egg beater about five minutes, and the chocolate is ready to serve.

BEEF TEA

The stimulating principle that we have noted in tea, coffee and chocolate, is duplicated in meats by a similar principle. This it is that gives color and flavor to the juices of meat. This principle in meats, as also the albuminous juices and minor compounds, are soluble in water, and when extracted make a valuable beverage in that it stimulates the appetite. Also being easily digested such a beverage is often desirable, when one is tired or indisposed. The pleasing aroma incidental to cooked meats can not be secured by means of cold water, but the albuminous juices (proteid) begin to harden or coagulate at about 134° F. The aroma is an essential aid to digestion and the hardening of the juices a hindrance; thus the temperature of the water should be regulated to fit both requirements, that is, the preservation of juices and flavor.

RECIPE FOR BEEF TEA

One pound of beefsteak from the round, two cups of cold water, salt to season.

Remove fat from the meat, wipe the steak with a damp cloth, then cut into small pieces. Have ready a fruit jar, scalded and cooled; put in the meat and two cups of cold water, cover the jar and let it stand twenty minutes in a cool place. Fold a newspaper to make a thick, smooth mat; put this into a saucepan, set the jar upon it and pour in cold water to surround the jar to the height of the liquid inside. Let the water heat gradually to 130° F. Keep it at this point for two hours, then increase the temperature to about 134° F., or until the color of the juice is darkened a little and the albuminous juices are slightly coagulated. Pour off the liquid, season and serve. A sprig or two of parsley, or a stalk of celery cut in pieces, may be put into the jar with the meat.

QUESTIONS

1. Think of two ways by which you can distinguish between boiling and simmering water.

2. Why is water heated more quickly when the saucepan is covered?

3. If you wish to make a thick syrup of sugar and water, should the pan be covered or uncovered, and why?

4. What difference do you note in the construction of an ordinary coffee and a teapot? Give reason for same.

5. Which is preferable, the first or last cup of tea, of coffee, and why?

6. Criticise the following menu for a dinner for a family of two young people: Broiled bluefish; baked potatoes; boiled onions, buttered; lettuce, French dressing; bread and butter; Boston cream cakes, cocoa.

CHAPTER IV

COOKING OF TRUE PROTEIDS, TISSUE BUILDERS, MILK AND CHEESE

WHEN we are to cook a new article, we should ask ourselves these questions: How will heat affect this? What is its composition? In our first lesson we found in milk an elastic, tenacious curd called casein, which was hardened by a high degree of heat. We also found a greenish liquid (whey), which we rightly suspect to be largely water. If we let a saucepan of milk remain over the fire for some time, a scum will form on the top; this is probably casein. Pour off the milk, and we find coagulated particles on the bottom of the dish. Albumin is coagulated by heat, and we conclude that, at least, a small quantity of albumin is found in milk. Let a cup or more of rich milk stand over night, and a thick (comparatively), yellowish substance will rise to the top of the milk; put a teaspoonful or more of this "top-milk" into your cup of hot coffee, and a few globules of *fat* will float on the top of the coffee. The whey holds in solution a little mineral matter and milk sugar. Thus, we have in milk proteid (in the form of casein and albumin), water, fat, carbohydrate (milk sugar), and mineral matter, the five food principles. Thus, cow's milk is often called a perfect food; it is for the young calf, but the food principles are not found in the right proportion to make it a perfect food for human beings. The calf, on milk alone, builds up a large, heavy framework of bone in a few months. Many years must pass before a child reaches a similar stage of physical development. Thus, to make cow's milk a perfect food for a child, the bone-making elements need to be reduced and other changes made, or the milk, as we say, should be "modified." An adult would not find it comfortable to take all his food in liquid form. The food elements in milk are combined with too large a proportion of water to make such a diet feasible; but when a glass of milk forms a part of any meal, the other proteid in the meal should be cut down accordingly. We should also keep in mind the quantity of milk used in cooking; as — if we provide a dish of cream toast (toast with thickened milk), we are supplying more proteid than when we have dry toast with butter.

COOKING MILK

We know that proteid is toughened by high heat, and that, in general, any process that hardens or toughens a food substance hinders the process of digestion; thus, when we consider the composition of milk, we would naturally conclude that milk, if cooked at all, should be cooked at a low temperature. However, there are people who seem to digest boiled milk better than that which has not been so treated, and, possibly, these are the exceptions that prove the rule. But while there may be some doubt on this point, there is no question but that the flavor of burned milk is absolutely unpalatable. Milk cooked directly over the fire burns very easily; also, when once the boiling point is reached, the bubbles, on account of the large proportion of solid material in the milk — do not break and scatter, but pile up, one above another, until the mass overflows the dish. Then, for this reason, if for no other, milk, whenever it is possible, should be cooked by some means that keep it from being heated to the boiling point. For such purposes we have the "double boiler." Two dishes are arranged, one inside the other, in such a manner that water surrounds the inner dish up to within, perhaps, two inches of the top. Thus, water stands between the article to be cooked and the heat, and the temperature of the cooking article never reaches that of boiling water. By this means, all risk of burning or overcooking is obviated.

After the water in the outer vessel has been boiling a few moments, small bubbles will appear close to the kettle, and at the surface of milk, in the inner boiler. These bubbles indicate that the milk is scalded, and that the temperature is about 160° F. As long as water is kept in the outer kettle, the temperature of the milk does not rise higher. A double boiler is easily secured by setting a small saucepan on two or three nails disposed in a larger saucepan.

CARE OF MILK

Milk is an article that offers conditions favorable to the growth of minute organisms, which may be introduced into it from the air or the utensils in which it is stored. Some of these organisms are harmful, others are not. Some cause the milk to sour. The growth of all organisms is hastened by mild heat, as the death of most is assured by boiling heat. Dealers, who supply milk to cities, are from necessity careful to chill the milk thoroughly as soon as it is taken from the cow; it is, also, kept chilled until the time of delivery. Half an hour in a hot kitchen, or in the sun, will undo all this careful treatment, and hasten the time of souring. Do not wait until after breakfast, but at once, as soon as the milk comes to your hand, set it aside in the coolest place at your command. Milk, cream and butter all readily absorb odors and flavors, and if kept in a refrigerator with other food should be closely covered. When possible, it is well to reserve a separate compartment of the refrigerator for these products. Receptacles, in which these are stored, should be made without seams, lest stale milk, etc., may find lodgment in them, and kept absolutely clean. When a portion of the milk is taken from a bottle, kept with other supplies, replace the stopper, or insert a fresh one before the milk is again set aside.

SOUR MILK

After milk sours it becomes thick; if it be cut with a knife or spoon, a greenish, watery liquid (whey) is seen. Sour milk is very useful in cooking. Some cooks fancy they get the best results by using simply the whey. This may be true in making certain dishes. But as the nutritious compounds of the milk are largely found in the thick, white part, it would seem advisable, in general, to use that also.

JUNKET

A similar thickening of milk takes place when it is acted upon by rennin; this thickening may be hastened by warming the milk slightly. When thus prepared, the sour taste is not present, and by the addition of appropriate flavors and a little sugar, milk may be presented in a variety of tasty and attractive dishes. These are junket or junket custards. Rennin is a ferment secreted in the glands of the stomach, and, for use in cooking, is prepared from the stomach of the calf. It may be obtained in liquid or tablet form; the latter is the most convenient for use.

PLAIN JUNKET WITH WHIPPED CREAM

Crush one-fourth a junket tablet and let it dissolve in a tablespoonful of cold water. Heat one cup of rich milk and two or three level tablespoonfuls of sugar to about 90° F. As milk heats to this degree very quickly, the safest way is to set a thermometer into it on putting it over the fire. Remove from the fire, take out the thermometer, and stir in half a teaspoonful of vanilla or a tablespoonful or two of sherry wine and the dissolved tablet. A few grains of salt, less than one-fourth a teaspoonful, may improve the dish for some. Pour the preparation into two glass cups; let stand in a warm place till it jellies, then set aside in a cool place, to become chilled. A short time before serving put a tablespoonful of sugar and a few drops of flavoring into one-third a cup of double cream and beat it solid to the bottom of the bowl. With a bag and tube, or a spoon, put the cream on to the top of the junket.

CARAMEL JUNKET

Stir two level tablespoonfuls of sugar over the fire until the sugar is dissolved and becomes a rich caramel color; add three or four tablespoonfuls of water and let cook to a thick syrup; add the syrup, a tablespoonful of sugar and a few grains of salt to a cup of milk and heat to 90° F.; add one-fourth a junket tablet, dissolved as above, and finish in the same way.

CHOCOLATE JUNKET

Dissolve one-fourth an ounce of chocolate over hot water; add three tablespoonfuls, each, of sugar and boiling water, and heat to the boiling point; add a cup of milk and half a teaspoonful of vanilla, test with the thermometer and, if the mixture is not at 90° F., heat it to that degree; add one-fourth a

Hot Toasted Wafers with Cream Cheese and Slice of Stuffed Olive — *Page 46.*

Cheese Toast with Bacon — *Page 49*

Cheese Ramequins — *Page 50*

Creamed Macaroni au Gratin — *Page 52*

Macaroni Croquettes — *Page 54*

junket tablet, dissolved as before, and finish in the same manner. These are simple, inexpensive desserts that admit of many variations. Coffee, crumbs of sponge cake or brown bread, spices, preserved ginger, cooked figs or dates, etc., etc., are among the articles suitable for this use.

Other recipes for use of junket will be given in the chapter on ices.

QUESTIONS

1. Why is milk called a "perfect food?"
2. Are cane sugar and milk sugar identical?
3. Is butter a tissue builder? Why?
4. Is butter a strength giver? Why?
5. What is the office of butter?
6. With what foods would you eat butter?
7. With which, rice or cornmeal, would you eat the most butter?
8. Would butter be needed with bacon and potatoes?
9. Which is preferable for making a sauce, second grade of butter, or fat from boiled poultry or beef?
10. Which do you consider the more economical form of fat to buy, cream or butter?
11. Why should milk be eaten from a teaspoon rather than drunk hastily from a glass?

CHEESE

The nitrogenous portion of the milk, as also some of the fat separated from the water (whey) and treated in a manner to preserve it for a longer or a shorter time is called cheese. Thus cheese is a compact, concentrated food, corresponding to eggs, lean meat and fish. On account of its density cheese is not always easy of digestion. It should never be given to young children. Some varieties of cheese, notably such as are soft or contain a goodly portion of the fat of milk, are more readily digested than others. Edam cheese, probably from the method of manufacture, rarely disagrees with any one. Most varieties of cheese, and particularly the common factory cheese, are more wholesome if grated or cut in thin shavings, mixed with cooked ingredients, and then softened with gentle heat. Vegetables, macaroni or bread crumbs, all foods of a starchy nature, are the articles usually introduced into cheese dishes, to lessen the density. As cheese, like all proteid substances, is hardened by high heat, care must be taken that the articles combined with it be thoroughly cooked before the combination is made.

HOT TOASTED WAFERS, CREAM CHEESE, ETC.

Mix such portion of a cream or Neufchatel cheese as is desired with cream, a few grains of salt and a dash of paprika to make a soft mixture but one firm enough to hold its shape. When ready to serve, toast some wafers or heat them in the oven, put a spoonful of the cheese on each with a slice of a pimola above. With a pastry bag and tube the cheese may be given a star shape.

SAVORY CHEESE

Beat one-fourth a cup (two ounces) of butter to a cream; gradually beat into this one-fourth a pound of common, factory cheese (grated), a tablespoonful of grated onion, a teaspoonful of Worcestershire sauce, a tablespoonful of tomato catsup, half a chilli pepper, chopped exceedingly fine, and a teaspoonful of fine-chopped parsley. Mix all together thoroughly, then press into a cup. Serve, turned from the cup, with toasted crackers or pulled bread and crisp celery, or, lettuce with French dressing.

CHEESE STICKS

Cut rye, whole wheat or graham bread into slices half an inch thick. Cut these into strips half an inch wide, after removing the crust. Grate two ounces of cheese; add a dash of paprika and beat into one-fourth a cup (two ounces) of butter, beaten to a cream. Spread this mixture on one side of the strips of bread and set them into the oven to melt the cheese. Serve with a fresh, green salad. Crackers may be used in place of the strips of bread.

CHEESE OMELET (BAKED)

2 eggs
6 tablespoonfuls of grated cheese
¼ teaspoonful of salt
¼ teaspoonful of paprika
1 cup of milk

Beat the yolks of the eggs until light and thick; fold in the cheese, salt and pepper; add the milk, folding it in, then fold in the whites of the eggs, beaten dry. Bake in a buttered dish or in cups. Serve in the cups with toast or wafers, a green salad or canned fruit.

CHEESE TIMBALES

1 tablespoonful of butter
1 tablespoonful of flour
¼ teaspoonful of salt
¼ teaspoonful of paprika
¾ cup of liquid (cream, milk or white broth)
¼ pound of cheese (grated)
2 whole eggs and 1 yolk

Melt the butter; in it cook the flour and seasonings, then add the liquid and stir until the sauce boils. Add the cheese and the eggs, beaten slightly. Turn into buttered timbale moulds, or, one mould of larger size. Set the mould or moulds into a pan on several folds of paper, surround with boiling water, and let cook in the oven until firm in the center. The water around the moulds should not boil during the cooking. Remove from the dish; let stand two or three minutes, then loosen the mixture at the edge of the moulds and invert them on a serving dish. Serve with a cup of sauce. Use milk, broth or tomato purée, as the liquid for the sauce.

SPAGHETTI CREOLE

½ cup of spaghetti or macaroni
2 tomatoes
1 slice of onion
½ pound of round steak
3 tablespoonfuls of butter
¼ cup of grated cheese
½ teaspoonful of salt

Break the spaghetti or macaroni into small pieces; cook these in boiling salted water until tender (See page 167), then drain and rinse in cold water. Peel the tomatoes and with a spoon empty them of seeds. Put the tomato pulp over the fire with the slice of onion, chopped very fine or grated, and let simmer, covered closely, until the macaroni is tender. Chop the meat fine; put it over the fire in a hot frying pan and stir while it turns from red to a brown color, then at once add it to the tomato and onion; add also the prepared macaroni, the butter, cheese and salt. Mix the ingredients by lifting them with a spoon and fork (or two forks), letting them stand meanwhile over hot water. Serve very hot. Cooked tomatoes pressed through a sieve, to exclude seeds, and dried or smoked beef (from one-fourth to a scant half pound) may be used in place of the fresh tomatoes and round steak.

CHEESE TOAST, WITH BACON

This dish may be made of any variety of bread, but it is particularly good when made of Boston brown bread. While the bread is being toasted, melt three level tablespoonfuls of butter; cook in it one level tablespoonful and a half of flour and one-fourth a teaspoonful, each, of salt and paprika; when frothy stir in three-fourths a cup of rich milk; stir until boiling, then set over hot water and stir in half or three-fourths a cup of grated cheese; continue stirring until the cheese is melted, then pour over the toast. A slice of crisp bacon is a good addition to each slice of toast. For bacon rolls, roll the bacon, pass a wooden toothpick through it, then fry in deep fat.

HOT CHEESE SANDWICHES

6 slices of bread ⅓ an inch thick
Butter
Grated cheese

1 egg
½ cup of milk
Salt

Remove the crust from the bread while trimming the slices, piled together, to a uniform size. Cut the slices in halves. Spread the bread with butter; grate cheese over the butter, using as much as can be pressed into the butter; press two pieces of the bread together, to form a sandwich, and continue until the six sandwiches are ready. Beat the egg, add the milk and salt, and mix all together, in this dip the sandwiches, first on one side and then on the other. Melt a little butter in a hot frying pan and in it set the sandwiches; when the bread is browned on one side, turn the sandwiches to brown the other side. Serve at once.

CHEESE RAMEQUINS

3 tablespoonfuls of melted butter
½ teaspoonful (scant) of salt
½ teaspoonful (scant) of paprika

¾ cup of fine soft bread crumbs
¼ pound of grated cheese
2 eggs, well beaten
1½ cups of milk

Melt the butter, add the seasonings, crumbs and cheese and mix thoroughly. Add the milk to the eggs and stir into the first mixture. Turn the mixture into buttered ramequins and let bake, surrounded by hot water, in a moderate oven. Serve very hot.

CEREAL WITH CHEESE

1 pint of boiling water
½ teaspoonful of salt
¼ pound of grated cheese
⅓ cup of Cream of Wheat or similar cereal
2 tablespoonfuls of butter

Put the upper part of a double boiler, holding the water and salt, over the fire, and when the water is again boiling, stir while sprinkling in the cereal; let cook vigorously five minutes, then set into boiling water, cover and let cook about forty minutes; then add the butter and the greater part of the cheese, beating them in thoroughly. Turn the mixture into a pan, rinsed with cold water, to make a thin sheet. When cold turn from the pan and cut into squares. Butter a serving dish that may be set into the oven. Put squares in the dish, leaving a little space between them, to cover the bottom of the dish; sprinkle these with cheese, then set other squares above and sprinkle with cheese. Set the dish into the oven to make all very hot.

MACARONI BAKED WITH MILK AND CHEESE

½ cup of macaroni
⅛ to ¼ cup of grated cheese
¼ cup or less of butter
Salt and pepper
Milk or thin cream

Cook the macaroni, broken in pieces, in boiling, salted water until tender; drain, rinse in cold water and drain again. Butter a baking dish (suitable for the table); put in a layer of macaroni, sprinkle lightly with salt, pepper, and grated cheese (Swiss, Parmesan or common factory) and dot it with bits of butter, then put in another layer of macaroni and add the other ingredients as before. Pour in rich milk, thin cream or skimmed milk mixed with a beaten egg, until it nearly covers the macaroni. Bake until the cheese is melted or the egg is set.

CREAMED MACARONI WITH CHEESE AND AU GRATIN

½ cup of macaroni
1½ tablespoonfuls of butter
1½ tablespoonfuls of flour
¼ teaspoonful of salt
¼ teaspoonful of pepper
¾ cup of milk
¼ cup of grated cheese

Prepare the macaroni as in the preceding recipe. Melt the butter; add the flour and seasonings and cook until frothy, then add the milk and stir and cook until the boiling point is reached; add the cheese and macaroni; mix by lifting the macaroni with two forks. Let stand over hot water until very hot throughout, or serve it *au gratin;* turn the mixture into a buttered baking dish, spread over it one-third a cup of cracker crumbs mixed with one tablespoonful and a half of melted butter and set the dish into a hot oven to brown the crumbs. Tomato purée or stock made of beef or veal may replace the milk.

RICE WITH CHEESE AND TOMATO

½ cup of rice
3 cups of cold water
1 cup of tomato purée
¾ cup of water or broth
½ teaspoonful of salt
¼ green pepper pod

1 small onion
3 cloves
1 parsley branch
¼ to ½ cup of grated cheese
2 tablespoonfuls of butter

Put the rice over the fire with the cold water and heat quickly to the boiling point; let boil five minutes, drain, rinse in cold water and drain again. To the blanched rice add all the other ingredients, save the cheese and butter, and let cook till the rice is tender, then with two silver forks mix in the cheese and butter. Serve as the main dish at luncheon or supper or as a vegetable dish, to add to a meagre proteid dish.

MACARONI, ITALIAN STYLE

½ cup of cooked macaroni
(See page 167 for cooking)
1½ tablespoonfuls of butter
1½ tablespoonfuls of flour
¼ teaspoonful of salt

¼ teaspoonful of paprika
½ cup of rich broth flavored
   with onion, carrot, etc.
¼ cup of tomato purée
¼ cup of grated cheese

Make a sauce of the butter, flour, seasonings, broth, and tomato. To the sauce add the cooked macaroni and the cheese; lift the macaroni with a fork and spoon to mix the ingredients thoroughly, cover and set over hot water to become very hot.

MACARONI CROQUETTES

½ cup of macaroni, cooked tender
2 tablespoonfuls of butter
3 tablespoonfuls of flour
½ teaspoonful of salt
2 tablespoonfuls of cheese
¾ cup of liquid (milk, cream, stock or tomato purée)
1 egg with 1 tablespoonful of water
Sifted bread crumbs

Make a sauce of the butter, flour, salt and liquid; add the cheese and the macaroni. Cut the macaroni in pieces half an inch long before adding it to the sauce. Mix thoroughly and turn into a shallow dish to cool. Remove the crust from half a loaf of bread, press the bread through a colander and then through a fine sieve. Beat the egg with the water. Spread some of the crumbs on a meat board. Divide the chilled mixture into four or six equal portions. Wet the hands, slightly, in cold water and roll each portion of the mixture into a ball; put the ball in the bread crumbs and roll it under the fingers, to lengthen it a little; carefully take up and pat the ends, first one and then the other, on the board, to make cylinder shape. When all have been shaped, begin with the one first shaped, and lift it by running a spatula under it lengthwise, dip over it the beaten egg, turn from one spatula to another and again dip egg over it, that the whole surface may be covered with egg, then roll a second time in the crumbs. Have ready a saucepan containing hot fat; drop a bread crumb into it and, if it browns as you count forty, take out the crumb and with a skimmer put into the fat two or three of the croquettes. Let cook until a golden brown — not too dark — then remove with the skimmer to a dish on which is laid soft paper. Let stand in the oven while the others are cooked. The croquettes will cook in about one minute. Serve with or without tomato sauce.

CHAPTER V

COOKING OF TRUE PROTEIDS CONTINUED: EGGS

Like woman, when an egg is good, there is nothing better; when it is bad, there is nothing worse. — Adolphe Meyer, M. C. A.

NINE times out of ten, deservedly or undeservedly, the market man must bear the odium when the meat is tough; for the young housekeeper is often not sufficiently posted in buying or cooking meats to lay the blame with certainty where it belongs. In the spring, however, meat is largely displaced by eggs, which are then fresh laid and plentiful. Fresh eggs are never disappointing, be they properly cooked; for, treated aright, they cannot be tough. Think of the wealth of variety in flavor, texture, and appearance that can be evolved in food by the use of eggs. They can be so treated as to give to a dish smooth solidity or an airy lightness and sponginess such as a breath will mar. They harmonize with savory no less than with sweet dishes, and may alike enrich and give character to a soup, a salad, or an ice. Verily, a certain famous chef was right, when he said that " without the aid of eggs the artistic cook would have to abandon his profession in despair."

But the use of eggs is by no means restricted to enriching or embellishing other dishes: their composition warrants service as *the* dish of the meal, bulk and dilution being provided in less nutritious articles.

Given fresh eggs, it matters not in what form they be presented, as *pièce de résistance* or garnish, and they will bear the hall mark of the cook. Properly cooked, eggs are never tough. Cooked in the shell and at a proper temperature, an egg, though firm enough to slice evenly, is a delicate morsel. Eggs, thus cooked, with crisp lettuce and well-seasoned mayonnaise, are, though frequently served, an ever-recurring pleasure to the palate. But how few of us know egg-salad at its best! Too often the white of the egg is a shiny elastic substance, elusive of the fork that would divide it. Eggs and boiling water should not form a continued partnership; for the result is always deplorable. On the breakfast table, in early spring, what can be more dainty or conducive to appetite than a fresh egg, carefully poached, and set above a round of bread, upon which each wire of the toaster is clearly marked on the brown of the otherwise evenly toasted surface. We are thinking of perfect home-made bread and an egg tender, though firm, with its golden heart dimly seen through a thin, filmy, veil-like covering. Give a finishing touch to the dish with a sprig of fresh, green parsley or cress from the near-by brook, just released from the winter's bondage, and the picture is complete, — a symphony in color.

Though poached eggs may be varied, by the use of salpicon mixtures, purées of meat, fish, or vegetables, or by sauces, these would become monotonous in time. Lest this happen, let us learn how to make really good omelets.

Much has been said in prose and verse in praise of omelets, and many a romantic incident is centred around the making of them. We refer, however, not to the light, puffy omelets, such as anybody can evolve, but to those subtle, tender, French creations, which monks and chefs of " ye olden time " were wont to concoct for the delectation of themselves or their fortunate patrons. These knights of the blue ribbon (for the term *cordon bleu* was not restricted to women) with dextrous hand are reputed to have flipped the tender omelet into perfect shape, and then to have tossed it onto the oval dish heated to receive it. The modern cook, unable to acquire the knack of sliding and tilting the pan to cook the egg evenly and delicately, picks up the cooked portion with a fork, thus letting the uncooked part touch the surface of the hot pan. It was probably in some such crude way as this that the Empress Maria Louise was manipulating the omelet when Napoleon, taking the omelet pan from her hand, and in vain attempt to imitate the deftness of the great Carême, flipped the omelet onto the floor. Chagrined at his failure, he is said to have retired, leaving the empress to complete the cooking in her own way.

In making the genuine French omelet, whole eggs

may be used; but a preponderance of yolks is preferable. Long beating is neither essential nor desirable: yolks and whites are to be simply well broken up and mixed. In cooking, great heat is serviceable; but the skill of the cook must be exercised to the end that the egg be subjected to it only for an instant.

Salpicon mixtures (cooked articles in bits, and mixed with a sauce) may be folded between or spread around an omelet, thus adding to its volume and character.

Omelet pans are made of various metals; but, all things considered, a thin steel pan is the best. Sheet iron is often used; but, as it soon warps from heat and does not then set level upon the stove, a new one is often in requisition. An agate pan, kept specially for the purpose, ranks next to steel.

Nor does egg-cookery end with poached eggs and omelets. Custards and soufflés, sponge cake and éclairs, as also the cup of coffee or consommé, and the thin-crusted croquette, are, one and all, good or bad according as to whether we have mastered the one great point in egg-cookery — temperature. Let us then make a careful study of this chapter, remembering that it is in just such little things as the cooking of eggs and the toasting of bread that our skill in cookery is shown.

COMPOSITION OF EGGS

The egg is another article of food that contains a goodly proportion of proteid, which is principally in the form of albumin. The white of the egg contains a higher proportion of albumin than does the yolk, while the yolk contains more fat than does the white. The other compounds are water and mineral matter. Three-fourths of an egg is water. The one food principle lacking is carbohydrate; thus foods rich in this principle — bread, potatoes, rice, etc. — are the ones to be combined with eggs to make a meal complete.

The shell of the egg is porous; on keeping, the water of the egg in composition evaporates, air enters to occupy the vacant place, and the egg soon (comparatively) spoils.

HOW TO TELL THE AGE OF AN EGG

Placed in the water, the egg, if fresh, will remain resting at the bottom of the vessel; if not quite fresh, it will rest with the big end raised higher than the small end, and the higher the big end is raised the older is the egg.

The reason why: As an old egg gets older, the water contained in the white of the egg evaporates, and this causes the empty space at the thick end of every egg to become enlarged. The larger that empty space becomes the more the egg rises in the water, till in course of time it floats.[1]

HOW TO BREAK EGGS IN COOKING

To break an egg, take it in the right hand and crack the shell by striking it, — near the centre of one ide, — upon the edge of a bowl; put the thumbs together at the crack, and gently break the shell apart. Take care to strike the egg only just enough to crack the shell. The shell of an egg, held in the left hand, may be broken by striking it sharply with a knife held in the right hand.

HOW TO SEPARATE THE YOLK FROM THE WHITE

Hold the egg lengthwise in the hand, over a bowl, while breaking the shell apart; turn the contents back and forth several times, keeping the yolk in one of the half shells, and letting the white slip over the edge into the bowl.

HOW TO STIR, BEAT, AND FOLD INGREDIENTS

If we put one or more articles, as flour, flour and egg, or flour, milk and egg into a bowl and move a utensil, like a spoon or fork, steadily round and round in the mass, each time in a widening circle, we call the process Stirring.

When we carry the utensil swiftly through a mass containing albumin or gluten in such a manner that

---

[1] *G. J. Hutchins in " Food and Cookery," London.*

a large portion is turned over at each stroke, a quantity of air, in minute bubbles, is entangled in the elastic proteid, thus making the mass very light. We call this process Beating.

After an egg, and particularly the white of an egg, is beaten, we may wish to incorporate it into other ingredients without loss of the air that has been beaten into it. To do this, turn the egg into the dish of ingredients, put in a spoon edgewise, turn it and lift up the ingredients and egg, and turn them over; repeat this until the mass is evenly blended together. We call this Folding. The principal articles that we wish to fold into others are the whites of eggs, beaten dry, and heavy cream, beaten solid.

BEATING EGGS

Whites of eggs alone may be beaten more firm than whites and yolks together, or yolks alone. Often if a small portion of yolk be left in a bowl containing several whites, it will be impossible to beat the mass to a firm consistency. Whites of eggs cannot be beaten dry unless the bowl and beater be perfectly dry and clean.

Slightly Beaten Eggs. For slightly beaten eggs the yolks and whites are not separated. Eggs are slightly beaten, when a full spoonful can be taken up.

Well Beaten Yolks. Yolks are "well beaten," when they are light, thick and lemon-colored.

Whites Beaten Dry. Whites are beaten dry, when

POACHING EGGS — *Page 64*

POACHED EGGS WITH TOMATOES AND BACON — *Page 65*

OMELET PANS — *Page 67*

the mass does not slip from the dish turned upside down.

Utensils for Beating Eggs. A fork, whisk, perforated spoon, or Dover egg beater are the utensils commonly used in beating eggs. When whites of eggs are beaten dry, the mass will be larger, if it be beaten with one of the first three utensils, but it will take a longer time to do the work than with the Dover egg beater.

COOKING EGGS

In our first lesson we noted that albumin was toughened by a high degree of heat. If you set a saucepan of cold water over the fire, put in a thermometer, and then break an egg into the water, you can note how the consistency of the egg changes as the water heats. As a study in the cooking of eggs, it might be worth while to cook several eggs, on different occasions, transferring them from the water, with a skimmer, to a slice of toast, when the thermometer registers 134°, 160°, 180° and 212° respectively. As far as solubility has a bearing on the subject, a raw egg is more digestible than one that has been cooked; but for other reasons, people in general prefer to have the albumin in eggs slightly coagulated by heat.

EGGS COOKED IN SHELL, SOFT, MEDIUM, ETC.

(1) Take a granite ware saucepan, holding rather more than one quart. In it heat one quart of water to the boiling point, remove the saucepan from the

fire, and lower an egg into it, cover closely and let it stand six minutes, for soft-cooked, and eight minutes, for medium-cooked eggs. With two eggs let stand eight minutes, for soft-cooked, ten minutes, for medium-cooked, and half an hour, if the eggs are to be used in salads, for a garnish, etc.

(2) Take two saucepans, the same as above. Heat the water in each to the boiling point, remove from the fire, and lower into one an egg from a refrigerator, and into the other an egg from the warm room; cook as before, six minutes, then compare the consistency of the two eggs. Why this difference?

(3) In a similar manner, we could learn that, in order to have uniform results, the conditions must not vary; i. e., the kind of saucepan, number of eggs in a saucepan, the quantity of water, as well as the temperature of the eggs, must be the same each time.

Poached Eggs, and Eggs Removed from the Shell and Cooked with White and Yolk Distinct and Separate

POACHED EGGS ON TOAST

Rub over the bottom of the frying pan with a bit of butter, and pour in about a pint of boiling water; add half a teaspoonful of salt and a teaspoonful of vinegar. Let this stand where the water will keep hot, but not boil. Break in two eggs, being careful to strike the shell only enough to crack it without disturbing the yolk. Let stand, until the eggs are set on the bottom, then loosen the egg from the pan, by carefully pushing beneath it a spatula or griddle-cake turner, to avoid too much cooking on the bottom, then let stand until delicately cooked throughout. Have ready two slices of bread, toasted to a golden brown. Wet the edge of each slice in salted, boiling water, set these upon the plates, made warm, dot with bits of butter, and with a skimmer remove the eggs from the pan to the toast. Add a bit of parsley or cress, and if desired a dash of black pepper to each, and place at once upon the table.

EGGS POACHED IN CREAM

Set a small frying pan containing a scant cup of thin cream into a dish of boiling water. When the cream shows tiny bubbles at the edge, add one-fourth a teaspoonful of salt and break in two fresh eggs. When the white becomes set a little, separate the eggs from the pan with a spatula, and when they are set throughout (this can be told by noting the condition of the eggs when the pan is gently shaken), remove them to two rounds of toast; pour the cream over the whole, and set at once upon the table.

EGGS "POACHED" IN FAT OR FRIED

When we remember the low temperature at which the albumin in egg is coagulated, it is evident that the fat in which an egg is to be cooked need not be very hot. Most housekeepers, whether young or old, fry eggs in too hot fat. Fat that sputters, when an egg is broken into it, is much too hot for the purpose. Olive oil, as it does not burn until heated to a very high temperature, is the best possible medium for frying purposes. Care must be exercised in its use, for there is no change in its appearance even when hot enough to brown any article put into it. Fat tried out, at a low degree of heat, from bacon, ham or salt pork, carefully poured from the sediment in the pan, is a particularly good medium for frying eggs. Break the eggs into the fat, and cook in the same manner as when poaching in water. If the fat does not cover the eggs, dip it over them with a tablespoon. If the fat used in this cooking be at the proper temperature and has never been raised to too high a degree of heat, the eggs will be discolored no more than when poached in water. Serve fried eggs with bacon, ham, spinach, etc.

Eggs Cooked with White and Yolk Mixed
Scrambled. Omelet (French, Puffy)

SCRAMBLED EGGS, REFORMED STYLE

Turn four tablespoonfuls of milk or thin cream into an agate frying pan, and add half a teaspoonful of salt. Beat four eggs with a silver fork just enough to break the yolk thoroughly. Then turn the egg into the hot milk. Cook over a gentle fire, stirring as the egg thickens, and adding, now and then, a bit of butter, until two tablespoonfuls have been used. When lightly set turn on to a hot serving dish and serve at once.

SCRAMBLED EGGS WITH VARIATIONS

Cooked ingredients, as chicken, ham, smoked tongue, sardines or anchovies, chopped or cut in bits, peas, asparagus tips, green or red peppers, parsley (the two latter chopped fine), small cubes of fried bread, and small cubes of hot bacon, may be added to eggs before scrambling. Peppers are usually cooked in butter until softened, before being added to the eggs.

GENERAL VARIETIES OF OMELET

Of omelets there are two general varieties — French and puffy — these are distinguished by the manipulation of the eggs, both in beating and in cooking. In the French omelet, the eggs are beaten simply to mix well the whites and yolks, no attempt being made to secure lightness; in the puffy omelet, all the air possible is beaten into the eggs, and the cooking is conducted in a manner to retain the air if possible to the moment of eating. For a particularly tender omelet use a greater number of yolks than of whites.

FRENCH OMELET

In making a French omelet, much depends on the condition of the pan. The inner surface needs be so smooth that, when the pan is shaken over the fire, the cooked mixture will slide upon it (forming creases where it doubles upon itself), thus letting the uncooked portion down upon the hot surface. A steel pan is preferable, and should be kept for this purpose alone. After using, rinse out thoroughly with hot water, and dry and polish with fine, soft tissue paper. Small omelets are handled more easily than large ones. Beat two eggs and the yolks of two more with a kitchen spoon or silver fork, until a full spoonful can be taken up. Add one-fourth a teaspoonful of salt, three tablespoonfuls of water, and a dash of pepper, if desired. Mix thoroughly, then strain into a bowl. Have a tablespoonful of butter melted in the omelet-pan. Bring this forward to a hot part of the range, let stand a minute, then turn in the egg mixture. Shake the pan back and forth with one hand, and, with a spatula or thin knife in the other, separate the cooked egg from the pan at the edge, so that in shaking, the uncooked egg may at this point run down on to the hot pan. Raise the side of the pan next the handle, in shaking forward, and lower it, when the pan is brought back. When nearly creamy throughout, roll the omelet, let stand a moment to color a little, then turn on to a hot serving-dish. A bit of butter, added at the last moment, will aid in giving color to the omelet.

PUFFY OMELET FOR TWO

Beat the yolks of four eggs until thick and lemon-colored; add a dash of pepper, one-fourth a teaspoonful of salt, and three tablespoonfuls of water. Beat the whites of two eggs until dry, then turn the yolks over the whites, and fold the two together. Have a tablespoonful of butter melted in the omelet pan; turn in the mixture, spreading it evenly over the pan. Let the pan stand, where there is moderate heat, about two minutes, then set it into an oven of moderate heat, to " set " the egg throughout. When a knife or spatula, thrust down in the centre of the omelet, can be removed without uncooked egg adhering to it, the omelet is done. Remove at once from the oven; score the centre of the top at right angles to the handle of the pan, fold at the scoring, and turn on to a hot platter. Much beating of eggs — as in the puffy omelet — especially if the number of yolks does not exceed the number of whites, causes dryness in the finished product. For this reason, a sauce of some kind improves a puffy omelet. Half or three-fourths a cup of tomato sauce poured around the foregoing omelet, after it is turned upon the platter, makes it much more acceptable. The two extra yolks may be omitted.

PUFFY OMELET WITH LEFT OVERS

One-fourth a cup — or even less — of cold, cooked peas, string beans, asparagus tips, mushrooms, chicken, ham, fish, oysters, lobster, etc., stirred into cream, tomato, or Bechamel sauce, are all admissible for adding flavor and juiciness, as well as bulk, to a puffy omelet.

COOKING A PUFFY OMELET ON THE GAS RANGE

On account of the air beaten into the eggs, a puffy omelet presents a braver appearance than does the French omelet, made of the same number of eggs; also the "knack" of making it successfully is easily acquired. But if the oven be not heated for some other purpose, it seems wasteful to heat the oven. To obviate heating the oven, manage in this way: Two stove "lids" are required. When the omelet is set, place the lid over the pan, which should not be too shallow, letting it rest on the edge of the pan, then set the other lid over the fire with the omelet upon it. Do not have the upper "lid" too hot.

QUESTIONS

1. The shell of an egg is porous. How does this occasion the spoiling of eggs?

2. Why are eggs packed with the small end downward?

3. Why can the freshness of an egg be determined by shaking it?

4. If tenderness be desired in a product (as doughnuts, cookies, etc.), should whites or yolks of eggs predominate in the mixture? Why?

5. Why is a larger number of yolks than of whites preferable in omelets and custards?

6. How may eggs broken into cups be poached in the oven and avoid overheat?

7. Should you add uncooked ingredients to an omelet?

ADDITIONAL RECIPES FOR COOKING EGGS

EGGS WITH CREAM IN RAMEQUINS

Butter ramequins holding one, two or three eggs as desired. For three eggs scald a scant half a cup of thin cream or rich milk. Scald the milk in the ramequin or use a saucepan and turn the milk into the ramequin. Break in three eggs, sprinkle a few grains of salt over the whites and set the dish into a moderate oven. If the dish is raised on little feet from the bottom of the oven, it may go directly into the oven. A ramequin, like the one shown in the illustration, holding three eggs, should be surrounded with hot water during the cooking. When the egg begins to set, sprinkle the surface with grated cheese and return to the oven to finish cooking.

A LATE-SUMMER BREAKFAST DISH

Peel three tomatoes, and cut out the hard piece around the stem end. Set in a well-oiled broiler, and cook over a rather dull fire until hot throughout, turning often to avoid burning. Dispose on a serving-dish. Set above each two pieces of tomato, an egg carefully poached in salted water, and dispose a slice of broiled bacon above and below the eggs. If preferred, the tomatoes may be cooked in the oven.

POACHED EGGS WITH ASPARAGUS

Have ready a small bunch of hot, boiled asparagus (See page 174) and two or three slices of toast.

Dispose the asparagus on the toast with the heads all the same way. Over the asparagus pour three-fourths a cup of white, Bechamel or drawn butter sauce and set an egg carefully poached in water above. For variety substitute cooked celery (stalks, cut in inch lengths), peas, string beans, chicken, fish, etc., for the asparagus. All of these should be stirred into the sauce and then set in place on the toast.

EGGS WITH SPINACH PURÉE
(Serve with bread or rolls at Breakfast or Luncheon)

Chop fine and press through a sieve half a cup of cooked spinach. Season to taste with salt, pepper, butter, and a dash of lemon juice. When thoroughly mixed and hot, use to line buttered egg-dishes or small casseroles. Break into each nest a fresh egg, sprinkle the whites of the eggs with a few grains of salt, and set to cook in a moderate oven. Serve when the egg is " set."

CHAPTER VI

COOKING OF TRUE PROTEIDS CONTINUED: FISH

FISH is neither palatable nor wholesome unless it be well cooked; it is cooked enough when the flesh will separate easily from the bones. When this condition is reached, the coagulation of the nitrogenous juices has been carried far enough and the fibers — under proper conditions of moisture — are reduced to a gelatinous consistency. The fibers of all varieties of fish being short, the flesh is always tender. The varieties that are deficient in fat, halibut, cod, haddock, bass, pickerel, etc. (we do not refer to shell fish), are easily digested. The main thing that claims our attention in the cooking of fish is the coagulation of the nitrogenous juices with as little loss of these juices as possible. When fish has been cooked in water, the water should be used or the process is extremely wasteful.

PREPARATION OF FISH FOR COOKING

Slices of fish require but little attention; wipe them with a damp cloth or let cold water from the faucet run over them, then wipe dry. Whole fish, even when cleaned at the market, will need more scrupulous care; wash thoroughly inside and out, then if any blood remains on the inside along the backbone, wash again and wipe dry. To skin, remove the head and cut down both sides of the fins, on the back, the entire length of the fish. Pull off this strip, loosen the skin below the head and pull it off, first on one side and then on the other. Then with a sharp knife scrape the flesh from the bones and nothing unedible will remain on the flesh.

BROILED FISH

Any fish that presents, when dressed, a thin flat appearance, as mackerel, bass, or bluefish, or a fish that may be cut in slices, as halibut, salmon or sword fish, may be broiled. While all the fish mentioned may be broiled, preference would be given to an oily fish as it is not easy to baste a fish while broiling, and a dry fish can ill afford to lose any of its juices. Mackerel, salmon, and bluefish are especially good for broiling. A whole mackerel, but slices of salmon and bluefish should be purchased. Sometimes it is possible to buy half a bluefish, cut lengthwise of the fish. Half a four-pound fish may not be too much for two, as the portion left over makes a most palatable salad.

BROILED BLUEFISH

Heat the broiler and rub over the wires on the inside with a piece of fat salt pork. Set the fish in place, and the broiler over the coals or under the gas

Cooking for Two 75

flame, with the flesh side towards the heat and rather close to it. After a few seconds, less than a minute, draw the broiler farther from the fire, to finish the cooking. Over the coals turn the broiler, occasionally, to cook the skin side of the fish. As the skin burns easily the cooking must be done, largely, on the flesh side. Whenever the flesh side is to be turned to the coals, brush it over with a little melted butter. Cook from fifteen to twenty minutes. When the fish is cooked, remove the broiler to a zinc-covered table or board (a labor-saving article the value of which in a kitchen can scarcely be estimated) or to a large agate or tin dish, then press the back of a four-pronged fork down upon the fish in such a manner that two prongs of the fork will be on either side of a wire of the broiler, now gently draw the fork down the wire the full width of the fish, thus separating the flesh from the wire of the broiler; repeat this with each wire on one side, then turn the broiler and repeat on the other side, when the fish may be slipped — skin side down — from the broiler to a platter made hot to receive it. Spread the fish with maître d'hôtel butter and serve at once.

BROILED HALIBUT OR OTHER SLICED FISH

Heat and oil the broiler as above; brush over both sides of the halibut with butter or salt pork fat, then set in place in the broiler; cook ten seconds and turn; repeat this for three or four minutes, then baste with fat and draw farther from the fire and let cook about fifteen minutes, turning each three or four minutes. Use a four-tined fork to separate the fish from the broiler (see preceding recipe) and slide to a hot platter. Spread with maître d'hôtel butter (page 196) and serve at once.

FRIED FILLETS OF FISH

Have thin pieces of fish freed from fat and bone; season with salt and pepper if approved and, if the flavor be agreeable, rub each fillet with the cut side of an onion. Have ready sifted bread crumbs from the center of a loaf of bread, and an egg beaten and diluted with two tablespoonfuls of water; dip the pieces of fish in the egg, then in the crumbs, to cover them completely, then shake off superfluous crumbs. Dip a frying basket into a kettle of hot fat, set it on a tin plate and in it dispose two or four pieces of fish; lower the basket into the hot fat, of which there should be enough to cover the fish, and let cook from three to six minutes. If the fish be not rolled, three or four minutes of cooking will be enough. Rolled fillets will take from four to six minutes.

TESTING FAT FOR FRYING

When the bowl (a Scotch bowl costing about 35c. is the best shaped and most durable utensil that can be had for frying) of fat has been over the fire for a little time after it has melted, drop in a crumb of bread; if the bread browns on one side while you count thirty as the clock ticks, it is of the right temperature for the fish. When the fish is cooked, let it drain in the basket, then remove it to a tin plate covered with tissue or blotting paper. Let stand at the door of the oven a moment, then serve. Do not let the pieces of fish touch each other, either in the basket or while draining on the paper, or they will lose their crispness. Fish may be fried in batter after the same manner as in egg and crumbs. The fish may be more easily covered with batter than with crumbs. Small fish, as brook trout and smelt, may be fried in the same manner. They will be cooked through when of a good golden color.

FISH FRIED IN BATTER

Season the pieces of fish as above; have them flat or roll them, turban shape, and run through each a wooden toothpick, dipped in melted butter, that it may be easily removed. Immerse the fish in batter, drain by holding it on a fork, and lower it into the fat, with or without a basket. Let cook from three to six minutes, or until nicely browned, then drain and serve. With fat at the proper temperature no appreciable fat will be absorbed.

SAUTÉD FISH. HALIBUT

A small slice of halibut or fillets of a white fish, bass or pickerel, or small whole fish, as brook trout and smelts, may be sautéd. Wash a slice of halibut and wipe it carefully. Dredge a board with Indian meal or white flour and shake on a little salt, then lay the slice of fish in the mixture; pat it a little, that it may take up the flour or meal and salt, then turn it over, that the other side may be covered in the same manner. Have ready a frying pan of such width that it will take the full length of the slice of fish; in this cook a slice of fat salt pork until the fat is well tried out; put in the fish and let cook over a steady fire until well browned on one side, then turn the fish and brown the other side. The fire must not be too hot, or the fish will be burned. If it is not hot enough, the nitrogenous juices will run from the fish, and the slice will not hold together. Properly cooked the fat will not be absorbed, and the fish may be easily turned and lifted from the frying pan in perfect shape.

SAUTÉD BROOK TROUT

Clean the fish by slitting them open in front, after the heads have been removed. After all have been cleaned, dip the fingers in salt and take hold of the top of the back bone with the left hand, then with a knife in the right hand separate the backbone and small bones attached to it from the flesh, by scraping or pushing the flesh from the bones. Wash in salted water, dry on a cloth, then roll in Indian meal, to which a little salt has been added; lay side by side in a frying pan, containing hot salt pork fat to cover the bottom of the dish; let brown on one side and then turn, to brown the other side. Properly cooked these will absorb no appreciable fat. Smelts may be cooked in the same way, though these are quite as often egged-and-crumbed and cooked in deep fat. The bones are not always removed, as they can be easily taken out after cooking.

SLICE OF SALMON, BOILED

Butter a piece of cloth large enough to take a slice of salmon; tie the cloth securely at the corners and lower it into a saucepan containing enough lukewarm water to cover the fish; add a teaspoonful of salt, cover the saucepan, and heat quickly to the boiling point, then let cook six or eight minutes. Lift up the cloth with a fork under the knot; let drain well, then remove to a tin plate, untie the knot and turn the fish on to a hot, folded napkin, set on a hot plate. Cook other fish in the same manner, the time of cooking depending upon the thickness of the fish. A thick piece of salmon weighing two or three pounds should be cooked nearly half an hour. Serve with boiled potatoes and egg or caper sauce.

ADDITIONAL RECIPES FOR COOKING FISH

From June to January black bass and pickerel abound in most of our inland ponds and small lakes. You or the other member of your family may enjoy fishing for them, and as they well deserve careful cooking we will notice them first.

FRIED PICKEREL

Remove the head and tail from the fish; with a sharp, pointed knife cut down the entire length of the front and empty the contents; cut off the fins, and with the back of the knife and the fingers work out the backbone and the small bones attached to it; cut the flesh down through the center of the back, then with the back of the knife push the flesh from the skin, thus making two long fillets. Leave these whole, or cut them in two or three pieces, each, according to the size of the fish. Lay them in an agate or earthen dish, pour over them one or two tablespoonfuls of oil and a tablespoonful of vinegar; sprinkle them with slices of onion and parsley branches, cover and set aside in a cool place for an hour or two, or until the next morning. Drain the slices, roll them in flour, season with salt and pepper, and set into a frying pan containing two or three tablespoonfuls of hot fat. Fat tried out of salt pork is particularly good for this purpose. Cook over a brisk fire until browned on one side, then turn and brown the other side. The fillets may also be egged-and-crumbed, and fried about five minutes in deep fat. They may, also, be baked in the oven, by the recipes given for cooking black bass. Serve with sliced tomatoes, or cucumbers, or with tomato sauce.

TOMATO SAUCE FOR FRIED PICKEREL

Cook a cup and a half of stewed or fresh tomato, half a green pepper pod, and half an onion, each

Fillets of Black Bass with Bread Dressing
Cucumber Salad — *Page 82.*

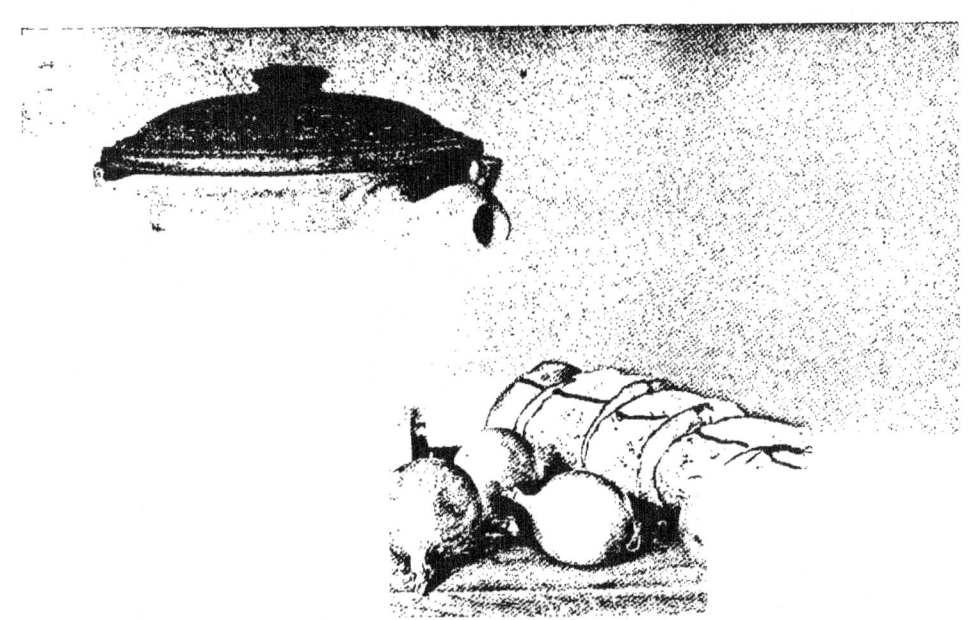

Fresh Fish en Casserole — *Page 88*

Halibut Steak — *Page 75.*

Rolled Fillets of Black Bass — *Page 83*

Truffled Fish Mousse — *Page 91*

sliced fine, also a bit of lean ham if at hand, ten or fifteen minutes, then strain and use the purée with two level tablespoonfuls, each, of butter and flour, in making a sauce. Season with salt and pepper as needed.

FILLETS OF BLACK BASS, WITH BREAD STUFFING

Remove the head of the fish; with a sharp-pointed knife cut through the entire length of the fish underneath, and thus empty the contents; cut the fish down the entire length of the back on both sides of the fins and take out this strip; loosen the skin all around the edge on one side of the fish, rub the fingers of the right hand in salt, — if they are damp the salt will stick to them, — then pull the skin from the side of the fish made ready. If at any place it does not separate from the flesh, push it with the knife. Remove the skin from the other side in the same way. Then commencing at the top push and scrape the flesh from the bones, keeping the flesh on each side as whole as possible. Wash and break up the bones, and put them in a saucepan over the fire, with cold water to cover; add two slices of onion, four of carrot and a sprig of parsley and let simmer an hour or longer. Wash the two fillets of fish and dry them on a cloth. Put some bits of butter (about a tablespoonful) in an earthen baking dish; on these lay a slice of the bass, put on this a layer of bread dressing, and above this the other fillet of fish; dot it with bits of butter, or strips of salt pork, and set into a hot oven. Bake about twenty-five minutes, reducing the heat after five or six minutes. Baste with some of the fish broth, in which a little butter has been melted, every six minutes. Just before the fish is baked, spread half a cup of cracker crumbs mixed with three level tablespoonfuls of melted butter over the top of the fish and return to the oven, to brown the crumbs. For the sauce melt two tablespoonfuls of butter; in it cook two level tablespoonfuls of flour and one-fourth a teaspoonful, each, of salt and paprika, then add three-fourths a cup of fish stock and one-fourth a cup of cream. Stir until boiling, then beat in a tablespoonful of butter. Serve cucumbers, French pickle or Philadelphia Relish at the same time. Two slices of halibut may be cooked in the same way.

BREAD STUFFING FOR BLACK BASS OR OTHER FISH

Pass enough bread, freed from crust, through a colander to fill a cup; mix with this two, crushed, sage leaves, a bit of thyme or sweet marjoram, one-fourth a teaspoonful, each, of salt and pepper and one-third a cup of melted butter.

CUCUMBERS TO SERVE WITH FISH

Let the cucumbers stand an hour or more in very cold or ice water. Remove the skin with a handy slicer, to give a channeled effect, and cut in thin, even slices. For one medium-sized cucumber rub over the salad dish with the cut side of a clove of garlic; put into a bowl three tablespoonfuls of oil, one tablespoonful of vinegar, and one-fourth a teaspoonful, each, of salt, pepper and onion juice; beat with a fork until thoroughly mixed, then pour over the cucumber slices disposed in a circle in the dish.

PHILADELPHIA RELISH

Chop very fine enough crisp cabbage to make a pint; chop very fine, also, two mild green or red peppers and mix the two thoroughly together, then set aside (covered) in a cool place until ready to use. Note that both peppers and cabbage are to be chopped exceedingly fine, as fine as it is possible to chop them. Mix together thoroughly one teaspoonful of celery seed, one-fourth a teaspoonful of mustard seed, half a teaspoonful of salt, one-fourth a cup of brown sugar and one-fourth a cup of vinegar, and let stand some time. When ready to serve mix the two together. This perhaps is not too much to prepare at once, as it is good, if kept chilled, as long as it lasts. Lemon skins (either whole or in halves) carefully freed from pulp, and with a thin slice cut from one end, to make them stand level, are often used as a receptacle for this relish.

ROLLED FILLETS OF BASS, BAKED

Remove the flesh from the bass in two fillets (as is described in the preceding recipe). Put the fillets in a dish, squeeze over them the juice of half a lemon, put slices of onion between, and set them aside in a cool place until ready to cook. Then roll the fillets, separately and loosely, into turban shapes, put bits of salt pork over them, and set to cook in a hot oven. After four or five minutes baste with salt pork fat and reduce the heat. Let cook about twenty minutes, basting five times. Leave two tablespoonfuls of the fat in the pan after the fish has been taken out; add to this two tablespoonfuls of flour and one-fourth a teaspoonful, each, of salt and pepper, and cook until frothy, then add a cup of broth made from the bones, bits of onion, parsley and a few slices of carrot, and cook until boiling. Add two tablespoonfuls of capers or fine-chopped cucumber pickles. Serve in a fish boat or bowl.

FISH BAKED IN CREAM OR MILK

A slice of halibut or fillets of bass or pickerel are particularly good baked and basted during the baking with cream or milk. Use an earthen baking dish. A particularly good dish, (sarraguemines ware), brown outside and white inside, is shown in the illustration of "Rolled Fillets of Black Bass." Rub over the bottom of the dish with butter; lay in the fish, put in a few thin slices of onion and pour in thin cream (milk will do) to nearly cover the fish. Let cook about fifteen minutes. Baste once or twice with the cream. Salt when nearly cooked. Do not have the oven too hot.

CREAMED FISH IN SHELLS, POTATO BORDER
(Luncheon or Supper, or course at Dinner)

Cook a pound of fresh haddock in a cup of water, to which a slice of onion and a tablespoonful of lemon juice have been added. Remove from the liquid, when the flesh separates easily from the bones, or in about ten minutes. Discard the skin and bones, and separate the fish into flakes. Use the liquid in which the fish was cooked, with one-fourth the measure of cream, in making a cup of white sauce. Allow a cup of sauce for each generous cup of the fish. Mix part of the sauce with the fish, and dispose it in buttered scallop shells. Spread a little more sauce over the top, then pipe mashed potatoes around the edge of the shells. Brush the potato with the yolk of an egg, beaten and mixed with a tablespoonful of milk, and set the shells in the oven to brown the edges of the potato. Serve at once with a slice of hard-cooked egg or a hot poached egg in the center of each.

Brushing the potato with the beaten yolk of egg is used mainly with an eye to the appearance of the dish; thus treated the potato will brown more quickly (yolk of egg is quickly affected by heat), but of course it may be omitted. This dish need not necessarily be made from fish cooked for the purpose. It is a particularly good way in which to use "left over fish."

FRESH CODFISH, BROILED

In ordering the codfish ask the dealer to remove the backbone. Heat the broiler very hot, oil it thoroughly, lay the fish upon it and let cook from fifteen to twenty minutes, the greater part of the time upon the flesh side, but turning several times and basting it with butter. When thoroughly cooked carefully loosen from the broiler and slide on to a hot platter; sprinkle with salt and spread over it the following butter.

RED PEPPER BUTTER

Beat one-fourth a cup of butter to a cream; gradually beat into it the pulp from cooked red peppers, scraped from the skin and seeds, to give the color and flavor desired. Finish with a tablespoonful of lemon juice, added a few drops at a time. For the dish shown in the illustration, chilli peppers, the length of the finger, were used. These come put up in small bottles, imported from England. They are of good flavor and may be used in preparing anchovy sandwiches or canapés, tomato sauce, rechauffés of meat or fish, or in Philadelphia relish or other recipes, where green peppers are called for.

SALMON STEAK, BAKED

Select a slice from near the middle of the salmon. Have it cut about three-fourths an inch thick. Such a slice will weigh from half to three-quarters of a pound. Butter an agate pan, lay the steak upon it, and pour around about half a cup of boiling water, to which a teaspoonful of lemon juice or vinegar and a scant half teaspoonful of salt have been added. Butter a piece of waxed paper and lay over the fish.

Set the pan directly over the fire and let stand until the water boils, then cook in the oven ten minutes. In the meantime, pare three or four large, round potatoes, and with a French scoop cut from them as many balls as possible. Put these over the fire, in boiling, salted water, to cook till tender. Melt a tablespoonful and a half of butter; in this cook a tablespoonful and a half of flour, then add half a cup of water and the liquid in the fish-pan and let cook until boiling. Set the fish on a platter with the potatoes, drained and rolled in the pan with a tablespoonful of butter and half a teaspoonful of salt. Put two slices of lemon at the base of the fish, and sprinkle the whole with fine-chopped parsley. Serve the sauce in a bowl.

FINNAN HADDIE, "BOILED"

Select a thick fish. Take half of it. Put flesh side down in a saucepan, cover with cold water, and set to cook on the back of the range. In about half an hour draw to a hotter part of the range, and gradually heat the water to the simmering-point. Let simmer from five to ten minutes, then drain the fish carefully. Serve on a hot platter. Pass at the same time hot, boiled potatoes and egg sauce.

FINNAN HADDIE, DELMONICO STYLE

Prepare the fish as above, then separate the flesh into flakes, discarding skin and bones. For each cup of fish prepare a cup of cream sauce; *i. e.,* melt two tablespoonfuls of butter, cook in it two level tablespoonfuls of flour, one-fourth a teaspoonful, each, of salt and pepper, and gradually add one cup of milk. Reheat the fish in the sauce. To serve au gratin, put the fish and sauce into a buttered au gratin dish, in alternate layers, having the last layer of sauce. Cover with cracker crumbs (one-third a cup to three tablespoonfuls of butter) mixed with melted butter, and set into a hot oven, to brown the crumbs.

FRESH FISH EN CASSEROLE

Any fish from which pieces about three inches square may be taken can be used for this dish. Salmon, cod, haddock and halibut are all available in most markets. Remove all skin and bone from the fish; put these over the fire in cold water to cover and let simmer. Meanwhile peel four small onions, cover with cold water and let boil ten minutes, then drain and add to the saucepan of fish trimmings to cook for an hour, or until nearly tender. Peel four potatoes and cut them in quarters, lengthwise. Cover with boiling water and let boil three minutes, then drain, rinse in cold water and drain again. Put the pieces of fish, of which there should be a pound or more, into the casserole, add the onions and the potatoes, a teaspoonful of salt and a dash of black pepper and strain the fish broth over the whole. A carrot, cut in quarters or slices, according to size, cooked half an hour and drained, may also be added. Cover and let cook half an hour.

FRESH FISH-BALLS

With a silver fork pick remnants of cooked fish into bits and sprinkle with salt and pepper. Pass through a vegetable ricer a few hot, boiled potatoes; to those add a little fish sauce, if at hand, or cream or butter, also salt and pepper, and beat as for mashed potato. To the fish add just enough of the hot potato to hold the fish together. Shape the mixture into balls; roll these in fine crumbs, then cover them with an egg, beaten and diluted with its bulk of milk or water, and again roll them in crumbs. Fry in deep fat; serve with Philadelphia relish or tomato catsup.

SALT CODFISH, CREAMED

1 cup of fish, flaked	1½ tablespoonfuls of flour
¾ cup of milk	1 egg
2 tablespoonfuls of butter	

Let the flaked or picked fish stand in cold water several hours or over night. Let heat gradually in the water. When the fish begins to shrink, drain and turn into a sauce made of the butter, flour and milk. An egg beaten slightly and another tablespoonful of butter (one or both) may be added at the last. Do not let the mixture boil after the egg is added. Stir constantly until the egg thickens the sauce a little.

SALT MACKEREL COOKED IN MILK

Let a mackerel lie, flesh side down, overnight in cold water. In the morning drain and dispose in an agate pan where it will lie flat; cover to the depth of one-fourth an inch with fresh, sweet milk and let simmer very gently, on the back of the range or in the oven, about twenty minutes. Serve with plain boiled or baked potatoes.

Often half a large mackerel will prove better than the whole of a small one. Left over bits of the fish are good in a potato salad or with yolks of eggs as a sandwich filling.

SHAD OR OTHER FISH ROE BAKED IN TOMATO SAUCE

Cut fine a small onion and a green or red pepper and cook in two tablespoonfuls of butter until softened and yellowed, then skim from the butter and sprinkle over the bottom of an au gratin dish. Above the vegetables set two fresh shad roe. Have ready a cup of hot tomato sauce; pour this over the roe and set the dish into the oven. Let bake about half an hour. Baste four or five times with the sauce, as roe is proverbially dry. Serve in the baking dish. White or brown sauce may replace the tomato.

FISH MOUSSE

3 tablespoonfuls of butter
3 tablespoonfuls of flour
¼ teaspoonful of salt
¼ teaspoonful of pepper
1½ cups of fish broth
½ cup of raw halibut
The white of 1 egg, unbeaten

The white of 1 egg, beaten dry
½ cup of double cream
½ teaspoonful of salt
The yolks of 2 eggs
2 tablespoonfuls of butter
1 teaspoonful of lemon juice

About half a pound of fish will be needed. Remove skin and bone; to these add a slice of onion with two cloves pressed into it, four slices of carrot, a branch of parsley and cold water to cover the whole. Let simmer an hour, then strain off the liquid. To the broth add milk as needed to make one cup and a half in all. Use this liquid with the butter, flour and seasonings in making a sauce. Cool one-fourth a cup of the sauce and keep the rest hot to serve with the mousse. Pound the fish, with a pestle, to a smooth paste. Measure out half a cup of the fish; to this add the white of one egg and the one-fourth a cup of sauce and pound again. When all is smooth, press through a gravy strainer set in part of a double boiler. To the fish mixture add the salt and then fold in the beaten white of egg and the beaten cream. Have ready four moulds thoroughly buttered and if wished decorated with figures cut from slices of truffle. Fill the moulds with the mixture. Set them on many folds of paper in a dish, pour in boiling water to reach to half the height of the moulds. Let cook in a moderate oven till firm in the center. The water should not boil during the cooking. When done remove the moulds from the water, let stand a few minutes, then loosen around the edge of the mould and turn upon a serving dish. Surround with the sauce, to which the yolks of the eggs, beaten into **two** tablespoonfuls of butter and the lemon juice, have been stirred.

FRESH FISH CHOWDER

A fish weighing about 2 pounds or about a pound of sliced fish	2 oz. of fat salt pork
	1 to 1½ cups sliced potatoes
	1 pint of hot milk
½ an onion	Salt and pepper

This dish is at its best when made of a whole fish, as the broth is richer when it contains the gelatinous matter from the bones. Fresh water bass and pickerel or cod and haddock from the salt water are all suitable. Skin and bones should be removed, to leave the fish in a solid piece, or pieces; cut the fish into pieces about two inches long and set aside. Cover the head and bones with cold water, heat slowly to the boiling point, then let simmer an hour or more. Cut the pork into quarter-inch cubes, and try out the fat; add the onion, sliced, and let cook until delicately browned; strain the water from the bones over the contents of the frying pan and let simmer a few moments, then strain this over the pieces of fish. Put the potatoes over the fire in cold water to cover; let heat quickly to the boiling point and boil three minutes; drain, rinse in cold water and add to the fish; cover and let cook about ten minutes or until the potatoes are tender. Add the hot milk and seasonings.

CHAPTER VII

COOKING OF TRUE PROTEIDS CONTINUED: MEAT

WE know that some cooked meat is tender and some so tough that it seems impossible to divide it with the teeth. We also know that some pieces of meat, naturally tough, may become tender if cooked in certain ways rather than in others, as a piece of round steak may be tough when broiled, and tender if braised or stewed. To know how to select tender cuts of meat, or to choose the method of cooking adapted to give the best results with the cuts at hand, one must know the situation, structure and use of the various parts of the creatures used for food. However, at this time we shall consider the subject only in the most general way.

Outside of game, we use for food, under the terms beef, veal, mutton, lamb, pork and poultry, the flesh of beeves, calves, sheep, lambs, swine and fowl. The general structure of all these is the same, viz.: a frame work of bone, encasing and protecting the vital organs, padded on the outside with fat and muscle or lean meat. This lean meat (muscle), rather than bone or fat, is the portion that interests us principally.

Perhaps we can best understand the construction of lean meat, if we observe, first, a whole joint of meat, as a shank of beef.

In structure the muscle seems to be composed of layers and bundles of small fibers; these, under the microscope, are shown to be tubes filled with matter in solution. The walls of these tubes are elastic albuminoid, and the contents, water holding in solution proteids, salts and extractives; these last give the characteristic flavor to the different varieties of meat. The fibers or tubes are covered and bound together by a very fine network of white connective tissue; the quantity of tissue varies with the length of the muscle fibers, long fibers needing more tissue to hold them in place than short fibers. In the breast of chicken, where the fibers are short, there is but little connective tissue. Connective tissue is largely made up of collagen, which, containing nitrogen and thus classed as a proteid, differs from true proteid in that it is softened by high heat, in the presence of moisture, and becomes gelatine.

In cooking meat we wish (1) to coagulate the proteids in solution in the tubes, and (2) to loosen the fibers, that they may fall apart easily, by changing the connective tissue, which holds them together, into gelatine.

We know that use strengthens muscle and makes it firmer; and we are wont to associate strength and firmness with the connective tissue; thus age and work thicken and harden connective tissue and render the process of loosening the fibers difficult. We would, then, expect to find tough flesh in the neck and leg of an ox, and would not choose cuts from these portions of a creature, when quick cooking is essential. The upper, back portion of four-footed creatures contains the tenderest meat and the least bone.

TO PREPARE MEAT FOR COOKING

Formerly it was necessary to remove meat from the wrappings the instant it was received, as the paper absorbed the juices of the meat. If the meat be first surrounded with waxed paper, this point is not essential. Store in a cool place till the moment of cooking, then wipe exposed surfaces with a damp cloth. Remove unsightly or bloody portions.

COOKING TENDER MEAT

From what has been said, it will be seen that tender meat contains but little connective tissue. The object in cooking is simply to coagulate the proteid substance in the tubes. This coagulation, we know, takes place at a temperature between 134 and 180° F. One thing must be looked out for during the time of this coagulation. When the muscle is cut and subjected to mild heat, the juices in the tubes on the exposed sides are drawn out and often lost. High heat will harden these juices at once. Then by subjecting the cut surfaces to high heat for a few moments, we may form a coating that will keep in the juices; then, by lowering the temperature, the juices within may be cooked just enough to jelly them, and change the color from bright red to a dull brownish hue.

BROILED SIRLOIN STEAK

Choose a small steak with tenderloin on one side, and have it cut one inch and a quarter thick. Wipe it carefully with a cloth wrung out of cold water, and cut off the flank end and any excess of fat. Heat the broiler. Rub the wires of the broiler with a bit of the fat, then put in the steak, having the rim of fat towards the open front of the broiler, that when the meat is held over the coals the melting fat may run down upon it, to baste it. Place the meat over and near the coals; let cook ten seconds, then turn, to cook the other side ten seconds; repeat for three minutes, then move the steak farther from the coals and cook from eight to ten minutes. Remove to a hot platter, and spread over the meat Maître d' Hôtel Butter. (See page 196.)

BROILED LAMB CHOPS

Prepare and cook as above, except shorten the whole time of cooking to from six to twelve minutes, according to the thickness of the chops.

BROILED BEEF CAKES

Put a small piece of steak, cut from the top of the round, upon a board; with a dull knife scrape the meat pulp from the connective tissue on one side, then turn and scrape the pulp from the other side, leaving the white fibrous mass on the board. Season the pulp with salt, mix thoroughly, then shape into small, flat cakes. Broil these in a hot, well-oiled broiler. Keep the edge of the cakes as thick as the center, or it will dry out too much in cooking. These require but a few minutes' broiling. They may also be pan-broiled.

PAN-BROILED BEEF CAKES

Have a cast-iron frying pan very, very hot; rub it over with a bit of fat, but leave no fat in the pan; put in the cakes, turn as soon as the outside is seared a little, keep the pan very hot, and keep turning the meat, until the outside is browned somewhat. Set on a hot platter and season as steak.

PAN-BROILED MUTTON CHOPS

Prepare the frying pan as above, and cook the chops in the same manner as the beef cakes. Cook from six to eight minutes, according to thickness. The outside should be brown, the center juicy and slightly red. If the chops are from a young creature, cook a little longer and do not leave the center red.

HAMBURG STEAK À LA TARTARE

Scrape the pulp from the nerves and fibers of a pound of choice round or rump steak and chop the pulp with one-fourth a pound of beef marrow very fine. Chop fine half a green pepper-pod and a slice of onion; cook these in a tablespoonful of hot butter until yellowed and softened; do not brown them. Add these to the meat and marrow with half a teaspoonful of salt, mix thoroughly, then shape into four balls; press the balls into flat cakes with a depression in the center. Rub over the bottom of a hot, iron frying pan with a bit of suet, then put in the meat, and break the yolk of an egg into the depression in each; baste the yolks with a little melted butter and set the frying pan into the oven; let the meat and eggs cook about five minutes, then remove them to a hot serving-dish, pour over a cup and a half of hot, brown or tomato sauce, and serve at once.

This will serve three or four people.

PLAIN HAMBURG STEAK

Prepare the meat as in the preceding recipe, or, pass the beef through a meat chopper; add the salt and, if approved, a little onion juice and mix thoroughly. Press the meat (this may be done nicely on a meat board) closely together into a flat, oval shape about three-fourths of an inch thick. Be careful to have the edges just as thick as the center. Heat the broiler and rub the inside of the wires with a bit of fat. Loosen the meat from the board with a spatula, then set it in place in the broiler. Cook about eight minutes. In the gas oven turn once. Over bright coals turn each ten seconds for half the time, then

Lamb Chops, Mashed Potato — *Page 96*

Lamb Chops, Planked — *Page 101.*

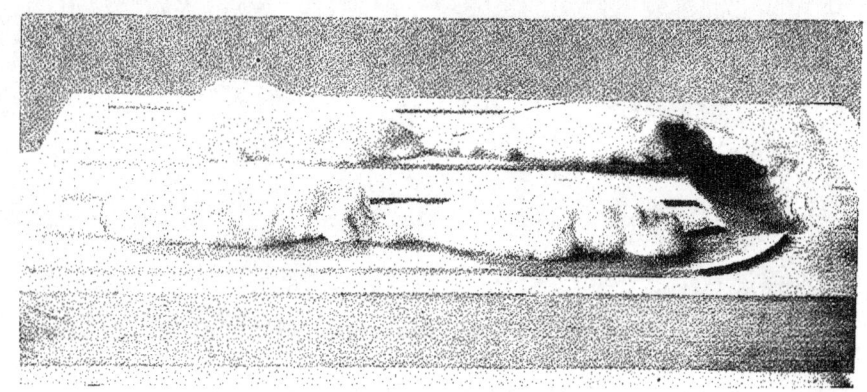

Two Sets of Sweetbreads — *Page 104*

Boiled Lamb for Two, Turnip and Carrot — *Page 113*

turn each two minutes. Spread with maître d' hôtel butter, page 196, or pour a cup of tomato or brown sauce over the meat on the platter.

BROILED CHICKEN

Cut the fowl down the back and through the breast. One of these pieces (half a chicken) will be enough for a family of two. Disjoint the wings and legs. Prepare the broiler as for beefsteak; put in the chicken and broil on the flesh side, three or four minutes (the skin on the other side will hold back the juice), then turn and broil on the skin side about one minute; repeat until the chicken is well marked with the wires of the broiler. Put the chicken into a baking pan, on a rack, and pour in half a cup of broth or hot water; baste the chicken thoroughly with melted butter, and let cook in the oven about twenty minutes, basting every five minutes. Serve with mashed potato, asparagus, hot or cold, and tomato salad.

BROILED BACON

Bacon may be broiled over a rather dull fire, but with a loss of fat, which is of value. To avoid this waste, the cooking may be done in the oven. Lay the bacon, cut in very thin slices, on the wires of a double broiler, close the broiler and set it into a moderate oven over a dripping pan. Let cook until the bacon is delicately browned and crisp, then serve at once.

This is one of the simplest and best ways of cooking bacon. That the bacon cook evenly, it must be sliced evenly. Lay the strip, skin side down, on a meat board, then with a strong, sharp, thin-bladed knife cut in slices as thin as possible, one after another, down to the rind; then run the knife between the slices and the rind, thus detaching them all together. Store the strip in a cool, dry place, that it may not mould and, also, that it may be sliced more readily.

WHEN A FRIEND COMES TO DINNER

If you use a gas range (in which things may be browned uniformly and very easily) try Planked Chops some day when a friend is to come home with your husband to dinner. This will not be when you first essay housekeeping, but after you have learned how to broil chops and make a dish of mashed potatoes, without fret or worry. The dealer will "French" the chops for you, but by the time you decide to make this dish, scraping the flesh from the rib bones of four chops will not seem a great undertaking. The feature of the pounded bacon and bread crumbs may be omitted.

Do not set the plank, when everything is in place upon it, too near the gas burner in the lower oven of your range. Do not hurry the browning of the potatoes and turn the plank, as needed, to color them uniformly. If the chops be underdone, at first, they will come out just right. Serve lettuce or celery salad with them, and finish with some sort of a sweet that you have made in the early morning and a cup of coffee.

LAMB CHOPS, PLANKED

Select four rib-chops and trim the meat from the bones, French fashion. Pound four slices of bacon, cooked crisp, to a powder; brush the chops lightly with bacon fat or melted butter, then roll them in the powdered bacon and then in soft bread crumbs (sifted). Broil the chops in a well-oiled broiler, *leaving them a little under done*. Have ready a cup of cooked peas, made hot and buttered, and about a pint and a half of mashed potato. Make a mound of potato on a hot, chop plank, set the chops against this and pipe the rest of the potato around them. Beat the yolk of an egg; add a tablespoonful of milk and with it brush over the piping of potato. Set the plank into the oven, to brown the edges of the potato and make all hot. To serve, set the plank on a chop plate, put frills on the ends of the bones and the peas between the chops and potato. This is to serve **two** or four individuals.

SIRLOIN STEAK EN CASSEROLE, RATHSKELLER STYLE

There is no object in cooking a choice sirloin steak in a casserole, for a round steak costing much less will give better results, from the fact that it contains more juice. On bills of fare in fine restaurants, we note the dishes, sirloin and tenderloin steaks, en casserole; but the cooking is not done in the covered casserole; the steaks are pan-broiled and then served in low, open casseroles in which they are easily carved.

For a sirloin steak large enough to serve three persons, make ready three or four small onions and a dozen, each, of raw carrot and potato balls. Cook these in a little hot fat, in a frying pan, until they are well browned on all sides, then cook in a pint or more of beef broth until they are tender; keep the vegetables hot. Melt three tablespoonfuls of butter and stir and cook until it becomes well browned, but not in the least burned; add four tablespoonfuls of flour and half a teaspoonful of salt and cook until it is also thoroughly browned, then set aside to become cold. When cold add a cup and a half of the broth in which the vegetables were cooked and stir until the mixture boils, then add the vegetables (also half a dozen or more of button mushrooms if convenient) and let stand in a dish of hot water until the steak is ready. Also heat a low, beefsteak casserole. Rub over the bottom of a very hot iron frying pan with a bit of suet, lay in the steak to cook one minute, then turn and cook the other side one minute and continue cooking and turning for six minutes, then transfer the steak to the hot casserole, season with salt and pour over it the sauce with vegetables; set the dish into the oven to remain about three minutes, then serve as above.

BROILING COOKED MEATS

We have said that only tender meat — meaning by this *naturally* tender meat — was suitable for broiling, but there are one or two varieties of meat that are first made tender by long, slow cooking, and then broiled to improve the flavor. The foremost of these are tripe and sweetbreads. Tripe is an inexpensive article of food that may be served in many appetizing ways. Perhaps the best of these, as it is certainly the simplest, is by broiling. Sweetbreads in some sections are considered a choice tid bit, and a great delicacy, and bring a high price, 75 cents and $1.00 per pair. In other localities they are given or thrown away, and in country places, where there is only a moderate demand for them, they sell for twenty to forty cents a pair. Both of these articles are well adapted to the needs of the family of two. Tripe may be purchased fresh or pickled. In buying fresh tripe get only enough for one meal, about a pound. More of the pickled article may be purchased, as it will keep in the refrigerator a week or longer. Presumably the tripe is tender when purchased. If this be not the case, it must be simmered until tender in boiling water. Sweetbreads spoil very quickly, and must be cooked as soon as purchased. Let stand in cold water an hour or more, changing the water often; remove veins, skins, etc., cover with boiling water and let simmer, nearly an hour. Drain and cover with cold water. When cold wipe dry and set aside until ready to use.

BROILED SWEETBREADS

Cut the sweetbreads in halves lengthwise, brush them with softened butter and broil over a rather dull fire, about five minutes, less rather than more, turning them every thirty seconds. Baste with butter once or twice. Set on a hot dish, spread them with Maître d' Hôtel butter and serve at once. Peas, asparagus tips, creamed potatoes or celery accompany the dish. Macaroni in tomato sauce with cheese is also good with this dish.

BROILED HONEYCOMB TRIPE

Brush over both sides of the tripe with melted butter or bacon fat, then pat on a board on which sifted bread crumbs have been spread, first on one side then on the other; set into a hot well-oiled broiler and cook over a bed of coals or under a gas flame from four to eight minutes. Under the gas flame turn but once. Over the coals turn every thirty seconds. Spread with Maître d' Hôtel butter. If the tripe be fresh, a teaspoonful of lemon juice should be gradually beaten into the butter.

ROAST MEATS

In broiling, a comparatively large extent of surface is presented to the fire. Sometimes we wish to cook tender meat that is in a compact form. A piece is often but a little less thick than broad. To cook such meat directly over the fire or in front of a fire (roasting) necessitates well-nigh constant attention. To simplify the cooking, we use a hot oven, in which heat is applied to all the surfaces uniformly, or approximately so. The first step is to sear over the surface, to keep the juices within the meat; then, as in broiling, the heat must be lowered. To aid in the outside searing and to convey heat into the meat, we pour hot fat over it (baste) every ten minutes. To sear over the meat, the oven should be at a temperature of 400 F. when the meat is set into it. After the initial searing is completed, the temperature should be lowered as soon as possible to about 240 F. Fat will not burn in the pan at this temperature. This is a guide in the roasting. The temperature of the roast at the center is much lower than 240° F., on account of the water in composition, and thus the juices are not overcooked or dried out.

Part of the fat used in basting may come from the meat itself, (dripping), but often this must be supplemented with additional fat left over from other roasts, or taken from the top of the soup kettle. If during the cooking a portion of the meat rests continuously in the hot fat, it will be overcooked, fried, not roasted or baked. To obviate this, set the meat on a rack, and always adapt the size of the pan to the size of the roast. If the pan be large, a large quantity of fat is needed to cover the surface of the pan, and keep it from burning. Water is sometimes used to obviate this trouble, but water changes the character of the product and should be discarded.

Roasts are preeminently for large families, still there are cuts of meat that are well adapted to the family of two.

ROAST BEEF TENDERLOIN

The tenderloin for a small family is cut from under the rump. It sells for thirty-five to forty cents a pound. It contains no bone and little waste. It weighs two and a half to four pounds; about three pounds is the average weight. Two or four slices may be removed for broiling, and the rest be cooked as a roast.

With the fingers and a sharp, thin knife, remove all skin and tendinous portions, and wipe the meat with a damp cloth. *When the oven is ready* (about 400° F.) rub a little salt over the surface and spread it with salt pork or bacon fat, or fasten strips of salt pork or bacon over it. Set it on the rack in a small pan, and into the hot oven; let cook five or six minutes, then turn, to sear over the other side; in about ten minutes baste with the fat in the pan, dredge with flour, reduce the heat and let cook from fifteen to twenty minutes longer, according to the thickness of the meat. Baste three or more times. When cut the meat should be dark on the outside to the depth of one-fourth an inch, and the center shaded from pink to red, but showing no signs of rawness; i. e., the juices should be coagulated throughout. Pour off the fat, to leave two tablespoonfuls in the pan, add two tablespoonfuls of flour and stir and cook until frothy; then add one cup of tomato purée, beef broth or cold water, or a mixture of these, and stir and cook until boiling. For a higher flavored sauce, a slice of onion and two of carrot may be cooked in the fat a few moments before the flour is added. This roast does not have the juiciness and full, rich flavor of a rib roast, and calls for a richly flavored sauce. Bananas baked in the skin, then removed from the skin and covered with a sultana sauce, are a choice accompaniment to this dish.

HAMBURG ROAST

Chop fine one pound of steak, cut from the top of the round, and two or three ounces of beef marrow, taken from the hind leg bone; a small slice of green or red pepper pod and half a slice of onion may be chopped with the meat or a teaspoonful of onion juice may be added after the meat is chopped. Add a scant half a teaspoonful of salt, the beaten yolk of an egg and one-fourth a cup of soft, sifted bread crumbs that have been soaked in cold water and wrung dry in a bit of cheese cloth. With the hand, mix all the ingredients together very thoroughly. Care must be taken to mix the marrow and bread evenly through the meat. Press the whole into a compact roll, of equal thickness throughout. Put a slice of pork or bacon on the meat rack (to hold up the meat), set the roast on this, put a second slice over the meat and set to cook in a very hot oven.

After six minutes reduce the heat, baste with the fat in the pan, and let cook about fifteen minutes longer. The roast should be brown on the outside and pink at the center. Serve with brown or tomato sauce.

TIP OF THE LOIN ROAST

The best of the small roasts of beef are two ribs cut from the extreme end of the hind quarter. This roast will weigh five or six pounds and will last a family of two nearly a week. The two ribs coming next to this cut (on the fore quarter, however) will weigh seven to ten pounds. As the hind quarter is hung up by the loop made by the tendon in the hind leg, the juices in this quarter naturally flow toward the tip, making it juicy, and, the roast being tender, is very desirable. Sear all over in a hot oven, then set the meat on the rack, skin side down, and when half cooked turn, to brown the skin. Cook from an hour and a quarter to an hour and a half, following the directions given for Roast Beef Tenderloin. Add extra fat if needed for basting. Select a pan but little larger than the roast. Use no water in cooking.

WILD DUCK, ROASTED

Truss the duck in the same manner as is given for Roast Chicken. Spread the outside with butter or bacon fat, and dredge with salt and flour. Put a dozen cranberries within, and roast in a hot oven from twenty to thirty minutes, basting three times with bacon fat. Remove the duck to a hot platter, and garnish with rounds of hominy, fried in deep fat, each holding a slice of bacon, rolled and baked at the same time as the duck, or better still fried in deep fat. Serve celery salad and currant jelly at the same time.

COOKING OF LESS TENDER MEAT

In cooking tender meat we took pains to secure a glossy, well-browned exterior and a delicate coagulation of the proteids in solution. In cooking less tender meat a rich-colored, high-flavored surface can be secured only indirectly. Our chief concern is to change the connective tissue into gelatine and to coagulate the proteids, delicately. To gelatinize connective tissue, moisture in the form of water is introduced and prolonged cooking is needful. As in roasting and broiling, the portion of meat is first subjected to high heat, that a coating may be formed to keep in the juices, after that the cooking is completed at a lower temperature. By experiments it has been found that the temperature in the center of meat during cooking is much lower than that of the liquid (or oven heat) surrounding it. Thus albuminous juices, which coagulate between 134° and 160° F. are not overcooked, though the liquid surrounding the meat be at the boiling point of water, 212° F. To give the best results, however, the liquid that supplies moisture for the cooking of meats containing much connective tissue should not exceed a temperature between 185° and 200° F. By lengthening the time of cooking, just as good results may be obtained and at a much lower degree of heat, as in the fireless cooker. In all cases the cooking is completed, when the fibers are tender and held together loosely yet compactly in a slightly gelatinous mass.

Without a thermometer, the proper temperature is assured, if the liquid " bubble " occasionally on one side of the kettle. A furious bubbling of the liquid hardens albuminous juices in solution; and in the cooking of meats, cut in small pieces, as joints of a fowl or pieces of round steak, cooked en casserole, or for beefsteak pie, the albuminous juices are hardened throughout.

CUTS OF LESS TENDER MEAT SUITABLE FOR FAMILY OF TWO

Beef is not as palatable when warmed over as is lamb, veal or fowl; thus pot-roast, boiled-and-braised beef, even in pieces of three or four pounds, are not recommended for the family of two. Other dishes of beef to take the place of these will be given. For stews, en casserole dishes, hashed beef and onions and beefsteak pies, meat from the round is the best; for beef tea, bouillon, cannelon of beef, or mince meat, select meat from the sticking piece. For corned beef, buy three pounds from the plate or the brisket. Carefully selected the lean and fat meat will be well proportioned. Either of these pieces, but more especially the brisket, will slice well when cold. Creamed corned beef is a dish that can be served with pleasure at least as often as once a week throughout the year, and well-made corned beef-and-potato hash never goes a begging. Corned beef, cut in tiny cubes and served with vegetables, potato cubes, peas and the like, and French or mayonnaise dressing, to which onion juice has been added, is easily prepared and deserves to be a favorite dish. Thus, with all these ways of presenting close, fine-grained brisket, four pounds may not be too much for an occasional purchase.

A fowl a year old may be cooked in moist heat until the fibers are tender, and the connective tissues are gelatinized, and then browned in the oven with much basting and dredging to approximate the glossy "carameled" appearance and flavor of a roast chicken.

A fowl a year old may be cooked to give quite a diversity of dishes. The breast, cut out neatly, may be cooked in a casserole for one meal; the rest may be stewed; of this the legs and wings may be fried, and on a third day the rest of the chicken, picked from the bones, with any of the breast left over, may be served in a pie.

Three pounds from the forequarter of yearling lamb provide a convenient piece for boiled lamb; the scrag, or neck end of the forequarter, is good for a stew, but the part containing the shoulder is preferable for boiling. This will serve for dinner and leave enough to be fine-chopped, when cold, and used for a second meal.

For veal stew, two or three pounds from any part of the forequarter may be selected; for other dishes of veal, the part of the hind leg that corresponds to the " round " of beef will be the choice.

For boiled ham, buy about three pounds from about the center of the ham; when cold cut in thin slivers across the grain of the meat. Very little of such a piece of ham will be left for chopping. Taking into account the very small quantity of waste in this piece and the large quantity of waste, when either the shank or the round end of a ham is selected, the higher price paid for the piece from the center will not prove an extravagance.

BOILED CORNED BEEF

Select three or four pounds from the plate or brisket; wash carefully in cold water, cover with cold water and heat slowly to the boiling point, then let simmer until the meat is tender. It will take about six hours. With a fireless cooker proceed as above, but, after simmering an hour and a half, set into the cooker to remain about ten hours. Serve with it boiled turnips or cauliflower.

NECK AND SHOULDER OF LAMB

The neck and shoulder of lamb, before referred to (see illustration, page 99), is an economical piece of meat, and capable of many variations in cooking. The whole piece shown in the illustration weighed about five pounds. The scrag, or neck end, — the fore leg is also on this part, — is the least desirable portion. This follows the rule that meat increases in value the further it is removed from the head. Either of these pieces (do not cut for a family of four or five) may be steamed, and the broth be thickened for a sauce; and they may be braised with vegetables or cut in pieces and cooked as a stew, a ragout, or a curry.

BOILED LAMB

Wipe the meat with a damp cloth, cover with boiling water, let boil five or six minutes, then simmer about three hours. Serve with caper sauce, boiled turnips, cauliflower or spinach, and potatoes.

SPANISH VEAL BALLS, EN CASSEROLE

About 1½ lbs. of veal (cutlet, from leg)
¼ cup of fat, salt pork or bacon
½ cup of fine, soft bread crumbs
1 egg, well-beaten
½ teaspoonful of salt

½ teaspoonful of paprika
1 teaspoonful of parsley (fine chopped)
1½ cups of cooked tomatoes
½ teaspoonful of salt
A slice of green or red pepper, chopped fine

Chop the veal, freed from skin, etc., and the pork very fine, add the other ingredients and mix all together thoroughly, then shape into balls by rolling portions of the mixture in the hands. Make about six balls. Roll the balls in flour, then sauté them in a little salt pork fat made hot in a frying pan. Heat about a cup and a half of canned tomatoes and turn into a casserole. Add the salt and chopped pepper, put in the veal balls, rinse out the frying pan with a spoonful of the tomato juice and pour into the casserole. Cover and let cook in a moderate oven an hour or more. Serve from the casserole, or from a platter, with a sprig of parsley in the top of each ball. Beef (from the round) may be prepared in the same way. Also a pound of veal steak or beef steak from the round, cut in pieces two inches square, may be browned and cooked with the tomatoes in the casserole. In this case two hours' cooking will be needed. The tomato may be strained, if desired, before it is set to cook.

CALF'S LIVER, HASHED

Cut from half to a whole pound of calf's liver into slices and pour over it boiling water to cover; let stand five or six minutes, then drain, wipe on a cloth and chop fine. Melt a tablespoonful of butter in a saucepan, put in the hashed liver, cover and let simmer very gently about one hour, stirring occasionally. Then add a dash of paprika, half a teaspoonful of salt and two or three tablespoonfuls of hot water or broth and serve when mixed thoroughly. Serve on rounds of buttered toast or with baked potatoes.

BREAST OF FOWL (ONE YEAR) EN CASSEROLE

With a sharp knife cut the breast, entire, from a fowl a year old and leave the rest of the flesh intact.

Have three or four tablespoonfuls of salt pork or bacon fat, butter or vegetable oil in a frying pan; when hot cook the breast over a brisk fire on the skin side until slightly browned, then set into an earthen dish; add about a dozen slices of carrot and an equal number of celery and pour in boiling water to half cover the chicken; put on the cover of the dish and let boil five or six minutes, then set to cook in a moderate oven for about two hours. Allow plenty of time for cooking, as the chicken may be kept hot in the dish after it is cooked enough. Renew the water as needed and add salt and pepper when about half cooked. Serve from the dish, or dispose the chicken on a platter with the vegetables around it.

HOW TO COOK AND SERVE REST OF THE FOWL

Separate the fowl at the joints, wash in cold water, drain, cover with boiling water and let boil six or seven minutes, then let simmer until tender. It will take about two hours, then add a teaspoonful of salt and cook longer if not perfectly tender.

FOWL SAUTÉD

Roll the legs and wings in flour seasoned with salt and pepper, then set them to cook in a frying pan containing three or four tablespoonfuls of hot, salt pork fat. When browned on one side turn the pieces and brown the other side. Serve garnished with celery tips and parsley. Serve also at the same time macaroni in tomato sauce, Turkish pilaf, plain boiled rice, curried rice, spinach a la crême, creamed potatoes, etc. Use some of the broth for a sauce. A partridge separated into joints may be cooked in the same way.

CHICKEN PIE FOR TWO

Pick the rest of the meat from the bones; add any bits left from the breast and chicken broth to cover the whole; add also salt and pepper to season. Heat to the boiling point, then turn into a small earthen baking dish. In the meanwhile sift together into a bowl a cup and a half of pastry flour, three level teaspoonfuls of baking powder and a scant half teaspoonful of salt. With the tips of the fingers work into the flour about one-third a cup of shortening, then with a knife mix the mass to a dough with sweet cream or rich milk in quantity as is needed. Turn the dough on to a floured board, turn it around with the knife, to flour it a little, then knead lightly and pat and roll into a sheet, a little larger than the dish. Cut out a round to fit the dish and make two crosswise slits in the center. Butter the edge of the dish, and set the crust in place. With a small round cutter stamp out several rounds from the rest of the dough. Use the same cutter and stamp the rounds into crescent and oval-shaped pieces; brush the under side of these with cold water and set them upon the crust in symmetrical fashion. Brush over the whole top with melted butter and bake about half an hour. If any

Chicken Breast, Cooked for Two — *Page 114*

Roast Chicken, Garnish of Cranberry Branches — *Page 117*

Chicken Pie for Two — *Page 116.*

chicken broth still remains, use it in making a sauce for the pie. To make a beefsteak pie, use small pieces of steak, simmered until tender, in the same way. For a partridge pie use the joints of the partridge, cooked tender, in the same way.

ROAST CHICKEN

We will suppose the chicken, weighing about three pounds and a half, has been picked and drawn. If long hairs remain upon it, take the legs in one hand, and the neck in the other, and thus turn the body in the flame from a tablespoonful of alcohol ignited on a tin plate or cover, to burn off the hairs. Cut off the feet at the knee joint. Turn back the skin on the neck, and cut off the neck itself on a line with the top of the wings. Do not cut off the skin. Wash the chicken inside and out and fill with bread stuffing. Sew up the opening through which the stuffing was put into the body of the chicken. Turn the third joints of the wings back over the neck skin, turned down upon the back. Run a threaded trussing needle through the flesh of the wing into the body, and let it come out through the skin of the neck, turned down on the back, and on a line with the place where it went in; put the needle back through the body and second wing an inch from where it came out, to leave a stitch in the back; now leave a stitch an inch long on the wing and run the needle through the body, to come out an inch from the place where it entered the first wing.

Tie the thread in a bow knot. Press the legs close to the body, drawing them up as high as possible. Run the threaded needle through the legs and body and return to the first side an inch from the place where the needle comes out. Tie in a bow knot. Spread a slice of salt pork over the breast of the chicken, set on a rack in a pan of suitable size and set to cook in a hot oven; after fifteen minutes, reduce the heat and let cook about two hours. Baste every ten minutes with the dripping in the pan, or with hot fat taken from the top of the soup kettle. Dredge with flour after each basting. An eight pound turkey requires at least three hours of cooking; often another hour is desirable. A fowl is cooked, when the joints may be easily separated.

BREAD STUFFING

Remove the crust from bread that has been baked at least twenty-four hours. Grate the bread or press it through a colander. To two cups of crumbs, add two fresh sage leaves, a sprig of summer savory, and a thin pepper-pod two inches long, all chopped fine, also a teaspoonful of onion juice, and half a teaspoonful of salt, with half a cup of melted butter. Mix all together very thoroughly and use to fill the chicken.

GIBLET SAUCE FOR ROAST CHICKEN

Pour the fat from the baking pan, to leave two tablespoonfuls in the pan; add two tablespoonfuls of flour, stir and cook until frothy, then add one cup of the water in which the giblets were cooked (these should be cooked while the chicken is being roasted), and stir until the boiling point is reached. Add the chopped giblets and serve.

BLANQUETTE OF VEAL

Have a pound and a half of the best end of a breast of veal; wipe the surface with a damp cloth and cut the meat into pieces two inches square; add water just to cover the veal, also a carrot, scraped and cut in quarters, two small onions, peeled and tied in a bit of cheese cloth, with a teaspoonful of celery seed, two branches of parsley, two cloves and a bit of bay leaf; cover and let simmer until the veal is tender (about an hour and a half); strain off the broth, discard the vegetables, and keep the veal hot. Melt three tablespoonfuls of butter; cook in it three tablespoonfuls of flour with a little salt and pepper, then add the broth and stir until the sauce boils. Beat the yolk of an egg; dilute with half a cup of cream and stir into the sauce; let cook, without boiling, stirring constantly until all is very hot, then stir in a tablespoonful of lemon juice and pour the sauce over the veal.

BEEF BALLS WITH SPAGHETTI OR MACARONI

Put over the fire half a can of red tomatoes, half a sweet green or red pepper, cut in shreds (after discarding the seeds), half an onion, cut in thin slices, two sprigs of parsley and a cup of water; let cook half an hour, then pass through a sieve into a casserole; add half a teaspoonful of salt and two tablespoonfuls of butter and the beef balls prepared as follows. Chop very fine half a pound of steak, freed from fat and stringy portions. Steak from the top of the round should be selected. To the chopped meat add one egg, beaten light, one fourth a cup of grated crumbs of bread, a grating of onion (about a teaspoonful) half a teaspoonful of salt and the same quantity of paprika; mix all together thoroughly, then divide the mixture into half a dozen portions; roll each into a compact ball. Have ready in a frying-pan two tablespoonfuls of hot fat (that from salt pork, bacon or the top of the soup kettle preferred); in this roll the beef balls until they are slightly browned on the outside, then drain on soft paper and put into the sauce in the casserole, cover the dish and let cook in the oven or on the back of the range about forty-five minutes. In the meantime cook half a cup of spaghetti, in whole or half lengths as preferred, in boiling, salted water until tender (it will take about half an hour); drain and rinse in cold water. When about ready to serve the dish, take out the meat balls, turn in the spaghetti and one-fourth a cup or more of Parmesan cheese and lift the spaghetti with a spoon and fork until it is thoroughly mixed with the sauce and cheese; return the beef balls, cover and let stand in the oven to become very hot, then serve in the casserole. Common American cheese may be used.

VEAL POT PIE, BAKED DUMPLINGS

Have about a pound and a half of veal from the breast or about a pound cut from the thick portion of the leg (cutlet or slice); cut the meat into small pieces, cover with boiling water and let simmer until tender. A slice of bacon or fat salt pork, cut in tiny strips, may be cooked with the veal and will improve the flavor. Turn the meat with broth to nearly cover into a baking dish. Season with half a teaspoonful of salt and a little pepper. Sift together one cup and a fourth of pastry flour, a scant half a teaspoonful of salt and two teaspoonfuls and a half of baking powder; into these work three tablespoonfuls of shortening, then stir in milk or water to make a dough that is not quite as stiff as for biscuits. Cut through and through the dough with a knife, then put it by the spoonful upon the meat, letting it rest upon the meat and cover the surface. Bake about twenty-five minutes.

CHAPTER VIII

LEFT-OVERS OF MEAT, FISH, ETC.

In families of two, it is often advisable, even during the summer, to prepare enough of certain articles of food for two or more meals at one and the same time; but, in general, the best results are obtained, both as regards palatability and digestibility, if just enough of each article be prepared for the meal and no more. Why bake three potatoes when only two are eaten? Why buy and cook six chops when four are just enough, and hot chops are more palatable and wholesome than cold ones? Plan to have everything so perfect that every morsel will be eaten, and nothing thrown away. If vegetables be left over and are to be used in salads, wait until the heat has left them, then cover securely, and plan for an early reappearance on the table. Serve cold meat cut in thin slivers; and, if made dishes are attempted, discard religiously all skin and gristle. Apply heat indirectly, by means of hot sauces and the like, lest strong heat impair the digestibility of the finished product.

CORNED BEEF HASH

Have ready an equal bulk of cold, corned beef and cold, boiled potatoes, chopped fine, and a hot frying-pan with two or three tablespoonfuls of straw-colored bacon fat. Turn in the meat and potatoes, add from three tablespoonfuls to a cup of broth, according to the quantity of hash, cover, and let become hot. Stir to mix thoroughly, make smooth in the pan, cover, and let stand, to crust over slightly next the pan. Roll as an omelet, and turn on to a hot platter. Garnish with slices of lemon and pickled beet. Two or three slices of cold crisped bacon if at hand may be chopped with the meat and potato.

HASH, CREOLE STYLE

1 slice of onion
¼ green or red pepper
2 tablespoonfuls of butter
1 cup of cooked meat (in cubes)
¾ cup of cold, boiled potatoes (in cubes)
½ cup of broth
¼ cup of tomato purée
Salt as needed.

Chop the onion and pepper very fine. Melt the butter in a hot frying pan (agate preferred) and in it cook the onion and pepper until they are softened; then add the meat and potato, both cut in tiny cubes; mix thoroughly, then add the broth and purée; mix again and set into the oven until hot throughout.

HASHED LAMB, WITH RICE AND PEAS

About 1 cup of chopped lamb
Broth, salt and pepper
½ cup of hot boiled rice
½ can or 1 cup fresh peas
Salt, black pepper, butter
½ teaspoonful sugar for canned peas

Remove all unedible portions from the meat before chopping. To the meat add broth and seasonings and let become very hot. Season the hot peas with salt and black pepper; add one or two tablespoonfuls of butter and, if canned peas are used, the sugar. Have all very hot. Dispose the meat in a mound in the center of a hot platter; surround with the hot rice and in turn surround this with the peas. Serve at once.

CREAMED HAM WITH POACHED EGGS

Put three-fourths a cup of milk in a double boiler with half a stalk of celery and a slice of onion; let cook fifteen minutes, then pick out the celery and onion and stir in a level tablespoonful and a half, each, of butter and flour, creamed together; stir until the mixture thickens, then cover and let cook ten minutes; stir in three-fourths a cup of fine-chopped ham (cold, boiled) and let stand to become very hot. Dip the edges of rounds of toast in boiling salted water. Set them on a hot serving dish, spread lightly with butter and then with the ham mixture. Finish with a carefully poached egg above the ham.

HAM-AND-MACARONI TIMBALES

½ cup of macaroni
Rapidly boiling water
Salt
½ cup boiled ham, chopped

1 egg, well beaten
¼ teaspoonful of salt
¼ teaspoonful of paprika
⅔ cup of milk or tomato purée

Cook the macaroni with salt in boiling water till tender, rinse in cold water and drain. Cut part of the macaroni into slices one-fourth an inch thick; take these, one by one, on the point of a skewer, dip in melted butter and use to line well-buttered moulds. As the melted butter cools, it will hold them in place. To the ham add one-fourth a cup of the tiny rings of macaroni, the egg, salt, paprika and liquid, mix thoroughly and use to fill the moulds. There will be about a cup and a half of material. Measure the moulds, then you will know how many to line. Let cook in hot water on folds of paper, either in the oven or covered closely on the top of the range or in a double boiler. Serve with a cup of tomato or white sauce, to which the rest of the macaroni has been added.

CREAMED CHICKEN

1¼ cups of cooked chicken cut in cubes
2 tablespoonfuls of butter
2 tablespoonfuls of flour
¼ teaspoonful of salt
¼ teaspoonful of pepper
1 cup of milk or thin cream

Make a sauce of the butter, flour, seasonings and milk. Add the chicken. Serve on toast or on corn fritters. Peas may be added with the chicken.

RECHAUFÉE OF HAM WITH BROILED APPLES

Melt about half a tumbler of currant jelly in a saucepan set over boiling water; lay in it some thin slices of cold, boiled ham and cover closely to become hot. In the meantime core three or more apples, cut them into slices or rings half an inch thick and remove the skin, also any of the seed cavities that may remain. Have ready a hot broiler; rub it over with a bit of fat ham or with a piece of butter in a cloth. Set the apples in the broiler and let cook over the coals about three minutes, on each side, or until the apple is softened throughout. With a spatula remove the apples to the edge of the dish on which the ham has been disposed. Put a tiny bit of butter on each ring of apple and serve at once.

CHICKEN BECHAMEL IN POTATO PATTY CASES

1⅓ cups of cold, cooked chicken in cubes
2 tablespoonfuls of butter
2 tablespoonfuls of flour
¼ teaspoonful of salt
¼ teaspoonful of paprika
½ cup of chicken broth
½ cup of cream
3 cups of well-seasoned mashed potato
1 yolk of egg

Make a sauce of the butter, flour, seasonings and liquid, add the chicken and heat over hot water. The potato should be just moist enough to flow through a tube easily. On a buttered baking sheet spread rounds of potato half an inch thick and nearly three inches across. Put the rest of the potato in a pastry bag and with star tube pipe potato on to the rounds, as if building a burr basket. Brush over the cases thus formed with the egg, and set into the oven, to make hot and brown the edges. Remove with a spatula or broad knife to plates, fill the open space in the centers with the chicken preparation and serve.

Cooking for Two 127

COTTAGE PIE

Cook remnants of cold roast lamb or veal, cut in thin slices, in stock made of the trimmings and bones, reinforced by chicken bones and remnants of uncooked meat, if at hand, until tender. Season with salt and pepper, and turn into a baking-dish. For a pint of meat with cup or more of broth, have ready about three cups of mashed potato, seasoned with salt and pepper and thoroughly beaten with butter and a little cream. Spread a layer of prepared potato over the meat, then put the rest on with a pastry bag and star tube. Brush over the potato with the yolk of an egg, beaten and diluted with a tablespoonful of milk. Set the dish in the oven, to brown the edges of the potato, then serve at once.

BOSTON BAKED BEANS, REHEATED WITH BACON

Have ready as many rounds of toast as individuals to serve. The toast may be made of any kind of bread preferred, with all crust removed. Put the beans in an agate dish; add two or three tablespoonfuls of boiling water, cover the dish closely and set into the oven to become very hot. In the meantime, roll strips of thin bacon (one for each service) into a compact shape, pass a wooden toothpick through each, to hold it in shape, put all in a frying basket, and let cook in deep fat about two minutes or until crisp; drain carefully. Dip the edges of the slices of toast in boiling, salted water and dispose on a hot dish;

spread each slice with butter, dispose the beans on the slices, and a roll of bacon on each. The bacon may be omitted.

RECHAUFÉE OF LAMB, CREOLE STYLE

Melt three tablespoonfuls of butter; in it cook one tablespoonful, each, of onion and green pepper, chopped fine; cook until softened and yellowed, but not browned; add three level tablespoonfuls of flour and cook until frothy, then add a cup of broth and half a cup of tomato purée and stir until boiling; add half a teaspoonful of salt, a dash of paprika, half a teaspoonful of grated horseradish, a teaspoonful of lemon juice and two cups of cooked meat, cut in small pieces and neatly trimmed. Serve in a border of plain, boiled rice.

RIZZOLETTI

½ cup of rice
1½ cups of stock milk or tomato purée
½ teaspoonful of salt
1 slice of onion
¼ cup of butter
¼ cup of flour
¼ teaspoonful of salt
1⅓ cups of milk stock or tomato purée
⅓ cup of chopped chicken
1 or 2 eggs

Blanch the rice in cold water, add the stock (that made from bones and giblets of fowl is good for this purpose) and the salt and let cook until the grains are tender but whole. Cook the slice of onion in the butter, add the flour and salt and let cook until frothy, then add the liquid and let boil. Remove the onion and stir one-third a cup of the chicken into one-third a cup of sauce. Into the rest of the sauce stir about a cup of the rice. The dish is at its best when each kernel of rice is surrounded with sauce. Turn both mixtures on to plates to cool. When cold form the rice into balls, make a depression in each ball and put in a little of the chicken mixture, cover with the rice mixture. Roll the balls in soft, sifted bread crumbs, then cover with beaten egg, and then roll in crumbs. Fry in deep fat.

QUESTIONS ON COOKING MEAT AND FISH

1. What compound is found in comparatively large quantity in meat, to which no particular reference has been made?

2. What causes the puffy appearance seen in a properly broiled steak, when it is taken from the fire?

3. Why have steak cut not less than an inch and one-fourth in thickness? If not able to answer this, cook a thick and a thin piece of steak, and compare the results.

4. Which contains the greater quantity of nutritious properties, 2 pounds of uncooked meat, or 2 pounds of meat weighed after being properly cooked?

5. What causes meat to shrink, when boiling water is poured over it, or when it is plunged into boiling water?

6. In broiling steak, etc., why for the first three minutes is the meat turned every ten seconds?

How does pan-broiling differ from sautéing and frying?

7. Which is the more easily digested, meat or fish, and why?

8. What is gained by frying fish in deep fat?

CHAPTER IX

GELATINOUS SOUPS AND JELLIES. PROTEID SPARERS

IN the first chapter we spoke of "the gelatinoids," a group of proteids that were not as important as the group containing albumin, gluten, etc., inasmuch as they cannot alone supply the nitrogen needed by the body. Though they be not the equivalent of true proteids, they may replace some of the proteid in the diet. They are easily digested and absorbed and tend to promote nutrition. They also furnish variety in diet. The gelatinoids, with which we have most to do in cooking, are found largely in the connective tissues of meat and in the ligaments and bones of veal and chickens. This gelatinous principle is dissolved by heat when moisture is present. The main point to keep in mind is that connective tissue and bone are both practically flavorless and, if this principle is to be made use of in cookery, flavor must be added to it. If the juices of the meat be used, then rich flavor is assured. When these can be had only in small quantity, then flavor must be secured from vegetables, herbs and the like. In making sweet dishes, we use the gelatine of commerce, and for flavor coffee, chocolate, wine, fruit juices, etc. Such dishes do not possess high nutritive value of themselves, but nutriment may be added, when advisable, by the use of eggs or cream.

SOUP STOCK FROM BONES OF A ROAST FOWL OR ROAST OF VEAL

Break up the bones, carefully, discarding any dressing that may be attached to them. If a few bits of raw lamb (ends of chops) or veal be at hand, these will give flavor to the soup. Also if uncooked giblets, heart, liver and gizzard, or the neck of the fowl be available, the soup will be much improved. Cover the materials to be used with cold water, and let heat slowly to the boiling point, then let simmer an hour, or longer, if uncooked material were added. Add now half an onion, cut in bits, half a small carrot, cut in bits, a stalk of celery or half a tablespoonful of celery seed, a sprig of parsley, six peppercorns and a scant teaspoonful of salt, and let cook nearly an hour, then strain off the broth. Set this aside in a cool place and when cold remove the fat. This fat may be used in making the thickening, if a thickened soup be desired.

SOUP 1

Have ready two or three tablespoonfuls of cooked rice and one-fourth a cup of bits of cooked chicken; reheat the soup, add the rice and chicken with salt and pepper as needed.

SOUP 2

Reheat the soup stock in a double boiler; beat the yolk of an egg — two are better — add half a cup of thin cream and stir into the soup. Season as needed and stir until the egg is set, then serve at once.

SOUP 3

To the stock add half to a full cup of tomato purée, serve in this way or finish as soup 1 or 2.

SOUP 4

Melt two tablespoonfuls of butter, or fat taken from the top of the stock; cook in it two tablespoonfuls of flour; add half a cup of cooked spinach, pressed through a sieve, and half a cup of the stock; stir until boiling, then stir into the rest of the stock. Season to taste. The yolk of an egg and cream may be added at the last moment. This is a most delicious soup.

SOUP 5

Cooked celery, onions, peas, or asparagus may be pressed through a sieve, and from half to a full cup be used in place of the spinach in soup 4.

CHICKEN STOCK OR BROTH FROM UNCOOKED FOWL

Have the fowl separated into pieces at the joints; wipe the pieces with a small piece of cheese cloth wrung out of cold water; put into a saucepan, and pour on cold water to cover well the pieces of fowl; heat slowly to the boiling point, then let simmer until the meat is tender. Pour off the liquid and set it aside to become cold, then remove all of the fat. Season with salt and reheat, or use in any of the soups given above. There should be a pint of broth for each pound of chicken taken. If less broth be secured, water may be added. Use the pieces of fowl in any of the dishes given for stewed fowl. If the broth jellies when cold, scrape off the fat, then wipe the surface with tissue paper or a piece of cheese cloth wrung out of hot water. A stalk of celery and half an onion may be cooked with the fowl for flavor.

SOUP FROM REMNANTS OF BEEF OR LAMB ROASTS

Prepare the stock in the same manner as when the bones and remnants of roast fowl are used. Tomato purée is a good addition to this stock. Cooked macaroni, cut in rings, makes a good garnish for the soup.

CHICKEN BREAST IN JELLY

Use broth from either cooked or uncooked fowl. If the broth makes a firm jelly when cold, gelatine is unnecessary. If the broth does not make a very firm jelly, add gelatine, about a level tablespoonful to a pint of broth. Soften the gelatine in one-fourth a cup of cold water, and dissolve in the broth, freed of fat and made hot. If cooked bones have been used freely

Chicken Potato Patty Cases — *Page 126.*

Boston Bared Beans on Toast. Bacon Rolls — *Page 127.*

Rizzoletti, "Left-over" Dish. — *Page 128.*

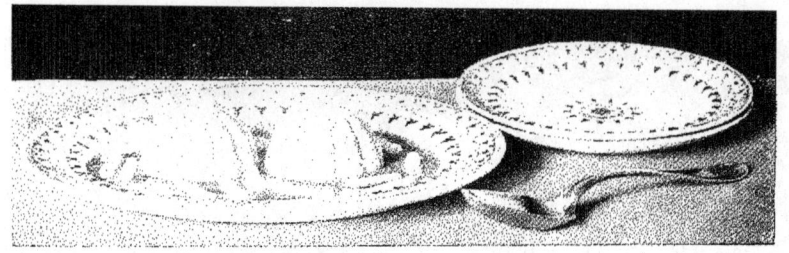

Ham and Macaroni Timbales, for Two — *Page 124.*

Cottage Pie — *Page 127.*

Veal Pot Pie, Baked Dumplings — *Page 121*

in making the broth, the jelly will not be very clear. It may be clarified a little by the use of the white of an egg. Crush the shell, nicely washed before the egg is broken, and beat the white slightly, mix these through the broth and heat the whole (broth, gelatine and egg) slowly to the boiling point, stirring constantly meanwhile. Let boil five minutes, then keep hot ten minutes (without boiling) while the mixture settles. Skim carefully, then strain through a table napkin, laid over a colander or strainer. Add seasoning as is needed. Put a little of the chilled broth into a mould, set in a pan of ice and water; when nearly firm put in some thin slices of cooked chicken, add more of the chilled-and-partly "set" broth and continue with chicken and broth, until the mould or moulds are filled. Serve when firm, with lettuce, cress or celery, and salad dressing.

COOKED CHICKEN, CHOPPED AND MOULDED IN ASPIC

Have ready a cup of clear soup (consommé, chicken broth or tomato and chicken bouillon) and a cup of fine-chopped, cooked chicken. Make the broth hot and in it dissolve half a level tablespoonful of gelatine that has been softened in three or four tablespoonfuls of cold water. Add a little of the gelatine mixture to the chicken. Set the moulds in ice and water, and put in the chicken and broth in alternate layers. Let each layer harden before another is poured in. Serve, turned from the moulds, with lettuce and French dressing. To unmold, immerse a mould in warm water to the height of the mixture within. With a sharp-pointed knife, loosen the mixture from the edge of the mould, then tip the mould first at one point, then at another, to let air in between the mould and the mixture, then invert over the center of the serving dish, when the mould should be lifted from the jelly. Repeat the process as needed.

COFFEE JELLY

In making the coffee for breakfast make one or two extra cups; strain all the coffee from the grounds when pouring the coffee at table. Let it settle, then pour off and use the top of the coffee. For two small cups (half a pint) of jelly, put half a level tablespoonful of granulated gelatine into four or five tablespoonfuls of cold water to stand about fifteen minutes; add a scant quarter of a cup of sugar and the cup of hot coffee; stir over the fire until the gelatine and sugar are dissolved, then strain into the cups. Serve with cream or a boiled custard. For fruit jellies see Chapter XIII.

EMERGENCY SOUP

½ cup of half-inch cubes of carrot
½ cup slices of celery
1 onion, cut in shreds
¼ cup of butter or fat from stock

1 cup of half-inch potato cubes
4 cups of water or broth
(2 tablespoonfuls of meat extract *with water*)
Salt and pepper

Melt the butter or fat and in it cook the carrot, celery and onion ten minutes. Cook the potato in boiling water five minutes, drain, rinse in cold water and drain again. Add the potato to the other vegetables with the water or broth and let cook one hour. Add the meat extract, if water was used instead of broth, with salt and pepper as needed.

CHICKEN-AND-TOMATO SOUP

1 tablespoonful of butter or fat from stock
2 slices of onion, chopped fine
2 sprigs of parsley, chopped fine
½ can of tomatoes
3 cups of chicken or veal broth
1 tablespoonful of cornstarch
2 or 3 tablespoonfuls of cold water
Salt and pepper

Cook the onion and parsley in the hot fat till yellowed. Add the tomatoes and broth and let simmer fifteen minutes. Press through a sieve. Reheat to the boiling point; stir in the cornstarch mixed with the cold water; let cook ten minutes. Skim and season.

SOUP MITOUNÉE

2 ounces of bread (2 or 3 slices)
5 cups of broth
Salt and pepper

Free the bread from crust, break it in pieces, add to the broth and let simmer about twenty minutes. Stir the soup occasionally with a wooden spoon. When all of the bread is reduced to a pulp and the soup is thickened uniformly, add salt and pepper as needed and serve.

LAMB - AND - TOMATO SOUP

1 pint of lamb broth (liquid in which lamb was boiled)	¼ carrot, cut in match-like pieces
½ cup of tomato purée (cooked tomatoes strained)	¼ green or red pepper, cut in shreds
½ an onion, cut in thin shreds	¼ cup of cooked rice
	½ teaspoonful of salt

Cook the pieces of onion, carrot and pepper in boiling water till tender; drain and add to the broth with the tomato, rice and salt. Let simmer five minutes.

CHICKEN - AND - TOMATO BOUILLON
(For a company dinner, Thanksgiving, etc.)

½ an onion	1 pint of water
¼ carrot	1 quart of chicken broth
3 tablespoonfuls of butter or dripping	Liquid drained from 1 can of tomatoes
1 soup-bag	Whites of 2 eggs
1 parsley branch	Crushed shell of several eggs
Yellow rind of 1 lemon	Salt and pepper

Cut the onion and carrot in thin slices, and cook in the butter until softened; add the " soup-bag " (bags of sweet herbs and spices prepared especially for soup) parsley, lemon rind and water and let simmer half an hour. Add the broth, liquid drained from the tomatoes, the whites of egg slightly beaten, crushed shells, salt and pepper. Mix all together thoroughly, then set over the fire and stir constantly until the boiling point is reached. Let boil five minutes, then draw to a cool part of the range and let stand ten minutes. Strain through a napkin laid over a colander. Reheat before serving. The liquid in which a fowl has been cooked, is preferable, but broth made from the remnants and bones of a roast fowl may be used.

STANDARD BEEF BROTH

2 lbs. of beef (one-fourth bone)
2 pints of cold water
2 tablespoonfuls, each, of carrot and celery
A slice of green or red pepper
Half a "soup-bag" or piece of bay leaf
8 peppercorns
½ small onion with 4 cloves
A branch of parsley

Two pounds of beef from the hind shank is a good selection. There should not be more than half a pound of bone. Wipe the meat and cut it into small pieces. If there is marrow in the bone, remove it and let it melt in a hot frying pan: into this or other fat, put about one-fourth of the meat and let cook, turning occasionally until well browned. Put this meat with the rest of the meat and the bone into a saucepan. Add part of the water. Pour the rest of the water into the frying pan, and let stand on the range until the browned juices are dissolved from the pan, then turn over the meat. Cover and let slowly heat to the boiling point; then let simmer three or four hours; add the vegetables and seasonings and let simmer another hour. Then strain and finish as other broth. When finished measure and if needed add water to make one quart of broth. This may be cleared with the whites of eggs as the "Chicken and Tomato Bouillon" was cleared.

FISH BROTH FOR SAUCES, SOUPS, ETC.

Cover the bones, skin and trimmings of fish with cold water. Add a tablespoonful, each, of carrot, onion and celery, a branch of parsley and a piece of pepper pod for each pint of water. Let simmer an hour or more, then strain off and use as meat broth.

QUESTIONS

1. What is the object of browning part of the meat used in making standard broth?
2. Why are vegetables, as onion, carrot, etc., sometimes browned in fat before adding them to soup stock? Think of advantages and disadvantages of doing this.
3. What dishes would you serve with Soup 4, made without egg or cream, to provide a perfect meal?

CHAPTER X

INTRODUCING THE COOKING OF CARBOHYDRATES, THE TRUE HEAT AND WORK FOODS

"Cooking is an essential preliminary to the ingestion of starch-containing foods, for uncooked starch cannot be utilized in any degree by man." — *Chittenden.*

SAUCES AND CREAM SOUPS

Up to this time we have been dealing with proteid food that is cooked delicately; but in the average diet of an adult only one part of proteid is needed for five and three-tenths parts of carbohydrate and fat, and of the carbohydrate the principal part is starch. Prehistoric and early man, endowed with strong digestive power, was undoubtedly able to digest, in some measure, crude starch. But the digestive power of civilized man has been gradually weakened by his habits of life, and, in order that his organism may convert starch into a form that can be made use of in his body, it must first be changed, by the action of strong heat, into sweet substances akin to sugar.

In this connection, it may be well to add that the mouth is the great starch-digesting organ of the body. The salivary glands of the mouth secrete a ferment, which continues the digestive process begun in cooking. It is well to lighten the labor of the stomach by dividing minutely in the mouth meat and other proteid substances, yet this is not obligatory. But when we come to the mastication of starchy food we are dealing with quite another matter. Starchy food *must* be chewed and chewed until it is impregnated through and through with ptyalin, the starch-digesting ferment of the mouth, or the chances are that the starch will be cast out of the system as waste material.

In some forms of cooking more starch is changed into sweet substances than in others. Thus in a baked potato the conversion of starch has been carried further than it has in a boiled potato, and in the brown crust of a loaf of bread than in the crumb at the center.

In general, the higher the degree of heat to which it is possible to subject the starch, the greater is the conversion, though heat at a lower temperature, long continued, brings about very nearly the same result. Let us see now how the cooking of starch may be carried out in the matter of sauces.

REGARDING SAUCES

Often richness or moisture, one or both, would improve an article of food, and, sometimes, we wish to add to the bulk of certain articles, to make them " go farther." In either case we may have recourse to sauces. Sauces are combinations of fat — usually butter or dripping — milk, broth, vegetable purées, or water and flavorings, with eggs or some form of starch, to give body or consistence to the mixture. The thing that interests us just now is the ways in which the starch in our dish may be cooked with the other ingredients, to produce the desired result. This may be done in three different ways.

PROPORTIONS OF THE INGREDIENTS IN SAUCES

Sometimes we may wish a very rich and buttery sauce; and, for some uses, a very thick sauce, as in making croquettes; for general use, however, no matter how the sauce is put together, the proportions of the various ingredients are the same, *i. e.*: For one cup of sauce, take

2 tablespoonfuls of fat   ¼ teaspoonful of pepper
2 tablespoonfuls of flour   1 cup of liquid
¼ teaspoonful of salt

1. Melt the fat in a small saucepan, set directly over the fire; add the flour, salt and pepper, and stir until frothy throughout, then add the cold liquid and stir constantly and vigorously until the mixture is smooth, thick and boiling. The liquid may be added hot, if the hot mixture of butter and flour be cooled before such addition.

2. Heat milk or cream over hot water (in double boiler), other liquids directly over the fire. Beat the butter to a cream; gradually beat into it the flour and seasonings; dilute this with a little of the hot liquid, and stir until the ingredients are evenly

blended; then turn into the rest of the hot liquid and continue to stir (over the fire) until the sauce boils and is smooth, or (in double boiler) until the sauce thickens and is smooth, then cover and let cook ten minutes or longer, stirring occasionally.

3. Use a little of the cold liquid in stirring the flour and seasonings into a smooth batter. Scald the rest of the liquid, if it be cream or milk, over hot water, or heat other liquids to the boiling point directly over the fire. Stir the batter into the hot liquid — dilute first with a little of the hot liquid, then when smooth stir into the rest of the hot liquid. If the double boiler be used, stir and cook until smooth, then cover and let cook ten or fifteen minutes, stirring occasionally; if cooked directly over the fire stir and cook until boiling. Just before serving, add the butter in little bits, beating in each bit thoroughly before the next is added.

THEORY OF THE THREE WAYS OF MAKING SAUCES

By the first method the sauce is very quickly made; thus, when time is an object, this way should be employed. The temperature of hot fat is considerably higher than that of scalding milk or boiling water or broth; thus, when the flour (starch) is cooked in hot fat, it is cooked more quickly and thoroughly than when it is cooked in liquid. But fat that has been heated to a high temperature is not very easily digested, and thus the first method of making a sauce should not be chosen, when the food is designed for children or those of weak digestion. What is gained in the thorough cooking of the starch is more than lost in the overheating of the fat.

In cooking starch in the liquid considerably more time must be allowed. In following the last method the flavor of the butter is more nearly retained. All sauces made by these formulas are known as white sauces. When milk or cream is used as the liquid, the sauce is called *cream sauce;* when tomato is used *tomato sauce.* When the broth (veal, chicken or fish) is flavored with vegetables the sauce is called *Velouté.*

HOW TO ADD YOLKS OF EGG TO A SAUCE

Any of these sauces may be enriched by adding yolks of eggs or butter. The yolks, well beaten, will curdle, if they be stirred into the sauce while it is boiling. Wait until the sauce is finished and it is time to serve it. Have it standing in boiling water, or on some part of the range where it will not boil. Put a few spoonfuls into the egg, mix thoroughly, then stir into the rest of the sauce. Continue to stir until the sauce thickens a little, which shows that the egg is cooked. Then serve at once.

DRAWN BUTTER SAUCE

⅓ cup of butter
2 tablespoonfuls of flour
¼ teaspoonful of salt

¼ teaspoonful of pepper
1 cup of cold water

Melt half the butter in a small saucepan; add the flour and seasonings and cook until frothy; add the water and stir constantly until the mixture thickens and boils; let boil three or four minutes, then gradually beat in the rest of the butter, a little at a time.

CAPER SAUCE
(For boiled lamb)

Prepare a drawn butter sauce, using lamb broth or water as the liquid. When ready to serve add one or two tablespoonfuls of capers drained from the liquid in the bottle. A teaspoonful of lemon juice may be added if desired.

EGG SAUCE
(For boiled fish)

To a cup of drawn butter sauce add a hard-cooked egg, cut in thin slices or chopped fine.

MOCK HOLLANDAISE SAUCE
(For boiled and baked fish, cauliflower, etc.)

1 tablespoonful of butter
1 tablespoonful of flour
¼ teaspoonful of salt
¼ teaspoonful of pepper
½ cup of white stock
Yolks of 2 eggs
¼ cup of butter
Juice of ½ a lemon

Use the butter, flour, seasonings and stock in making a sauce in the usual manner. The stock should be flavored with onion, etc. Cream the four tablespoonfuls of butter and beat the yolks into it, then gradually beat the mixture into the sauce. Finish with the juice of half a lemon.

BROWN SAUCE

There is another general variety of sauce that differs from the white sauce principally in color. The liquid in this sauce may be vegetable purée, fish, or meat broth, but it is usually beef broth made dark by browning the ingredients of which it is made in hot fat. For this sauce, cook the fat until browned but not burned; add, for a high-flavored sauce, one or two slices of onion, two slices of carrot, a bit of parsley and half a stalk of celery, all chopped rather coarse; let these brown in the fat, stirring constantly that they may not burn; now add three level tablespoonfuls of flour, and the usual quantity of salt and pepper and continue stirring and cooking until the flour assumes a reddish brown tint; then add the cold liquid, and stir and cook until smooth and boiling, then strain. You will note that the proportions remain the same as for the white sauce, save that more flour is used. By the long cooking in the hot fat the conversion of the starch in the flour is carried farther than in the white sauce and the thickening property of the starch is lessened, thus more flour is required.

For a brown tomato sauce proceed as in making the brown sauce, but use tomato purée as the liquid.

THICK SAUCE FOR FOUNDATION OF CROQUETTES

4 tablespoonfuls of fat
⅓ cup of flour
¼ teaspoonful of salt
¼ teaspoonful of pepper
1 cup of liquid

Prepare in one of the three ways given previously, page 143.

THIN SAUCE FOR FOUNDATION OF CREAM SOUPS

1 tablespoonful of butter
1 tablespoonful of flour
¼ teaspoonful of salt
¼ teaspoonful of pepper
1 cup of milk, thin cream or white broth

CREAM SOUPS

It is but a step from cream sauce to cream soup. Use milk or thin cream in making the cup of sauce, then add from half to a whole cup of any kind of purée at hand. By purée is meant any food substance cooked (usually in water, though in some cases, as with tomatoes, water is unnecessary) and pressed through a sieve. Sometimes more and sometimes less of the article may be pressed through the sieve; dilute the portion in the sieve with some of the liquid that has already dripped through so as to push through as much of the article as is possible. The larger part of tomatoes, onions, spinach, peas and beans will pass the sieve; less of celery, green corn and asparagus may be pressed through, on account of the tough cellular structure of the latter vegetables. Cooked fish and meat, free from skin and bone, then pounded smooth and passed through the sieve may be used in these soups. The fish and meat should be diluted with fish or meat broth, or the resulting soup will be too thick. Salt and pepper, and, occasionally, a little more hot milk or broth are needed. A gravy strainer, set into one of the parts of a small double boiler, and a wooden pestle are indispensable in reducing the cooked material to the purée form. With these soups serve croutons, toasted crackers, or pulled bread.

CROUTONS FOR CREAM SOUPS

Cut stale bread into slices from one-fourth to one-third an inch thick; remove the crusts, spread the surfaces with butter, and cut the slices into pieces an inch square. Set these into the oven to brown, turning to brown both sides.

TOASTED CRACKERS

Split the common Boston or soda cracker, toast over the fire or in the oven, spread lightly with butter and serve. These may be spread with butter and then browned in the oven, but they are more wholesome spread with butter after they are browned.

PULLED BREAD

Remove the crust from a loaf of fresh-baked bread and cut and pull the loaf into halves, lengthwise; repeat this cutting and pulling until the pieces are about an inch thick; they may be the length of the loaf or shorter. Dry these in a slack oven until they snap when broken. They should be amber in color. Reheat before serving.

CREAM-OF-PEA SOUP

Press half a cup of peas and the liquid in which they were cooked through the sieve. Melt a tablespoonful of butter; add a tablespoonful of flour and one-fourth a teaspoonful, each, of salt and black pepper and cook until frothy in the butter; add one cup of milk and cook, stirring constantly, until smooth and boiling; add the pea purée and stir until smoothly blended and again boiling. If too thick add a little hot milk or broth with additional salt and pepper and serve at once. If canned peas be used, add to them half a teaspoonful of sugar. Canned or fresh peas may be substituted for the corn in the "Cream-of-Corn Soup." These soups provide a nutritious luncheon.

CREAM-OF-CORN SOUP (TO SERVE FOUR)
(Formula with variations)

Press enough canned or fresh corn, chopped fine, through a sieve to yield one-third a cup of purée. Beat one egg and the yolk of another; add one-fourth a teaspoonful, each, of salt and black pepper, three tablespoonfuls of cream and the purée. Mix thoroughly and turn into four buttered timbale moulds. Set these in a pan on several folds of paper, surround with water at the boiling point, and let cook in a slow oven until firm. Serve hot, one in each plate of soup. Slice half an onion fine; add a sprig of parsley (fresh or dried) and let cook in two tablespoonfuls of butter until the onion is softened and yellowed; then add one cup of the chopped corn and a pint of broth or hot water (broth from chicken giblets and bones is good) and let simmer ten or fifteen minutes. Pour the liquid through a sieve and pound the corn with a pestle, then press as much of the corn as is possible through a sieve, diluting it, meanwhile, with the hot liquid; then reheat the purée. Melt two tablespoonfuls of butter; in it cook two tablespoonfuls of flour, half a teaspoonful of salt and a little pepper, then add one cup of milk; stir until thickened and boiling, then add the purée and one-fourth a cup of cream.

DELICATE CELERY SOUP

1 large slice of onion
3 stalks of celery
3 cups of milk
3 tablespoonfuls of butter
3 tablespoonfuls of flour
1 teaspoonful of salt
½ teaspoonful of pepper
1 cup of cream

Break the stalks of celery in pieces and pound these in a wooden bowl; add to the onion and milk and set to cook in a double boiler. Let cook twenty minutes. In the meantime melt the butter and in it cook the flour and seasonings; add the cream and stir until the sauce thickens and boils, then strain into it the celery and milk.

CREAM-OF-TOMATO SOUP

1 cup of tomato purée
2 cups of thin white sauce
Additional seasoning, if needed

CREAM-OF-CHICKEN SOUP

½ cup of chicken purée
2 cups of chicken broth seasoned with vegetables
1 cup of thin cream sauce
1 yolk of egg with 2 tablespoonfuls of cream

CREAM-OF-STRING BEAN SOUP

½ cup of string bean purée
1½ cups thin white sauce
½ cup of milk scalded with a slice of onion, and half a stalk of celery
Salt and pepper as needed

CREAM-OF-SPINACH SOUP

¼ cup of spinach purée
1½ cups of thin white sauce
½ cup of milk scalded with a slice of onion and 3 slices of carrot
Salt and pepper as needed

CREAM-OF-OYSTER SOUP

1 cup of oysters (half a pint)
½ cup of cold water
1½ cups of thin white sauce
½ cup of hot cream

Pour the cold water over the oysters; take each oyster in the fingers, rinse in the water and remove bits of shell that may be attached to it. Chop the oysters fine and press as much as possible through a sieve. Scald whatever does not pass the sieve with the water (strained through a cloth to remove sand) and add to the purée; stir the whole into the hot sauce and add the cream with salt and pepper as needed.

CREAM-OF-OYSTER SOUP, NO. 2

1 cup of oysters
½ cup of cold water
1½ cups of thin white sauce

CHOPPED CHICKEN MOLDED WITH ASPIC — *Page 135.*

STRAINER, CLOTH AND COLANDER, READY TO STRAIN LIQUID ASPIC OR CONSOMMÉ — *Page 135*

HARD COOKED EGGS MOLDED IN ASPIC.

One Service of Cream of Corn Soup — *Page 150*

Utensils needed to make Purées for Cream Soup — *Page 142*

Pour the water over the oysters and remove bits of shell. Strain the water through two folds of cheese cloth. Heat it to the boiling point, add the oysters and again heat to the boiling point; stir into the hot sauce. A slice of onion and stalk of celery, scalded in the sauce, make a variation of flavor.

OYSTER STEW

½ cup of cold water
1 pint of oysters
1½ cups of hot milk or water
½ teaspoonful of salt

½ teaspoonful of white or black pepper
3 tablespoonfuls of butter
¼ cup of cracker crumbs

Pour the cold water over the oysters, rinse each and remove bits of shell; add the hot liquid and bring quickly to the boiling point; add the butter, seasonings and crumbs and serve at once.

CHAPTER XI

CARBOHYDRATES (WORK FOODS) CONTINUED

"Few things show the difference between comfortable and slovenly housekeeping more quickly than the dressing of vegetables." — *Mrs Rorer*

THE COOKING OF VEGETABLES (INCLUDING CEREALS, MACARONI, ETC.)

In cooking vegetables the questions most often asked refer to:

1. The temperature of the water in which the vegetables are set to cook.
2. The temperature of the water during cooking, *i. e.*, Shall the water simmer, simply boil, or boil rapidly?
3. The quantity of water (much or little).
4. The time to add salt, also the quantity.
5. Is soda ever added to the water, and, if so, for what purpose?

Save for the first item, no rule can be made that will apply to all vegetables.

TEMPERATURE OF WATER IN WHICH VEGETABLES ARE SET TO COOK

All vegetables are set to cook in water that is boiling at the time they are put into it.

All wilted vegetables should be revived in cold water before cooking.

All dried vegetables should be soaked in cold water several hours, or over night, before cooking.

A knowledge of the composition of a vegetable gives the key to the way in which it is to be treated during the cooking.

COMPOUNDS IN VEGETABLES

Starch is the dominant principle in most vegetables, though protein, sugar, fat, mineral matter and water (one or all) are combined with the starch. In some vegetables the starch is largely in the form of cellulose or woody tissue, but, in whatever form it may be, starch must be thoroughly cooked or it is unwholesome.

Vegetables containing a good proportion of starch sugar or fat have a corresponding high food value, and in selecting food supplies are classed by themselves. Green vegetables and all those deficient in the above compounds are eaten for flavor and variety as also to secure bulk in food so necessary for perfect elimination of waste products. Whatever the vegetable may be, the cooking is to be carried out in a manner to retain the particular compound which makes it valuable.

VEGETABLES WITH ONLY SLIGHT TRACE OF STARCH

Vegetables, like lettuce, endive, celery (inner blanched stalks), tomatoes, cucumbers, and small, quickly-grown radishes, contain but a slight trace of starch. They are mostly water and mineral salts, both of which would be lost largely during cooking, unless the cooking be done at a gentle simmer, and the water be retained as food. These vegetables, then, might be exempt from cooking, save for variety. When cooked, no more water should be used than can be served with them, and the cooking should be at a gentle simmer.

VEGETABLES CONTAINING SUGAR, PROTEIN AND SOME STARCH

Green peas and asparagus contain so much starch that cooking is a necessity, but, to retain the sugar and other compounds, the cooking should be at a gentle simmer, in a small measure of water, and the water should form a part of the finished dish. The same is true of spinach; the water that clings to the leaves in washing being sufficient for the cooking.

VEGETABLES WITH STARCH AS CELLULOSE

Parsnips, salsify, carrots and turnips contain but little starch other than that found in their cellular structure; this fiber, like animal fiber, is hardened by high heat, and cooking should not be carried on at a temperature higher than the boiling point of water. The cooking should be prolonged until the fiber is tender, but no longer. All vegetables should be removed from the fire as soon as they are cooked.

VEGETABLES WITH MUCH STARCH

Potatoes, breakfast cereals, rice, samp, macaroni, noodles and other pastes, used as vegetables, are rich in starch. A good potato, properly cooked, is mealy. A potato, no matter how good it may be, cooked in simmering water is water-soaked and soggy. If potatoes be cooked in furiously boiling water, the outside becomes softened and washed away, while there is "a bone in the center." To cook in perfection, keep the water just at the boiling point until the potatoes are cooked. The same is true, practically, in respect to the cooking of other starchy vegetable products, but in cooking rice and macaroni, *rapidly* boiling water is necessary, in order that the grains or pieces be kept moving and separate from each other. A light, flaky dish of rice cannot be secured in a double boiler, where the water is of necessity below the boiling point.

WHEN TO USE A LARGE QUANTITY OF WATER

Some varieties of onions are strong flavored; when such, and also members of the cabbage family, are to be cooked, the use of a large quantity of water will insure a more delicate flavor.

USE OF SALT AND SODA

Hard water has a tendency to harden cellulose or woody fiber, and thus keeps sweet juices or other valuable compounds within the article cooked; soft water acts in the opposite way. Salt added to water makes it hard, raises the boiling point a little, and intensifies the color of green vegetables. Soda softens water and causes green vegetables to assume a faded look. As the appearance of food has much to do with our taste or distaste thereof, certainly, for æsthetic reasons, the use of salt in the cooking of green vegetables would be a gain. Again, as green vegetables contain little woody tissue, but often sugar that we wish to retain in the article, the cooking of these in salted water would seem advisable. In general, salt should be added to the water in which all vegetables, except those containing much cellulose, are to be cooked. Potatoes and onions never taste just right unless the water in which they are cooked be salted. A teaspoonful of salt to each generous quart of water will be found about right. Soft water is called for when the cellular structure of dried peas, beans and lentils is to be made tender. If such water be not available, a teaspoonful of bicarbonate of soda, added to each two quarts of water in which the vegetable is to be cooked, will soften the water.

VEGETABLES CONTAINING MUCH STARCH
POTATOES
PREPARATION OF POTATOES FOR BOILING

New potatoes: Scrape off the skin, scrub with a vegetable brush, then wash thoroughly. Old potatoes: Pare the potatoes, remove the eyes and, if they be large, cut them in halves, lengthwise; let lie in cold water — no salt — an hour or longer before cooking.

BOILED POTATOES

Add a teaspoonful of salt to a generous quart of boiling water; put in the potatoes and let cook until tender. It will take from twenty to thirty minutes. Drain thoroughly, sprinkle lightly with salt and shake the pan back and forth on the hot stove lid. If they cannot be served at once, move to the back of the range and cover with a cloth. Salt sprinkled on the hot, moist potato, on account of its affinity for water, tends to draw it out and make the potato mealy.

MELTING POTATOES

Pare four or five potatoes of the same size and cook them in boiling, salted water; when done, drain, sprinkle with salt, and cover with a towel, to take up the moisture; then take the potatoes, one by one, and press each firmly in a towel, to give it a round shape, and set them, side by side, in a well-buttered baking dish; turn in consommé or milk and cream, half and half, to surround the potatoes to one-third their height. Set half a teaspoonful of butter on each potato, or brush over the tops generously with melted butter, and let bake from fifteen to twenty minutes or until the liquid is absorbed and the potatoes are browned a little on top.

MASHED POTATOES

Boil the potatoes as above and pass through a vegetable press into a hot saucepan. For about a pint, or four or five potatoes, add two level tablespoonfuls of butter, a little hot milk (one-fourth a cup) and half a teaspoonful of salt. Beat with a perforated wooden spoon until very light and fluffy, then turn into a hot vegetable dish and serve at once.

MASHED POTATO CAKES

Roll mashed potato, left from a meal, in the hands into balls and flatten into cakes. Set to cook in a frying pan containing hot bacon fat or dripping; let brown on one side, then turn and brown the other side. The cakes may be patted down in a little flour before cooking. For baked cakes, set the cakes on a buttered dish, put a small piece of butter on the top of each and let cook in the oven until hot and lightly browned.

BAKED POTATOES

Scrub the potatoes, either white or sweet, with a brush. Bake in a hot oven. The oven should be at a temperature that will render potatoes of medium size soft in about forty-five minutes. The skins should not be blackened. If the potatoes are to be eaten at once, take them from the oven to the dining-room. If there is to be a delay of five minutes, make two gashes in the top of each potato, one at right angles to the other. Gently squeeze the potato to let out the steam, partially wrap in a napkin and take to the table.

POTATOES ANNA

Butter the inside of two or three English muffin rings and set them on a baking sheet, also buttered. Fill the rings compactly with pared, raw potatoes, sliced very thin and dipped in melted butter, bacon fat, or dripping. Also season the potatoes with salt and pepper as they are set in place. Put half a teaspoonful of butter on the top of each ring of potatoes. Let cook on the floor of a hot oven about ten minutes, then with a spatula turn ring and potatoes together, and let cook ten minutes longer. With the oven at a proper temperature the potatoes will be browned on both sides and well cooked throughout in twenty minutes. Remove the potatoes and rings (with a spatula or broad knife) to the serving dish, then discard the rings.

HASHED POTATO IN RAMEQUIN

3 or 4 cold, boiled potatoes
½ teaspoonful of salt
3 or 4 tablespoonfuls of butter
3 or 4 tablespoonfuls of boiling water

Chop the potatoes, sprinkling them with salt meanwhile. Butter a ramequin; into it put the potato, disposing it evenly to the depth of an inch or more. Dot here and there with bits of butter, then pour in the water distributing it evenly over the potato. Let cook in the oven until hot throughout and a bit of potato here and there is lightly browned.

SAUTÉD POTATOES

Cut the potatoes into halves, lengthwise. Have a little hot fat in a frying pan. The fat from bacon just cooked is preferable. Lay the potatoes in the fat and let cook until nicely browned, then turn and brown the other side.

POTATOES AU GRATIN

2 cups of chopped, cooked potato
1½ cups of white sauce
1 to 4 tablespoonfuls of grated cheese
¼ cup of cracker crumbs
2 tablespoonfuls of melted butter

Stir the potato and cheese into the sauce and turn the whole into a buttered au gratin dish; stir the crumbs into the butter and spread over the top. Set into a hot oven to brown the crumbs.

POTATOES WARMED OVER IN MILK

Melt three tablespoonfuls of butter in an agate frying-pan. Put in a cup and a half of sliced, cold, boiled potatoes. Sprinkle with about half a teaspoonful of salt, and turn carefully over and over, to mix them with the butter. When the butter is absorbed, turn in nearly three-fourths a cup of milk, cover and let cook, not too rapidly, until the milk is partly absorbed.

LYONNAISE POTATOES

2 tablespoonfuls of butter or dripping
½ small onion, chopped fine
2 tablespoonfuls of butter or dripping
2 cups of cold, boiled potatoes, in slices
½ teaspoonful of salt

Cook the onion in two tablespoonfuls of butter until softened and slightly browned. Skim the onion from the frying pan to free it from the butter. To the butter in the pan add two tablespoonfuls. Turn in the potatoes and cook until they are browned slightly, adding the salt meanwhile. Add the cooked onion, and toss the onion and potato together thoroughly. Serve on a hot dish.

POTATOES, AMERICAN STYLE

1¼ cups of cold, boiled potatoes
1 cup of milk
1 slice of onion
1½ tablespoonfuls of butter
1½ tablespoonfuls of flour
¼ teaspoonful of salt
¼ teaspoonful of pepper
1 tablespoonful of butter creamed
1 yolk of egg

Scald the milk with the onion, cream the 1½ tablespoonfuls of butter and beat the flour into it; dilute with a little of the hot milk, then stir into the rest of the hot milk; let cook ten minutes, stirring occasionally. Remove the onion, add the potatoes, cut in slices, let become hot throughout, then carefully beat in the tablespoonful of butter, creamed and mixed with the beaten yolk. A little fine-chopped parsley sprinkled over the potato is a good variation.

SARATOGA POTATOES

Select smooth potatoes of same size and long rather than round, and pare and cut them into thin, even slices. The slices must be of uniform thickness throughout, or they will not cook evenly. Cover the prepared potatoes with cold water to which a piece of ice has been added. Let stand an hour or longer, to become cold and crisp. Dry on a soft cloth, a few at a time, and cook at once in hot fat, keeping the slices separated with a skimmer. Take, for frying, fat that has not been previously used for frying. Cook to a pale straw color, drain on the skimmer, then on tissue paper. Keep hot at the mouth of the oven until all are cooked. Sprinkle with salt before serving.

BREAKFAST CEREALS

Cereals are in a dry form and much water needs to be added during cooking; they also contain considerable tough cellulose. A high degree of heat is needed, to soften the cellulose, or they may be cooked at a lower temperature, if the time of cooking be lengthened. Some " breakfast foods," as those to which the term " rolled " is applied, are partly " steam-cooked " and half an hour's cooking will generally suffice for these. Wheat germ meal and other similar preparations need an hour's cooking; oatmeal and corn meal call for six to eight hours and if cooked in a double boiler longer cooking is advisable. Rice boiled in water, as potatoes, will cook in about the same time as potatoes, from twenty to thirty minutes. It will take about forty-five minutes to cook rice in a double boiler. *Salt* — a teaspoonful to a pint — should be added to the water in which cereals are to be cooked. *Proportion of water needed:* Cereals containing a goodly proportion of gluten call for less water than those in which gluten is replaced by starch. In general four times the weight of the cereal in water is needed. Thus, one cup of cereal, weighing half a pound, would call for two pounds, or a quart, of water. When cooking Vitos and other cereals, rich in gluten, cut down the water to three or three and one-half cups.

METHOD OF COOKING CEREALS

Turn the requisite quantity of boiling water — as a pint — into the upper part of a double boiler, add a teaspoonful of salt (to the pint) and wait until the water reboils; then stir vigorously while slowly turning half a cup of cereal into the water. Do not add the cereal fast enough to stop the boiling of the water. Stir and let boil five minutes, then set it into the lower part of the double boiler in which boiling water has been poured to one-third the height, cover the cereal and let cook over the boiling water the requisite time. Add boiling water to the outer kettle, as needed to surround the inner kettle, without its boiling over. Do not stir the cereal after the first five minutes. When cooked the cereal should be rather stiff. If it be soft and mushy, it is not readily masticated.

RICE, SOUTHERN STYLE

Put half a cup of rice over a quick fire in a quart of cold water and stir while heating the water to the boiling point; let boil rapidly three minutes, then turn the whole into a sieve and pour cold water through the rice, left on the sieve, and return it to the kettle. The rice is now "blanched" or cleaned. Add to the rice a quart of boiling water and a teaspoonful of salt and let cook rapidly until the grains are tender. Drain the rice from the liquid and dry in a hot oven, shaking the dish occasionally, to separate the grains. A little salt sprinkled over the top of the rice will absorb any water remaining on the rice and help to make it flaky. Use the rice water for a soup. Add it to lamb or chicken broth.

RICE COOKED IN DOUBLE BOILER

Following the general rule a pint of water would be called for when half a cup of rice is to be cooked in a double boiler. If the rice be from a fresh or late gathered crop — thus not very dry — this may be a generous measure. If the cooking is to be done in stock or tomato purée, the above proportions will be about right. Rice cooked with tomato and cheese is given under cheese dishes. To cook in the double boiler, blanch the rice as in the first recipe; add the milk, stock or purée, preferably hot, in the upper part of the boiler, half a teaspoonful of salt and let cook until the liquid is absorbed. Do not stir during the cooking.

MACARONI

Break half a cup of macaroni into pieces about an inch long. Have ready over the fire a saucepan containing a quart or more of rapidly boiling water; add a teaspoonful of salt and when the water reboils, sprinkle in the macaroni. Do not cover. If at first any of the macaroni sticks to the bottom of the saucepan, stir with a fork. Keep the saucepan boiling, adding boiling water to replenish the supply when needed, and the pieces of macaroni will not stick to the pan or to each other. When the macaroni is tender, turn it into a colander, to drain off the water, then let cold water run through it, to rinse off the pasty exterior. The macaroni is now ready to be finished after any formula desired; but no matter how the macaroni (and other similar preparations) is to be served, the initial cooking is always as above. For recipes for cooking macaroni with cheese, see chapter on Cheese. In any of the recipes in which macaroni is combined with cheese, the cheese may be omitted.

SWEET POTATOES AND SQUASH

In sweet potatoes and squash, besides much starch, we have sugar to deal with. The sugar is best retained if both be cooked without paring.

BOILED AND BAKED SWEET POTATOES

Scrub the potatoes with a brush, cover with boiling water, bring quickly to the boiling point and let boil gently until they are just cooked through, and are not in the least soft. Drain off the water and set them into the oven. Take them out, one by one, to peel, returning them to the oven as soon as peeled. Bake sweet potatoes in the same manner as white.

BROILED SWEET POTATOES

Cut boiled or baked sweet potatoes in halves, lengthwise, spread the flat sides with butter and set to cook in a well-oiled broiler (bars rubbed with a buttered paper) over hot coals or under a gas burner. Do not set too near the heat, and turn during the cooking, to avoid burning. When hot throughout set onto a hot dish. Spread with butter, sprinkle with salt or salt and sugar.

SQUASH

Squash is better when baked or steamed than when boiled. When boiled set to cook without removing the skin, but carefully remove the seeds and strings connected with them. One fourth a squash, often much less, is all that should be cooked at one time. Let boil until tender, then drain off the water and set the squash, on a tin plate, skin side up, in the oven, to dry off. Scrape the pulp from the shell, and press it through a ricer into a saucepan; add half a teaspoonful (for a pint) of salt and two or three tablespoonfuls of butter, also a little black pepper if approved. Stir the squash over the fire until well mixed, then turn into a hot dish.

STEAMED SQUASH

Prepare as for boiling. As the squash is cooked over and not in the water, a longer time for cooking is required. Season and finish as Boiled Squash.

BAKED SQUASH

If the shell is not too hard, the squash may be cut in pieces about the size of a potato. Remove seeds and stringy portions, then set to bake on the grate of an oven suitable in temperature for baking potatoes. The squash will bake in about forty minutes. Remove to a hot dish. Serve and eat as baked potatoes. Baked squash is particularly good with beefsteak.

VEGETABLES CONTAINING LITTLE STARCH

CELERY, HOLLANDAISE STYLE

1 cup of cooked celery (nearly a pint of uncooked)	¼ teaspoonful of salt
2 tablespoonfuls of butter	¼ teaspoonful of pepper
2 yolks of eggs	1 teaspoonful of lemon juice

Use trimmed stalks of well-bleached celery; cut these into pieces half or three-fourths an inch long. Let simmer in water to cover until tender. Renew water as is needed during the cooking; when the celery is tender there should not be more than a cup of water with it. Cream the butter; add the salt, pepper and one yolk; beat in this yolk, then add the other, and when evenly mixed, stir into the cooked celery; let stand over hot water or on the back of the range while the mixture is being added; add the lemon juice. Serve at once in a hot dish or on slices of toast. The lemon may be omitted.

CREAMED CELERY

1 cup of cooked celery
2 tablespoonfuls of butter
2 tablespoonfuls of flour
¼ teaspoonful of salt
¼ teaspoonful of pepper
1 cup of milk, less the celery water
2 slices of toast
Boiling salted water
Butter

Cook the celery as above, but reduce the water till but little remains. Measure the water and use this with milk or cream to fill a cup as the liquid in making a sauce. Stir the cooked celery into the sauce. Dip the toast in boiling, salted water, set on plates, spread with butter and pour the celery and sauce over the toast. For a more hearty supper or luncheon dish set poached eggs above the celery.

SPINACH

Carefully cut off the roots, discard discolored leaves, but retain the inner heart-leaves that are not fully opened. Wash in many waters; wash from one pan to another as long as sand is seen in the bottom of the pans. If the spinach is wilted, let it freshen, after it is trimmed, by standing in cold water, before beginning to wash it. Finally rinse from a pan of clean water into a saucepan. Sprinkle a teaspoonful

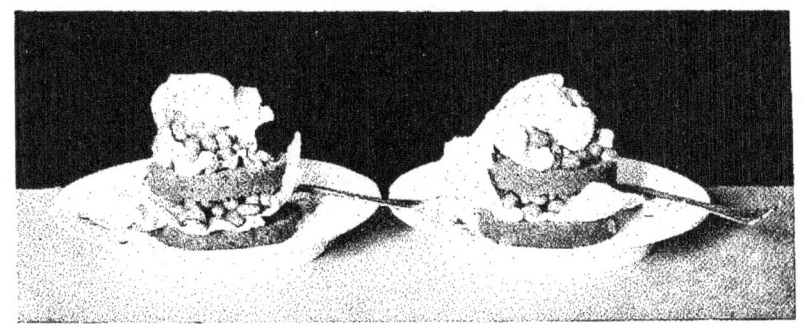

Cold Baked Bean Sandwich, Club Style — *Page 183.*

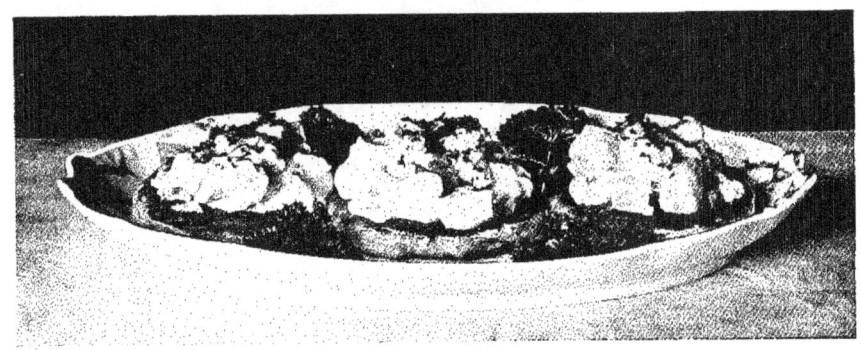

Corn Fritters with Creamed Chicken — *Page 179*

Mashed Potato — *Page 160*

Lima Beans Baked with Salt Pork — *Page 182*

Frying Saratoga Potatoes — *Page 164.*

Baked Potatoes — *Page 160*

of salt over the top and set to cook. Press the spinach down in the saucepan as it becomes heated, and turn it over, that all the leaves may become heated, and cook without adding other water than clings to the leaves from the washing. When done turn into a colander, press out the juice and dispose in a mound on a serving dish. Serve as " greens." One-fourth a peck is enough to buy at one time.

CHOPPED SPINACH

Prepare, cook and drain the spinach as above, then chop very fine (in a wooden bowl); add a tablespoonful of butter, one-fourth a teaspoonful, each, of salt and pepper and return to the saucepan; stir over the fire until the spinach is hot throughout; turn into a vegetable dish and dispose on it a hard-cooked egg, shelled and cut in halves lengthwise.

LEFT OVER SPINACH

Press the chopped spinach very compactly into two small cups and set aside in a cool place. Turn from the cups onto lettuce leaves. Serve with French dressing or with oil and vinegar.

GREEN SHELL BEANS
(Lima, Cranberry, Kidney, etc.)

Put the shelled beans over the fire in boiling, salted water to cover; let boil five minutes, then simmer until tender. It will take an hour or an hour and a half. When tender the water should be nearly evaporated. Add salt (half a teaspoonful to a pint), black pepper and two tablespoonfuls of butter or one-fourth a cup of cream.

STRING BEANS

Snip off the ends, at the same time pulling off the strings if present, break into two or three pieces or put several beans together on a meat board and with a sharp knife cut all at once into about three pieces. Wash in cold water, drain and set to cook in boiling, salted water. It will take about two hours. String beans should be cooked when freshly gathered, otherwise make ready for cooking and let stand an hour or more in cold water. When cooked season with salt and pepper and add butter or cream. They are good in cream sauce, and, cold, make a good salad when dressed with oil, vinegar and a little onion juice.

STRING BEANS WITH BACON

Cut one or two slices of tender bacon in tiny cubes and cook in a frying pan to a delicate brown. Add a pint of hot, cooked-and-drained string beans and if liked a grating of onion or a few drops of onion juice. Shake the frying pan, to mix thoroughly. Add half a teaspoonful of salt and one-fourth a teaspoonful of pepper and turn into a hot dish. Peas and Lima beans (fresh or dried) may be prepared in the same way.

VEGETABLES CONTAINING SUGAR WITH LITTLE STARCH

For general directions in regard to cooking, see first pages of the chapter.

GREEN PEAS

If possible do not shell the peas until just before it is time to cook them. Add boiling water to just cover the peas; add salt, half a teaspoonful to a pint of water, and let the contents of the saucepan simmer until the peas are tender. It will take about twenty minutes. When the peas are cooked the water should be reduced to a few spoonfuls. Add one or two tablespoonfuls of butter, a little black pepper and serve at once.

GREEN PEAS, CREAMED

Cook as above and pour over a cup and a half of peas a scant cup of white sauce. Make the sauce after the usual formula, but as there will be a little liquid in the peas, use a little less liquid in making the sauce. Rich milk or thin cream may be used for the sauce.

CANNED PEAS

Turn the peas from the can into a sieve and let the water from the cold water faucet run through them. Drain, add a few spoonfuls of boiling water, a teaspoonful of sugar, half a teaspoonful of salt and one-fourth a teaspoonful of black pepper. Cover close and let become very hot; then serve at once. Canned peas may also be stirred into cream sauce.

ASPARAGUS

Scrape the scales and skin from the lower end of the asparagus stalks, then shorten (cut off) each stalk at the point where it begins to be tough. Tie the stalks in a bundle and set to cook in a small quantity of boiling, salted water. In the upper part of a double boiler the stalks may stand upright, the tender tips, which require the least cooking, being out of the water, will cook in the steam. Thirty to forty minutes' cooking is needed. If the stalks lie flat in water, they will cook in twenty or twenty-five minutes. Have ready two slices of toasted bread; dip the edges of the toast in the asparagus water and set them on the serving dish; dispose the asparagus on the toast and set into the oven. Beat two tablespoonfuls of butter to a cream; beat in two tablespoonfuls of flour, dilute with a little of the asparagus liquid, then stir into the rest of the liquid; let boil five or six minutes; add another tablespoonful of butter, salt if needed, and pour over the asparagus and toast.

ASPARAGUS AS PEAS

Prepare the asparagus stalks as before, then cut them into half inch pieces. Cook in boiling, salted water to cover. Do not add water unless necessary to keep the vegetable from burning. When cooked add, for a pint, one-fourth a teaspoonful of pepper, salt if needed and two or three tablespoonfuls of butter.

STEWED TOMATOES

Pare two ripe tomatoes, cut in slices, and set over the fire in a small saucepan; cover and let cook while one-fourth a cup of cracker or soft bread crumbs are made ready; add these to the tomatoes with half a teaspoonful of salt and a dash of pepper. Let cook until the tomatoes are soft; add two tablespoonfuls of butter and mix thoroughly. One-fourth a green or red pepper pod, cut in thin slivers, may be put with the tomatoes when they are set to cook.

STEWED TOMATOES WITH CORN, MEXICAN STYLE

3 tomatoes
1 tablespoonful of butter
½ sweet pepper
½ teaspoonful of salt

1 cup of fresh boiled corn, cut from the cob
1 tablespoonful of butter

Peel the tomatoes and cut in quarters, discarding the seeds. Melt the butter in a frying pan; add the pepper, chopped fine, and let cook without browning. Add the tomato and salt and let cook until very hot throughout, add the corn, the last tablespoonful of butter and more salt if needed.

BROILED TOMATOES

2 or 3 firm, ripe tomatoes
Salt and pepper

Butter
Sifted bread crumbs

Cut out the hard center around the stem end of the tomatoes, then cut each in two slices. Dip the cut side of the tomatoes in melted butter, dredge lightly with salt and pepper — then press into soft, sifted bread crumbs (taken from center of stale loaf), broil over coals or under a gas burner until soft throughout. In broiling under a gas burner, have the skin side of the tomato down. Dispose on a hot dish; put a bit of butter on the top of each slice and serve at once.

BEETS

Young and tender beets are very palatable, they contain a large proportion of sugar, which should be carefully retained during cooking. Scrub and wash with great care, to avoid breaking the skin. If the skin be broken, the juices of the beet will pass into the water and nothing but fiber be left for serving. Old beets or beets that have been slow in growing can rarely be cooked tender. Young beets should cook in three or four hours. When tender drain and cover with cold water; push the skin from the beets with the hands, then cut in slices. Sprinkle with salt and pepper and add bits of butter, here and there. The beets may be chopped rather coarse instead of sliced.

PICKLED BEETS

Cover the left-over beets sliced for dinner with cold vinegar, cover and set aside. In cool weather pickled beets may be kept two or three days. Figures may be cut from slices of pickled beet and used to decorate cabbage, potato, fish and other salads.

GREEN CORN

The principal compound in green corn is sugar, and great pains should be taken to preserve this. If the sugar be lost, the corn is tasteless. Probably there is no vegetable that requires such careful handling as green corn. It should go from the parent stalk to the saucepan or fire. Left husked or unhusked in a hot kitchen an hour or two and the sweetness has departed.

BOILED CORN

Have the water boiling and salted; put in the ears, from which the husk and silk have been taken, heat quickly to the boiling point and let boil rapidly five minutes. Remove from the saucepan with a fork or skimmer.

CREAMED CORN AU GRATIN

2 tablespoonfuls of butter
2 tablespoonfuls of flour
¼ teaspoonful of salt
¼ teaspoonful of black pepper or a slice of green or red pepper, chopped fine
¾ cup of milk
1½ cups of green corn pulp
⅓ cup of cracker crumbs
2 tablespoonfuls of melted butter

Make a sauce of the butter, flour, salt, pepper and milk; stir in the corn, fresh cut from the cob, and turn into a buttered baking dish. Mix the cracker crumbs with the melted butter and spread over the corn mixture. Let bake until the crumbs are brown. To get the pulp, with a sharp knife cut down through the center of the kernels, lengthwise of the rows, then with the back of the knife scrape out the pulp, or, if the corn be very tender, cut off and reserve the tops of the kernels, then press out the pulp and use both together.

GREEN CORN, CREOLE STYLE

2 tablespoonfuls of butter
1 slice of onion, chopped fine
1 slice pepper pod, chopped fine
2 tablespoonfuls of flour
½ cup of tomato purée
½ teaspoonful of salt
1 cup of corn pulp
1 teaspoonful of fine-chopped parsley
1 or 2 yolks of eggs, when desired

Melt the butter and in it cook the chopped onion and pepper until softened and yellowed; add the flour, stir until blended, then add the tomato purée and salt; stir until smooth and boiling, then add the corn and parsley; stir until boiling throughout, then serve at once. For a more substantial dish add at the last, the beaten yolks of one or two eggs. Do not boil after the egg is added. If more convenient the flour may be omitted and two tomatoes, peeled and cut in small pieces, may replace the purée.

GREEN CORN CUSTARD

1 egg
1 cup of corn pulp (fresh or canned)
½ cup of cracker crumbs
⅓ cup of sugar
½ teaspoonful of salt
2 cups of milk

Beat the egg and add the other ingredients in the order enumerated. Bake nearly an hour in a very slow oven. Serve hot with butter at luncheon or supper.

GREEN CORN CUSTARD, No. 2

1½ tablespoonfuls of corn meal
¼ cup of cold milk
1 cup of scalded milk
1 tablespoonful green pepper (chopped fine)
½ teaspoonful of salt
1 tablespoonful of butter
1 cup of corn pulp (generous measure, canned or fresh)
1 egg, well beaten

Stir the corn meal with the cold milk and cook in the hot milk (over hot water); stir until the mixture thickens, then remove from the fire, add the other ingredients and mix thoroughly and turn into a dish suitable to send to the table.

Set on several folds of paper, in a baking dish, surround with boiling water, and let cook until the center is firm. Serve hot as a vegetable with meat or with bread and butter at luncheon or supper.

CORN FRITTERS

1 egg, beaten light
1 cup of corn pulp (fresh or canned)
½ teaspoonful of salt
⅓ cup of milk or cream
½ cup of pastry flour
½ teaspoonful of baking powder
Salt pork fat or olive oil

To the beaten egg add the corn pulp and milk or cream. Sift together the flour, salt and baking powder and mix thoroughly. Fry as griddle cakes in a little salt pork fat or olive oil. Or, have hot fat in a Scotch bowl, dip a tablespoonful in the hot fat, drain carefully, then take up a spoonful of the mixture and with a second spoon push it into the hot fat; fry to an amber color.

CORN CHOWDER

1 slice of fat salt pork	1½ cups of hot milk
1 small onion	3 tablespoonfuls of butter
1½ cups of corn pulp	¾ teaspoonful of salt
1 cup of sliced potatoes	Black pepper

Cut the pork in tiny bits and cook the fat from it in a frying pan; add the onion, peeled and cut in very thin slices, and let cook until yellowed. In the meanwhile pour boiling water over the potatoes, heat quickly to the boiling point and let boil three or four minutes, then drain, rinse in cold water and drain again. Pour a cup of boiling water over the onion and pork and let simmer three or four minutes, then strain this water over the potatoes, squeezing out all the juice; then discard the onion and pork. After the potatoes have been boiling five minutes add the corn and let the whole boil till the potatoes are tender, then add the hot milk, salt, pepper and butter. Serve with crackers.

SUCCOTASH

1 cup of stewed beans (preferably Lima)	3 tablespoonfuls of butter
	¼ teaspoonful of pepper
1½ cups of corn pulp	¼ to ½ cup of cream
¾ teaspoonful of salt	

Succotash may be made from fresh or dried beans. In both cases the beans should first be cooked until tender, then add the corn pulp and cook about five minutes after boiling begins. Add the butter and seasonings. If there be enough liquid with the beans, the cream may be omitted. Succotash is eaten with a spoon, but it should not be at all sloppy.

DRIED VEGETABLES CONTAINING NITROGEN (PROTEIN)

DRIED LIMA BEANS

½ cup of dried Lima beans
Cold water
½ teaspoonful of salt
2 tablespoonfuls of butter
¼ teaspoonful of black pepper

Soak the beans over night in about a quart of cold water. Wash and set to cook in boiling water to cover well; heat to the boiling point, then let simmer (covered) until tender, replenishing the water as needed. When cooked there should be only a little thick liquid in the pan. Add salt about half an hour before the beans are cooked. Cook three or four hours. Add the butter and pepper and shake the pan to distribute through the beans. Cooked Lima beans make excellent salad and soup.

BOSTON BAKED BEANS

1 pint of pea beans
1 teaspoonful of bi-carbonate of soda
¼ pound of salt pork
2 tablespoonfuls of molasses
1 teaspoonful of mustard
1 teaspoonful of salt

Let the beans stand in cold water over night; wash and rinse in several waters. Parboil until a pin will pierce the beans. Change the water during the parboiling, adding the soda with the last water. Rinse thoroughly. Put half the beans in the bean pot. Pour scalding water over the pork, scrape the rind thoroughly, wash in the water, then score the rind in half inch strips (for cutting in slices when cooked). Put the pork on the beans in the pot, and pour in the rest of the beans. Mix the molasses, salt and mustard with hot water to pour and turn over the beans. Then add boiling water to cover. Bake about eight hours in a moderate oven. Keep the beans covered with water and the cover on the pot until the last hour. Then remove the cover, and bring the pork to the top, to brown the rind. Less than a pint of beans can not be baked very successfully.

LIMA BEANS BAKED WITH SALT PORK

Parboil one quart of lima beans with half a pound of salt pork. Take out the pork, and score it in slices for serving. Then turn the beans into a baking-dish. Set the pork in the center, and bake until the beans are tender. Do not have the beans too moist when ready for the oven. Cover the dish for a time with an agate plate, then remove the plate to crisp the beans and pork. Use with the pork beans that are rather old and require at least two hours' cooking. Dried beans soaked over night in cold water may be used after an hour of parboiling. Parboil young, tender beans about twenty minutes. Add butter, pepper, and salt, and bake nearly an hour. Do not use pork with young beans, unless it be first cooked by itself two or more hours.

COLD BAKED-BEAN SANDWICH, CLUB STYLE

Butter two slices of Boston brown bread; on one of these dispose a heart-leaf of lettuce holding a teaspoonful of salad dressing; above the dressing set a generous tablespoonful of cold, baked beans, then another lettuce leaf and dressing; then finish with a second slice of bread, a tablespoonful of beans, a floweret of cauliflower, and a teaspoonful of the dressing over the cauliflower.

VEGETABLES WITH STARCH IN FORM OF CELLULOSE

For general directions see beginning of the chapter.

BOILED PARSNIPS, BUTTERED

Parsnips are much sweeter in the spring than in the fall. To prepare wash and scrape until clean. Set to cook in boiling water and continue the boiling until nearly tender, then add salt and finish cooking. Cut in halves, lengthwise, the parsnips will cook in about half an hour; left whole it will take nearly an hour. Drain carefully, sprinkle with salt and add plenty of butter.

BOILED PARSNIPS, SAUTÉD

Scrub the parsnips with a brush, without scraping or cutting them in halves. Let boil until tender, then drain, cover with cold water and with the hands slip off the skin. Cut into slices three-fourths an inch thick and set to cook in a frying pan containing about three spoonfuls of fat tried out from salt pork. Let cook until browned on one side, then turn, to brown the other side.

PARSNIP FRITTERS
(Left over parsnips)

1 cup of parsnip purée	1 egg, beaten light
¼ teaspoonful of salt	Salt pork or bacon fat
¼ teaspoonful of pepper	

Press the cooked parsnips through a gravy strainer, set into part of a double boiler (into which it fits). Use a wooden pestle; to the purée add the salt, pepper and egg (often the white may be omitted, the yolk being sufficient to hold the pulp together) and mix thoroughly; shape into small flat cakes. Have ready a frying pan containing a little hot fat; cook the cakes until brown on one side, then turn to brown the other side.

BOILED TURNIPS

Pare the turnips and cut them in slices from half to a whole inch thick. Set to cook in boiling water without salt. When nearly tender add salt and cook until tender. Serve with butter, or, drain carefully, then mash with a pestle, add salt and butter and stir over the fire until very hot.

BOILED TURNIPS, CREAMED

Cut the boiled turnips into half inch cubes. For a generous cup of cubes prepare a cup of cream sauce. Pour the sauce over the cubes and let stand over hot water until very hot.

STRONG JUICED VEGETABLES
ONIONS

Hold the onions under the water from the faucet while peeling. Set to cook in a large saucepan of boiling water. After boiling half an hour, pour off the water and again add a generous quantity of boiling water. Let cook rapidly, uncovered, until tender. Add salt when the water is changed. Season with salt, black pepper and butter. For Creamed Onions, pour over four hot boiled onions about three-fourths a cup of hot cream sauce.

CHAPTER XII

INTRODUCING THE GREAT FUEL FOODS: FATS (CREAM, BUTTER OLIVE OIL AND SALADS)

Fats form the third great class of food stuffs; these are represented in our bodies in the form of fatty tissue. Fatty tissue is made up of a mass of albuminous cells, containing oil and held together by a slight framework of connective tissue. The oil in nuts, olives and seeds is, in the same way, held in cells connected together by a framework of connective tissue. Fat and oil are practically the same thing, fat being oil in a solid state and oil being fat in a liquid state.

THE USES OF FATS IN THE BODY

As fat contains about eighty per cent. of carbon, largely available as a source of heat, fats would seem to be indicated for use in cold rather than in warm weather, and in a cold climate rather than in the reverse. Still this compound is a necessity for people even in hot climates; for growth and proper nutrition are dependent upon the ingestion of a due proportion of all the food principles. Fats lubricate the human machine and aid in building up fatty tissue, which serves as a cushion for the nerves, and provides a reserve store of material to furnish heat and energy in time of need. During convalescence from severe acute disorders, and while suffering from chronic wasting diseases, fats in larger measure are a necessity. In both cases an easily digested form of fat is called for.

FORMS OF FATS USED AS FOOD

1. Fatty tissue in the form of bacon, the exterior of roasts, steaks and chops, or of boiled ham, corned beef or mutton.

2. The fat that is cooked from bacon and meats (drippings), the kidney fat of beef (suet) and pork, removed by heat from the fatty tissues and clarified.

3. Oil expressed from vegetables and seeds, as olive and cotton-seed oil.

4. Combinations of suet and vegetable oil, as cottolene and cotosuet.

5. Butter and cream.

DIGESTION OF FATS

Starch is digested, largely, in the mouth, proteid in the stomach, but fats are changed but little until they reach the small intestine. Here the pancreatic juice, bile and intestinal juice divide the fat into smaller and still smaller droplets; these minute droplets are then taken up by the cellular lining of the intestine and carried to the blood. Anything that aids in the division of the oil is helpful to its digestion and assimilation. Thus, with fat and oil, we masticate food that is deficient in these compounds; as lean meat, bread, potato and other vegetables, which tend to separate the masses of fatty tissue (bacon and the like). Or, we spread butter upon steak or bread, or toss hot vegetables in butter, to coat them with it, or turn lettuce and other green vegetables over and over in oil, that each leaf may glisten with it.

WHY PASTRY AND DOUGHNUTS ARE NOT EASILY DIGESTED

From what has been said above, it would seem that pastry, in which starch is surrounded by fat, and doughnuts, which are largely starch, cooked in fat, would form ideal ways of presenting fat to the system. But fats are not affected by either saliva or gastric juice, and, if starch be permeated through and through with fat, how is the saliva to get at the starch to digest it? If the doughnuts be so made and fried that the fat does not penetrate the dough, the principal objection to this form of food is removed, but pastry cannot be called a hygienic form of food. It should be reserved for occasional use and not presented in daily bills of fare.

DIGESTIBILITY OF FATS AND OILS

In health all forms of fat, in moderation, are usually well digested, but they produce satiety earlier

GERMAN APPLE CUP — *Page 209.*

BEETS STUFFED WITH CABBAGE-AND-NUT SALAD — *Page 206.*

HOW TO BEAT CREAM — *Page 194*

Potato Salad, French Style — *Page 206.*

Egg Salad for Two — *Page 204.*

in a meal than do other food compounds. Good butter, cream and cod liver oil are the forms of fat most easily digested. All fats heated to a certain temperature (*i. e.*, to the smoking point), which varies with the kind of fat, become decomposed, and some of the products evolved, when the fat is ingested, occasion irritation of the mucous membrane throughout the digestive tract, and, consequently, indigestion. Hence, the greatest care must be taken that fats be not overcooked. This is one reason why fried foods *may* be harmful, and why butter, which is quickly affected by heat, is more wholesome when uncooked than when cooked. Used with steak, vegetables, etc., the heat of the article, upon which it is spread, is all that should be applied to it.

EFFECT OF HEAT ON FATS

Melt butter or drippings over the fire and they will foam and bubble, as if boiling; continue the heating, and the bubbling ceases, the fat becoming still. If we tested the fat with a thermometer we should find that, when it was still, the temperature was considerably above the boiling point of water (212° F.), and that, when it was bubbling, the temperature was about that of boiling water. When fat bubbles, as if boiling, it is because there is boiling water in it; when the boiling ceases, water is no longer present. Fat or oil will burn before the boiling point is reached. When all the water present in fat or oil has evaporated and the fat is still, it grows hot very fast, rising to 300° or 400° F. Olive oil may be heated even to 600° F. If we put a piece of dough into fat that is bubbling, we find that it absorbs fat and does not take on any color; but, if we put the dough into fat that is still, it becomes brown in a few moments, and, if properly mixed, does not absorb fat. In reality, the higher the temperature to which we can raise the fat without its burning, the more quickly will the exterior of the article to be cooked be browned and hardened so as to exclude the fat. Olive oil can be heated to a temperature of about 600° F. before it burns, and thus it is the ideal fat for frying purposes. On account of the cost it is not generally used for this purpose. Lard is the fat that is next best for frying, then comes drippings from meat, then suet, while butter is the least desirable medium for frying.

HOW TO TEST THE TEMPERATURE OF FAT FOR FRYING

We have noticed that we do not speak of *boiling* fat, nor do we wish to speak of smoking, hot fat; for, when fat smokes, it is burning and is too hot for use; nor can such fat be restored to proper condition for future use. Food cooked in it, especially if it has been overheated a long time, or several times, will not take on appropriate color, and whatever fat is absorbed by the article will not be wholesome. When the fat becomes still, have ready some inch cubes of stale bread and drop one of these into the fat. If the cube of bread becomes a golden brown, while you count forty, *as the clock ticks,* the fat is at the right temperature for croquettes, fish-balls, small fish, like brook trout and smelts, or small fillets of fish and oysters. If it takes sixty seconds to brown the cube of bread, the fat is at the proper temperature for frying fritters, doughnuts and other similar mixtures of uncooked ingredients. You may think the fat should not be as hot for frying fillets of raw fish and oysters as for croquettes, made of cooked ingredients, which are simply to be reheated. But fish and oysters, being cold, will cool the fat so that longer cooking will be needed to secure the right color for the exterior, and the proper cooking of the article.

PREPARATION OF FOOD FOR FRYING

Heat, as we know, coagulates and hardens albuminous substances; thus, if we cover an article to be fried with a substance rich in albumen, as eggs, or even less rich, as milk, and plunge it into hot fat, a covering will be produced that will keep out the fat perfectly. With the egg, we use sifted bread crumbs; with the milk, we use flour or meal. The starch in the flour, meal or crumbs, is changed by the heat to caramel, and a well-tasting crust is formed. A thin coating is all that is essential. The juices of chops and oysters, thus protected, can not pass out into the fat any more than the fat can enter, thus such articles when properly fried are particularly juicy and well-flavored. It should be needless to add, that the covering must be complete at every point, and that the fat must be deep enough to *cover* the articles to be cooked in it.

The dough for fritters, doughnuts and the like, must contain enough egg to keep out fat heated to the proper temperature for frying. Croquettes, oysters and the like, are often placed in a basket, so that three or four may be lowered into the fat and removed from it at the same time. The articles must not touch each other, or steam will be produced, which will moisten the crisp crust. Drain carefully, in the basket, over the kettle of fat, then remove to soft paper for the final draining.

TRYING OUT AND CLARIFYING FATS

Cut the fat in small pieces, cover with cold water and let stand over night; pour off this water, add fresh water or milk — a cup to each two pounds of fat — and let cook very slowly until the pieces are light brown in color, and the fat is clear and still (no sound of bubbling or cooking). Strain through a cloth and press the fat from the pieces for a second quality of fat.

FAT FROM COOKED MEAT, THE SOUP KETTLE ETC.

When the liquid is cold, remove the fat to a saucepan, add part or a whole cup of cold water and let cook slowly, until the water has evaporated and the sound of cooking has ceased, then strain through a cloth. Much of the flavor and odor of the fat passes off in the water during its evaporation. Slices of raw potato may be used instead of water to clarify fat. It is probably the evaporation of the water in the potato that is responsible for the clarification.

HOW TO TREAT FAT AFTER FRYING

After the frying is finished, remove the fat to a cool place and let it settle. Crumbs or flour, left in fat and reheated with it, will burn long before the fat is hot enough for frying, and spoil the fat. When the fat is cool, pour it carefully from the sediment in the bottom, through one or two folds of cheese cloth laid over a colander or sieve, add cold water or slices of potato and clarify as above. Wipe out the kettle with soft paper, wash and dry, and when the fat is again cool, return it to the kettle. A round-bottomed Scotch bowl (iron) is the best utensil for frying.

FATS AND OILS USED IN THE PRESERVATION OF FOOD

Fats and oils may be used to advantage in the preservation of many kinds of food; these by excluding air prevent the drying or decomposition of the food that is covered with them. After a bottle of olives or pimentos has been opened and a part of the contents used, the remainder may be kept as long as the oil remains in good condition — often six months or longer — by simply putting into the bottle or can a few spoonfuls of oil that may float — a thin layer of oil — on the top of the liquid. So a layer of oil over fish — as sardines — preserves them for a long time. Potted meats and pâté-de-foie-gras are kept by means of lard or butter, which is melted and poured over the articles, when they are put up. Of course all articles preserved in this way should be stored in a cool place.

CREAM

Both cream and cream transformed into butter are considered particularly digestible forms of fat. The volume of a certain quantity of cream is increased by beating. This process, probably, renders the cream a little more digestible, as it also makes it more attractive. Cream taken from the top of the milk can, or after the milk has stood about twelve hours, is called thin, or single cream. Such cream cannot be beaten very firm; it contains too much milk and is not thick enough. Cream taken from milk that has been standing twenty-four hours is called double, heavy or thick cream. This may be beaten " to stand alone," or until it is solid to the bottom of the bowl. Thin cream is beaten with a whip churn; this contains a dasher, which is moved up and down in the cylinder. The froth is removed as it rises to the surface. Thick cream may be beaten most quickly with a Dover egg beater. To keep the cream from " spattering," cover the bowl with a circular sheet of paper, and let the top of the beater emerge from a hole in the center.

TO THICKEN THIN CREAM

Pasteurized or other thin cream may be thickened by a solution of lime in sugar (viscogen) and then whipped to a stiff froth with a Dover egg beater.

To make the viscogen, dissolve five ounces of sugar in ten ounces of water. Add six ounces of cold water to two ounces of quicklime, and let it gradually slake; then strain through a fine sieve to remove unslaked particles; combine the two liquids and shake occasionally for two hours. In three hours set the mixture aside to settle, then siphon, or pour off, the clear liquid. Store in small bottles, filling each full and stoppering tight as the liquid absorbs carbonic acid from the air, thus darkening the color and reducing the strength. Use one-fourth a teaspoonful of viscogen to three-fourths a cup of chilled cream. Stir the cream while adding the viscogen to it.

BUTTER

The cooking of butter detracts from its digestibility; thus, when it is to be used on vegetables, broiled meats, fish, etc., the heat it receives from the article upon which it is served will suffice. Butter is very quickly affected by heat, and will burn more quickly than other forms of fat; on this account, great care needs to be taken in its use for frying purposes. For this reason, and also on account of expense, some other form of fat is usually selected for cooking articles in the frying pan. When butter is to be used for frying, let it heat until all froth has subsided, the casein, salt, etc., has been deposited on the bottom of the dish, and the water has evaporated. The liquid fat may then be poured from the sediment and will keep almost indefinitely.

By beating butter with a perforated wooden spoon or a silver fork, air is incorporated, which lightens it. In cake making this is an important item. For quickest and best results, when butter and sugar are to be creamed together, make the butter smooth and light before any of the sugar is added, then gradually beat the sugar into the butter. Butter is beaten to a cream, when it is of a smooth, cream-like consistency, and the edges look whitish.

Creamed butter is preferable for spreading over steak and chops.

MAÎTRE D' HÔTEL BUTTER
(For Broiled Meats and Fish)

Beat two tablespoonfuls of butter to a cream; beat in one-fourth a teaspoonful of salt, a dash of pepper and half a teaspoonful of fine-chopped parsley; then add a teaspoonful of lemon juice, a few drops at a time. For *red pepper butter,* add in the place of the parsley one or two chilli peppers, chopped fine. A few drops of onion juice may be added.

USE OF OLIVE OIL

Our largest use for olive oil is in the form of salad dressings. Occasionally butter or cream is taken for this purpose. Cream is well adapted for use in salad dressings, but as butter is too solid to coat cold vegetables, it is usually made into a dressing by cooking; this detracts from its digestibility, and thus it is preferable not to consider it in this connection. The dressings that a family of two will oftenest elect are called French and mayonnaise dressings. French dressing is preferable with fruit and green vegetables, and, also, to season fish and meats that are afterwards to be served with mayonnaise dressing. A mayonnaise dressing is rich, and thus is used principally at luncheons or banquets, while the lighter French dressing is selected for the more hearty meal of dinner.

Cream, beaten solid, is added to a mayonnaise dressing, or, with seasonings and a little lemon juice, is used by itself as a salad dressing.

FRENCH DRESSING

3 tablespoonfuls of oil
1 to 3 tablespoonfuls of lemon juice or vinegar
¼ teaspoonful of salt
⅛ teaspoonful of pepper

The ingredients for the dressing may be mixed and poured at once over the salad materials, which are then turned over and over until the dressing has been taken up by them, or, the condiments, mixed with the oil, may be first used, then, after each leaf or separate piece has been thoroughly coated with the oil, the acid may be poured on and the salad turned over and over until the acid is evenly mixed throughout.

MAYONNAISE DRESSING

⅛ teaspoonful of paprika
¼ teaspoonful of salt
Yolk of 1 egg

1 cup of olive oil
1 tablespoonful of lemon juice
1 tablespoonful of vinegar

Mix the salt and pepper, add the yolk of egg, and beat until thickened a little; add the lemon juice and vinegar gradually. Use a Dover egg beater, and beat in the oil, a teaspoonful at a time. After a time the oil may be added by the tablespoonful. Beat thoroughly after each addition of oil, as also during the time the oil is being taken up by the mixture.

Cover the dressing with an earthen or glass dish, and let stand in a cool place until ready to use.

Half this quantity of dressing may be made by dividing the yolk of egg. The main point to be noted in making this dressing is, *that all of the acid is to be added to the yolk of egg before beginning with the oil.* By this method all danger of curdling is avoided.

COOKED SALAD DRESSING

The yolks of 2 eggs
½ teaspoonful of salt
½ teaspoonful of sugar
¼ teaspoonful of mustard
¼ teaspoonful of paprika

2 tablespoonfuls of vinegar *or* lemon juice
The white of 1 egg, beaten dry
2 tablespoonfuls of butter
⅓ cup of double cream

Beat the yolks very light, add the seasoning and acid and stir, while cooking over hot water, until the mixture thickens; turn the white into the mixture and return the dish to the hot water (remove it while beating the white dry) while the two are folded together; continue the cooking until the whole is very hot, then beat in the butter, a little at a time, and set aside to chill. When ready to serve fold in the cream. Remove the dressing from the fire before adding the butter. Use in place of mayonnaise. If to be used with fruit let the acid be lemon juice.

CLEANSING AND CARE OF SALAD PLANTS

Green vegetables and salad herbs are a main dependence in salad making. By themselves they are dressed as salads and are an important part of most salads made of cooked materials. Cooked materials may, with advantage, be mixed with dressing some hours before service, but green vegetables and herbs are palatable and wholesome only when fresh and crisp; thus if wilted, when purchased or brought in from the garden, they must be revived in water, and as all dressings tend to wilt them, dressings must not be added until the moment for eating the salad has actually arrived. Great care must be taken in washing salad plants that are to be eaten raw; each leaf of lettuce must be examined closely, to rid it of minute life; celery also and cabbage must be scrutinized with care. Each stalk of celery and leaf of lettuce should be washed in water and inspected separately. Lettuce, especially that grown in a hot house, will not bear rough treatment; handle the leaves delicately, rinse them in a pan of water, shake in a lettuce basket or a piece of cheese cloth, then wipe dry with a soft cloth. Oil will not adhere to a wet surface. Lettuce may be made ready to serve some hours in advance, if it be set aside in a cool place, in a receptacle tightly closed. A tin pail of suitable size answers the purpose well.

LETTUCE SALAD

1 head of lettuce
¼ teaspoonful of salt (generous measure)
¼ teaspoonful of pepper
4 tablespoonfuls or more of oil
2 tablespoonfuls of vinegar

When ready to serve put the carefully washed and dried leaves in a salad bowl; shake over them the salt and pepper and pour on the oil; with a fork and spoon, turn the leaves over and over until they glisten with oil. If the lettuce takes up all the oil, add another tablespoonful, and still another if it seems needed. Pour on the vinegar, and again turn the lettuce over and over. A few drops of onion juice may be added with the vinegar, or, before putting the lettuce into the bowl, rub over the inner surface of the bowl with the cut side of half an onion or clove of garlic. Pepper grass may be dressed with the lettuce, or mustard leaves, chopped fine, may be sprinkled over the lettuce after it has been dressed.

CABBAGE SALAD

Let the cabbage stand some time in cold or ice water. Slice very fine, season with salt and paprika, or, omit the paprika and use a green or red pepper, sliced fine, or small preserved peppers, chopped fine. Remove the seeds from the peppers before chopping. Mix mayonnaise or a boiled dressing with the cabbage when it is ready to serve.

TOMATO SALAD

Peel the tomatoes, cover closely, and set aside in a cool place, to become chilled. Before serving, cut large tomatoes in halves, crosswise. Any dressing may be used.

PEPPER-AND-ONION SALAD

Plunge a green or red pepper into boiling water, remove at once and rub off the thin outer skin; set the pepper aside in a cool place, to become chilled and crisp. Cut out a piece around the stem, and take out the seeds and veins. Then cut the pepper round and round in the thinnest rings possible; cut half a small, mild and tender young onion in exceedingly thin slices and separate these into rings. Sprinkle the whole with a little salt and pepper, perhaps one-fourth a teaspoonful of each, then pour on two tablespoonfuls of oil; mix and crush the vegetables in the oil, adding another tablespoonful if needed. Lastly add about half a tablespoonful of vinegar and mix again. Serve on heart leaves of tender lettuce. Serve with roast beef, lamb, etc.

ASPARAGUS SALAD

½ head of lettuce
1 dozen stalks of cooked asparagus
1 hard-cooked white of egg (Use hard-cooked yolk for another dish)
4 slices of pickled beet

3 or 4 tablespoonfuls of olive oil
1 or 2 tablespoonfuls of vinegar
¼ teaspoonful of salt
⅛ teaspoonful of pepper
½ a clove of garlic

Put the washed, dried and crisped lettuce onto a serving dish, and dispose above the asparagus with heads all the same way. Cut the shelled egg in slices, and use these as they are as a band over the asparagus, or, remove the yolk for another dish and set in its place figures cut from slices of pickled beet. Rub a bowl with the garlic; in it mix the dressing and pour it over the salad and serve at once.

RUTABAGA TURNIP SALAD

1 cup of cooked turnip cut into half-inch cubes
½ tablespoonful of fine-chopped parsley or capers

½ head of lettuce
½ the recipe of French dressing, with a teaspoonful of onion juice

Mix the French dressing in a bowl; add the onion juice and mix again; pour over the turnip and mix with fork and spoon. Set aside to become chilled. Serve on the lettuce, sprinkling the top with the parsley or capers.

LIMA BEAN SALAD

1½ cups of cooked Lima beans (fresh, canned or dried)
1 teaspoonful of grated onion
1 tablespoonful of fine-chopped parsley
¼ teaspoonful of salt
½ a chilli-pepper, chopped exceedingly fine
3 or 4 tablespoonfuls of oil
1 to 2 tablespoonfuls of vinegar

To the beans add the onion, chilli-pepper, salt and parsley, and mix thoroughly; add the oil and mix, and then the vinegar and mix again. This salad may stand some time before serving.

STRING BEAN SALAD

Prepare as above, substituting cold, cooked string beans for the Lima beans.

BAKED BEAN SALAD

1½ cups of cold, baked beans
3 or 4 tablespoonfuls of olive oil
2 tablespoonfuls of vinegar
2 teaspoonfuls of fine-cut chives or
1 teaspoonful of onion juice
¼ teaspoonful of salt
¼ teaspoonful of paprika
2 tablespoonfuls of fine-chopped olives
2 tiny gherkins, sliced thin and spread like fans

In slicing the gherkins do not cut the slices apart at the stem end; spread the slices to give the effect of a fan and dispose them on the salad, at the ends of the plate. Mix the beans with the other ingredients, by tossing them, or turning them, over and over, with a spoon and fork. For a change use fine-chopped mustard pickles in the place of the olives.

POTATO SALAD

1½ cups of cold, boiled potatoes cut in half-inch cubes
½ teaspoonful of salt
¼ to ½ teaspoonful of paprika
  or
1 slice of red or green pepper, chopped fine
1 slice of onion, chopped fine
2 tablespoonfuls of capers, chopped fine
2 tablespoonfuls of parsley, chopped fine
2 tablespoonfuls of mustard pickles or piccalilli, chopped fine
4 to 6 tablespoonfuls of oil
2 to 3 tablespoonfuls of vinegar when desired
2 hard-cooked eggs, chopped fine *or*
½ cup of sardines, picked in bits, *or*
½ cup of anchovies, picked in bits

Sprinkle the salt over the potato and mix thoroughly; then add the chopped ingredients and mix again; add the oil and turn the potato over and over until the oil is taken up; then add the vinegar and turn the ingredients again. Cover and set aside in a cool place until ready to serve. This salad should stand some time after mixing before it is served. When adding eggs, sardines or anchovies add them with the chopped ingredients.

EGG SALAD

2 or 3 hard-cooked eggs
½ head of lettuce
½ the recipe for either French or mayonnaise dressing

Cook the eggs in the shell. See page 64. Cool the eggs in cold water, shell and cut them in even slices. Dispose the slices on the lettuce, carefully washed, dried and crisped, and pour over the dressing. Serve at once.

CHICKEN SALAD

1 cup of cooked chicken, cut in ½ inch cubes	¼ cup of cucumber, cut in half-inch cubes
½ cup of tender celery, cut in ¼ inch slices *or*	½ the recipe for French dressing and
¼ cup of cooked peas and	About ⅓ the recipe for mayonnaise dressing

Mix the chicken with the French dressing, cover and set aside in a cool place for some time. When ready to serve drain the dressing from the chicken — if any be present — add the celery or the peas and cucumber (when celery is out of season) and mix with the mayonnaise dressing. Serve either with or without lettuce.

TOMATO JELLY SALAD, MACEDOINE STYLE

¾ cup of canned tomato	¼ cup of cold water
1 thin slice of onion	¼ cup tiny bits of green string beans
½ stalk of celery or a few celery leaves	1 olive, chopped fine or sliced
1 small piece of bay leaf	1 teaspoonful of capers
1 slice of red or green pepper or ½ chilli pepper	1 hard-cooked yolk of egg, sifted, or the equivalent of cold chicken, veal or lamb, chopped fine
¼ teaspoonful of salt	
¾ tablespoonful of granulated gelatine	

Simmer the tomato, onion, celery, bay leaf, pepper and salt ten or fifteen minutes; add the gelatine, softened in the cold water, and strain. Let the mixture cool, stirring occasionally, until it begins to thicken, then stir in the string beans (or peas), olive, capers and yolk of egg or the meat and turn into small cups or moulds. It is often convenient to make this salad one day (as Saturday) and serve it the next day. To unmold see page 136.

POTATO SALAD, FRENCH STYLE
(To serve four or five)

3 cups of cooked potato cubes
Scant tablespoonful of grated onion
2 tablespoonfuls of fine-chopped parsley
½ teaspoonful (generous) of salt
½ teaspoonful of paprika
1 cup of double cream
2 tablespoonfuls of tarragon vinegar

To the prepared potato add the onion, parsley, salt and pepper; turn the ingredients over and over until well blended; let stand in a cool place until ready to serve. Beat the cream and vinegar until firm throughout, then mix through the potato.

BEETS STUFFED WITH CABBAGE-AND-NUT SALAD

Have ready young beets, boiled tender and skinned, heart leaves of a head of lettuce, washed and thoroughly dried, cabbage, chopped fine with pecan nut meats, and either boiled, French or mayonnaise dressing. Cut out the centers of the beets and trim them, as needed, to make cases one-fourth an inch in thickness. Reserve the trimmings to be chopped fine, to garnish a salad for the next day. Mix the prepared cabbage and nuts with the dressing and use to fill the

Astoria Salad — *Page 210.*

Celery - and - Apple Salad — *Page 208.*

Asparagus Salad — *Page 202.*

beet cups. Dress the lettuce with French dressing, and on it set the cups. Serve at once.

Celery, cut fine, may replace the cabbage. The boiled dressing given on page 198 is particularly good with this salad.

TOMATO-AND-CHEESE BALL SALAD

Peel the tomatoes and cut each into two slices, or, if smaller tomatoes be at hand, scoop out the centers, to make cases. For one-third a Philadelphia cream cheese take two or three olives and half a chilli pepper; chop these very fine and mix through the cheese. Roll the cheese into small balls half an inch in diameter and dispose two or three balls on a slice of tomato, resting on two heart leaves of lettuce. Pour two or three tablespoonfuls of French dressing over the articles on each plate and serve at once.

PRUNE-AND-PECAN NUT SALAD

¼ pound of prunes
¼ pound of pecan nut meats
½ head of lettuce
4 tablespoonfuls of oil
2 tablespoonfuls of lemon juice
¼ teaspoonful of salt (or more)

Soak the prunes over night in cold water; let cook on the back of the range until tender (and no longer), when the water should be pretty thoroughly evaporated. When cold cut from the stones in neat lengthwise pieces. Cut the nuts in slices, lengthwise. Mix the oil, lemon juice and salt and pour over the prunes and nuts. Mix and turn onto the lettuce. Serve with roast meats or with bread and butter.

ORANGE-AND-DATE SALAD

2 oranges
¼ pound of dates (scant weight)
½ head of lettuce
3 tablespoonfuls of oil
1 tablespoonful of lemon juice
¼ teaspoonful of salt

Pour boiling water over the dates to cover them and stir with a silver fork while the water is reheated to the boiling point. Skim the dates from the water to an agate pan and set into the oven a few moments to dry them. Watch carefully, as they burn easily. When cool enough to handle, take out the stones, and cut the flesh into narrow strips. Wash and dry the lettuce, which should be very crisp. Dispose the lettuce in a salad bowl; mix the salt, oil and lemon juice and pour over the dates. Let these stand while the oranges are peeled and cut in thin slices, lengthwise of the orange, then mix the orange through the dates, adding a fourth a tablespoonful of oil, if the dates have absorbed the dressing poured over them. Dispose the fruit on the lettuce leaves and serve at once. Sliced figs may replace the dates. Serve with bread or with roast meats.

APPLE-AND-CELERY SALAD

1 cup of apple (peeled and cut in half-inch cubes)
½ tablespoonful of lemon juice
½ to 1 full cup of tender celery (inner stalks cut in one-fourth inch slices)
French or mayonnaise dressing as desired

Mix the apple and lemon juice, to keep the apple from discoloring, then mix the apple and celery with French dressing. Use lemon juice instead of vinegar, in making the dressing, and allow for the lemon juice poured over the apple when it was cut. Instead of French dressing, mayonnaise may be used. One-fourth a cup of walnut meats, broken in pieces, may be added with the celery.

GERMAN APPLE CUP (BOSTON HOTEL)

Select fine-grained apples, one for each service; core and pare, leaving on a section of the skin, in the shape of a ring, near one end of the apple. Cut heart-stalks of celery very fine, but do not chop it; mix the celery with mayonnaise dressing, to which half the bulk of whipped cream has been added; add also more salt and pepper. Use this mixture to fill the hollow centers of the apples, rounding it up above the apple a little; in the center of the mixture in each apple set a tiny heart-leaf of lettuce. Dispose the apples on heart-leaves of lettuce and serve at once. The ring of apple skin gives a little color to the dish; the end of the apple on which it is left should be upward. To serve in perfection, when coring the apple, remove all the seed cavities. If the apples must stand after paring, rub over the exposed surfaces very lightly with the cut side of a lemon. This will prevent discoloration.

FLEUR-DE-LIS SALAD, MURRAY'S RESTAURANT, NEW YORK

Cut either oranges or grapefruit in halves, crosswise. With a sharp-pointed knife cut around the pulp in each section of the fruit. Also cut the membrane separating the sections and the core from the skin and remove all the membrane and core in one piece. Sprinkle over the pulp, thus left in the fruit skin, a few sliced walnut or pecan meats and a little French dressing. Set the halves of the fruit, thus prepared, on individual plates and in the center of each set half a dozen heart-leaves of French endive in an upright position, to imitate the fleur-de-lis.

ASTORIA SALAD, REVISED

1 head of endive	A narrow strip of red pepper
½ grapefruit	2 tablespoonfuls of olive oil
½ an orange	The juice of the fruit
2 halves of fresh or canned pear	¼ teaspoonful of salt
A narrow strip of green pepper	Paprika if desired

Remove the pulp from the grapefruit and orange without taking the membrane. Cut the pear in lengthwise slices. Cut the endive in halves, lengthwise, discard outer coarse leaves, wash with great care and wipe each leaf. Dispose the halves of endive on individual plates (these will resemble a spread fan), set the slices of pear, one almost overlapping another, lengthwise, at the root end of the endive; back of these, in the same way, the sections of orange pulp, with the sections of grapefruit just above the tips of the leaves. To the juice add the olive oil and salt; beat together vigorously, pour over the salad and serve at once.

CHAPTER XIII

FOODS SUPPLYING MINERAL SALTS AND ORGANIC ACIDS, MORE PARTICULARLY FRUIT

THE foods that supply us with mineral salts and organic acids are found largely in the vegetable kingdom. Some of these are in the form of roots, leaves, blossoms and stems of plants; others are the seed vessels of the plants, and still others are the fleshy coverings of the seeds intended by nature as a protection for the latter until maturity, or for the early sustenance of the young plant which sprouts from the seed. We speak of these foods as fruits and vegetables. Properly, however, all the seed vessels are fruits, while the others are vegetables, but we are not accustomed to think of a squash or a tomato as a fruit, and so the distinction we make between fruits and vegetables seems to be largely a matter of custom.

COMPOSITION AND FOOD VALUE OF FRUITS

Most fresh fruits contain a large proportion of water, from eighty to ninety per cent. being not an unusual proportion. There is also considerable cellulose in fruit; this, with other starch present in unripe fruit, is largely changed by the ripening process into sugar and gums. One of these gums, pectin, corresponds to the gelatine in meats. It is this gum that causes fruit juice to jelly when it is cooked with sugar.

The quantity of proteid in fruit is very small; as a rule less than one per cent. is found.

From a dietetic point of view fruits are valuable on account of the relatively large proportion of mineral salts and organic acids which they contain; of the salts, potash, found also in many vegetables, is the most important.

The organic acids in fruits (tartaric, malic, citric, etc.) impart to them an agreeable acid flavor and tend to keep the blood in an alkaline condition, a state on which good health depends. The water in fruits may be considered as distilled, than which no better source of pure water exists.

DIGESTIBILITY OF FRUIT

The digestibility of fruit depends largely upon the nature of the variety and its degree of ripeness. An apple has a firmer cellular structure than a peach and thus the latter is the more easily broken up and acted upon by the digestive fluids. Thus the peach is very properly called " the children's fruit." As sugar is more easily digested than starch, and as the starch and cellulose in ripe fruit have been largely changed to sugar, ripe fruit is more easily digested than that which has not reached this condition. When the banana is in a fit condition to eat (uncooked) the skin has become dark, at least in spots, and the pulp is dry and mealy. Bananas left in a paper bag will ripen more quickly than when left uncovered in the light. Cooking is a ripening process, and bananas, pears and apples, not sufficiently ripe to eat raw, are palatable and wholesome, cooked.

FLAVOR FRUITS AND FOOD FRUITS

Hutchison and others divide fruits from a nutritive point of view, into two groups, food fruits and flavor fruits. Under food fruits are classed such as contain more than twenty per cent. of solids. The best example of this group is the banana. This, in its fresh state, contains a little proteid and considerable carbohydrate. Figs, dates and raisins all belong to this group. Weight for weight, dried figs are said to be more nourishing than bread. Flavor fruits have little claim to be called foods; they are largely composed of water and are sweet and agreeable in flavor. Grapes constitute a class between these two groups, as the juice of the grape contains from ten to thirty per cent. of sugar.

NUTS

Nuts are fruits that possess high nutritive value. Their general composition is about as follows:

Water	4 to 5 per cent.
Proteid	15 to 20 "
Fat	50 to 60 "

Carbohydrates . . .	9 to 12	per cent
Cellulose . . .	3 to 5	"
Mineral Matter . . .	1	

The high percentage of fat in nuts and their dense cellular structure tend to make them difficult of digestion. To render nuts desirable as an article of food, artificial grinding, supplemented by cooking, is necessary. Walnuts, chestnuts and almonds are the varieties of nuts in most common use. Chestnuts deserve to be better known and more widely used in this country; they contain a high percentage of carbohydrate, much proteid and fat, while almonds have a high percentage of nitrogenous matter and but little of the carbohydrate principle; thus chestnuts would be used in the place of bread or potatoes, and almonds in the place of fish or meat.

EFFECT OF COOKING ON FRUITS

Cooking, as we have previously noted, softens the cellulose in fruit and converts such starch as is present into sugar, thus making the fruit more digestible. At the same time heat drives out the mineral salts and the acids in the watery juices, and, if these juices be not retained, cooked fruit is not as valuable as uncooked. Fruits preserved by drying need to be soaked several hours or over night in cold water, to soften and fill out the dried tissues.

PREPARATION OF FRESH FRUIT FOR SERVING

Fruit exposed for sale in a market is apt to collect dust and should be thoroughly washed before it is eaten. Hull strawberries, raspberries and blackberries, then rinse quickly in cold water and drain at once. Rinse grapes in cold water, to which a small quantity of salt has been added, then rinse again in pure, fresh water. All fruit, except that freshly gathered and thus warm from the heat of the sun, should be chilled before serving. When possible leaves of the trees on which the fruit was grown should be put beneath the fruit, on the plate. Pass sugar or sugar and cream with berries; do not add either to them before serving. It should be needless to say that the tough skins of apples, plums, pears, grapes, etc., are not wholesome.

SERVING OF GRAPEFRUIT AND ORANGES

A grapefruit is cut in halves crosswise, and serves two persons. With a sharp, pointed, French knife remove the seeds, then cut around the pulp in each section, that it may be removed with a spoon. Set halves of grapefruit on small plates covered with paper doilies or leaves. Oranges may be served in the same way. Or, simply cut in halves, the pulp may be removed with a spoon without the preliminary use of a knife. Or, the sections of fruit pulp, either grapefruit or orange, with all the juice, may be disposed in glasses. A little sugar may be sprinkled over the top if desired.

GRAPEFRUIT WITH BAR-LE-DUC CURRANTS

Cut a chilled grapefruit in halves. Remove the seeds, and cut around each section of pulp close to the membranous walls or partitions. With a sharp knife carefully free the membrane from the sides and bottom of the skin, and lift it out, leaving the pulp in place. Put a spoonful of Bar-le-duc currants in the center. Serve as a first course at luncheon or dinner.

SERVING PINEAPPLES

After the skin and "eyes" have been removed, the flesh may be picked from the core with a silver fork and served with or without sugar. Or the fruit may be cut in slices, crosswise or lengthwise, and eaten from the hand. A tender, well-ripened pineapple needs no sugar; less choice fruit may be sprinkled with sugar and left standing in a cool place two or three hours before serving.

SLICED PEACHES

Peel the skin from the peaches, cut the flesh through to the stone in even slices and lengthwise of the fruit and sprinkle with sugar at once, to keep the fruit from discoloring.

SLICED ORANGES

Slit the peel, lengthwise, on one side of the orange, then remove with the fingers; carefully remove every vestige of the white pith on the outside, then place the orange on a board and with a sharp knife cut in thin slices, lengthwise of the fruit, removing seeds if any are present. Sprinkle lightly with sugar, or serve without sugar.

DATES

Take about half a pound of dates. Cover the dates with boiling water; stir and separate them in the water with a silver fork; skim them from the water to an agate pan, and set them into the oven for three or four minutes to dry off. Cut each date in halves, removing the stones. They are now ready to serve with a cereal and cream or without a cereal.

MACEDOINE OF MIDWINTER FRUIT

For each service take:

5 or 6 dates	½ or ¼ grapefruit
½ small banana	

Prepare the dates and remove the pulp of the grapefruit as indicated above. Peel and scrape the bananas, then cut in even slices. Retain all the juice of the grapefruit. Dispose the prepared fruit in glass or china saucers, dividing the juice among them. Dispose a few slices of banana and halves of dates on the top of the fruit in a symmetrical manner; sprinkle with powdered sugar and serve when thoroughly chilled either as an appetizer before luncheon or as a dessert dish at dinner or luncheon.

QUICK APPLE SAUCE

Pare, quarter and core three or four tart apples. Put over a quick fire with about one-fourth a cup of sugar and half a cup of boiling water; cover and let cook until tender. Serve hot or cold.

STRAINED APPLE SAUCE

Pare, quarter and core three or four tart apples; add half a cup of boiling water, cover and let cook till tender. With a pestle press the apples through a sieve; add about one-fourth a cup of sugar (a grating of nutmeg if desired) and let cook three or four minutes.

STEWED PRUNES

Wash one-third or one-half a pound of prunes, rubbing them between the hands, rinse in cold water and drain; then cover with cold water and let stand several hours or over night. Set to cook in the water in which they were standing, adding more if needed. Let simmer until they are tender and the water is reduced. Just before removing from the fire add from one-fourth to one-half a cup of sugar and let simmer six or eight minutes. The sugar may be omitted and often be unmissed. The juice from half a lemon, a little candied orange or lemon rind, or a tablespoonful or two of sherry, may be added occasionally, to give variety to the flavor. The blanched pits from the stones also give a pleasing flavor.

EVAPORATED PEACHES

Prepare and cook the peaches in the same manner as the prunes; one-fourth a pound is enough to cook at one time. These are particularly good, served with cream.

DRIED FIGS

Use figs that come in small baskets, or such as have a thin, silky skin. Wash the figs, pour boiling water over them and let cook until the skins are tender. For half a dozen figs, add a scant quarter a cup of sugar and let boil five minutes. Flavor with lemon or orange juice, or sherry, for a change. Serve with or without cream.

CRANBERRY JELLY

Cook one quart of cranberries and one cup of water in a covered dish five or six minutes. Then with a pestle press them through a fine sieve. Stir in two cups of sugar; and, without reheating, turn the mixture into a mould. Do not return to the fire after the sugar is added or the mixture will not jelly. The strong acid of the cranberry in connection with high heat " splits " the sugar and interferes with the jellying process.

Cooking for Two

STRAINED CRANBERRY SAUCE

Prepare as jelly in the recipe given above, *except* cook the cranberries in *two* cups of water.

CRANBERRY SAUCE, UNSTRAINED

Heat two cups, each, of sugar and water to the boiling-point. Add one quart of cranberries. Cover the saucepan, and let stand on the back of the range five minutes. Then move to the front of the range, and let cook five minutes after boiling begins. Set the sauce aside, covered, in the saucepan, until cold. The shape of the cranberries is well preserved in this sauce.

APPLES STUFFED WITH DATES AND BAKED

Select tart apples, core neatly, pare, and fill the cavities with stoned dates (prepared as above). Bake until tender throughout in a hot oven, basting once or twice with a little hot, sugar-and-water syrup. Serve with the morning cereal, or as a dessert dish at luncheon or dinner, with cream or milk.

APPLES, PRALINEE

4 apples
¾ cup of sugar
1 cup of water
⅓ cup of blanched almonds chopped fine
8 level tablespoonfuls of sugar

Core and pare the apples; dissolve the sugar in the water, then let cook about five minutes; in this syrup cook the apples until tender, turning them often to keep them in shape and to cook throughout the apple. Remove to a serving dish. Stir constantly while cooking the eight spoonfuls of sugar and the almonds over a hot fire until the sugar becomes caramelized. Turn the nuts and caramel upon the apples, taking care that none falls on the dish. Have the syrup in which the apples were cooked boiled till quite thick, pour this around the apples. Serve at once or when cold with or without cream.

LEMON JELLY

1 tablespoonful of granulated gelatine
¼ cup of cold water
1 cup of boiling water
½ cup of sugar
½ cup of lemon juice

Let the gelatine stand in the cold water fifteen minutes or longer (until all the water is absorbed); add the boiling water and sugar and stir until the gelatine and sugar are dissolved; let cool a little, add the lemon juice and turn into cups. Set aside to become cold and firm. Serve with cream or boiled custard. Preserved peaches or pears, cooked prunes or figs, or nut meats, also sections of orange, from which the membrane has been removed, or slices of banana, may be moulded in the jelly. A tablespoonful of gelatine is needed to each scant pint of liquid.

ORANGE JELLY

1 tablespoonful of granulated gelatine
¼ cup of cold water
½ cup of boiling water
½ cup of sugar
1 cup of orange juice
1 tablespoonful of lemon juice

Prepare in the same manner as lemon jelly. Grapefruit jelly may be made by the same recipe.

ORANGE SECTIONS IN JELLY

"Blood" oranges are very juicy and make a pretty colored jelly. Remove the sections from peeled oranges in such a manner as to leave no trace of membrane on the pieces. Set these, lengthwise, into individual moulds (some moulds are well adapted to this purpose), and gradually fill the moulds with the fruit mixture. Serve, when set and cold, turned from the moulds. The filling of the moulds may be expedited if the moulds are set in a pan of water and crushed ice. Then put in a tablespoonful of the mixture; when this hardens the sections of orange will be held in place and the moulds can be half filled and then completely filled.

PRUNE JELLY

1 tablespoonful of granulated gelatine
¼ cup of cold water
¼ pound of prunes, cooked tender
Grated rind of 1 orange or lemon *or*
1 tablespoonful of candied peel, cut very fine

2 tablespoonfuls of orange juice *or*
1 tablespoonful of lemon juice
⅓ cup of sugar
2 or 3 tablespoonfuls of sherry wine if desired
Hot water to make 1½ cups of material

Remove the stones and cut the cooked prunes in pieces. The meats from the stones (cracked) or one-fourth a cup of sliced almonds or walnuts may be added. Soften the gelatine in the cold water, and dissolve in the hot prune juice; add the other ingredients and measure the whole. There should not be more than one cup and a half. If not that quantity hot water may be added. One tablespoonful of gelatine is supposed to be needed for each pint of liquid, but in summer time or if the mixture is heavy with fruit or prunes, the quantity of liquid must be cut down.

PRUNES STUFFED WITH CHEESE

Let choice prunes soak over night in cold water; steam until tender; slit down at one side and remove the stone from each. Grate Edam or other cheese; add a little fine-chopped red pepper, or a dash of paprika, and enough mayonnaise dressing to mix the cheese to a soft and smooth consistency. Fill the open spaces in the centers of the prunes with the cheese mixture. Serve with lettuce salad, over which French dressing has been poured, and toasted crackers. Philadelphia or Neufchatel cheese may be used; also, French dressing in the place of the mayonnaise.

STRAWBERRY SANDWICHES

Bake sponge cake of any variety in a sheet; cut the cake into pieces of a size suitable for individual service and split each piece. Have ready some hulled-and-washed berries, mixed with sugar. Put the prepared berries between and above the pieces of cake.

Baked Bananas, Sultana Sauce — *Page 225.*

Macedoine of Midwinter Fruit — *Page 218*

Grape Fruit — *Page 216.*

Grape-fruit Jelly — *Page 226.*

Apple, Pralinée — *Page 221.*

Sliced Figs in Sherry Wine Jelly — *Page 227*

Serve with a pitcher of cream. The cake may be hot or cold, but it is best when freshly made.

BANANA WHIP

1 banana
¼ cup of sugar
1 tablespoonful of lemon juice
⅓ cup of double cream
2 pistachio nuts

Peel the banana, scrape off the coarse threads and press the pulp through a sieve; add the sugar and lemon juice and cook over the fire, stirring constantly until the mixture boils; remove from the fire and let become chilled. Beat the cream till firm to the bottom of the bowl. Fold the chilled banana and cream together and turn into two glasses. Pour boiling water over the nuts, let stand about two minutes, pour off the water, add cold water and push off the skins from the nuts. Chop the blanched nuts fine and sprinkle over the mixture in the glasses.

BAKED BANANAS, SULTANA SAUCE

2 bananas
¼ cup (or less) of Sultana raisins
1 cup of boiling water
⅓ cup of sugar
1 teaspoonful of cornstarch
1 teaspoonful of butter
½ teaspoonful of vanilla *or*
1 tablespoonful of lemon juice or sherry

Pull down a section of a banana skin, then loosen the pulp from the rest of the skin; remove all coarse threads and replace the fruit in its original position in the skin. Set the bananas, in an agate dish, in a moderate oven, to bake until the skin is blackened and the pulp is soft. It will take about ten minutes. Take the pulp from the skins without injury to the shape and dispose in saucers in half circles. Pour over the sauce. Serve hot as an entrée with meat or as a dessert dish. Cook the raisins in the water until tender. Stir in the cornstarch and sugar mixed together, let simmer six or eight minutes, add the butter and flavoring and the sauce is ready to serve. The water will evaporate during the cooking of the raisins. Add more as needed but do not have more than half a cup in the dish when the cornstarch is added.

GRAPEFRUIT JELLY

- 1 tablespoonful of granulated gelatine
- ¼ cup of cold water
- ¼ cup of boiling water
- ⅓ to ½ cup of sugar
- 1 tablespoonful of lemon juice
- 1½ cups of grapefruit, pulp and juice together
- 2 or 3 tablespoonfuls of sherry or maraschino at discretion
- 6 or 8 candied cherries

Soften the gelatine in the cold water and dissolve in the hot water; add the sugar and stir occasionally until cold, then add the fruit and juice, also wine if used. Set five small moulds in a pan of ice and water to become chilled. Cut the cherries in slices to form rings. With a steel skewer dip the cherry rings in the grapefruit mixture, and set them on the chilled sides and bottoms of the moulds, to which they will adhere. Then fill the moulds, little by little, with the grapefruit mixture.

SLICED FIGS IN SHERRY WINE JELLY

1 tablespoonful of granulated gelatine
¼ cup of cold water
¾ cup of boiling water
½ cup of sugar
½ cup of sherry wine
Juice of ½ a lemon
5 or 6 figs
Whipped cream

Soften the gelatine in the cold water and dissolve in the boiling water; add the sugar and stir occasionally until cold. Add the wine and lemon juice. Let a mould holding a scant pint become chilled in cold or ice water. A fluted mould is good for this dish. Cut the figs in slices, dip some of these in the jelly mixture and use them to decorate the mould; then fill the mould, alternately, with slices of figs and the mixture, letting the jelly " set " partially, each time, before adding the slices of figs. When the jelly is unmolded garnish with whipped cream, put on with bag and tube, and bits of fig.

SWEET-PICKLE JELLY

(To serve with roast chicken, lamb or beef)

¼ package (1 tablespoonful) of granulated gelatine
1 cup of syrup from sweet pickle jar (scalded)
1 cup of sweet pickle, cut in small pieces (peach, pear, melon or pin-money mangoes)
¼ cup of cold water
1 orange (juice, and pulp in bits)
2 tablespoonfuls of maraschino cherries in small pieces, at discretion
3 tablespoonfuls of liquid from the cherries, at discretion

Soften the gelatine in the cold water and dissolve in the hot syrup; let cool, then add the other ingredients; if mangoes be used add both outside and filling. Carefully discard the orange seeds. Stir the mixture in a pan of ice water until it thickens enough to hold up the bits of fruit, then turn into small molds or one of larger size. This recipe will serve six people.

CHAPTER XIV

SUGAR: A GREAT SOURCE OF HEAT AND ENERGY

BOILING OF SUGAR: CANDY MAKING

THERE are certain grasses, stems and roots that yield sweet juices, which are valuable to us not only for the mineral salts and organic acids contained in them, but also on account of the large proportion of the carbohydrate principle that is present in a comparatively assimilable form. These juices are separated from the water, fibrous and other matters with which they are combined, and are known commercially as sugar. See also chapter I.

Sugar being readily changed to a liquid passes quickly into the circulation, and its stimulating effects are quickly felt; but it lacks " staying " qualities, and thus articles in which much sugar is used should be eaten after the substantial dishes rather than before them.

Sugar changed by cooking to caramel gives to many dishes a flavor that is unequaled. It may be made into a syrup and thus stored for use as needed. Caramel syrup may be used on fried mush or griddle-cakes, as a sauce for custards and puddings, or to flavor cake, icing or ice cream. Sugar and water, or sugar and cream or milk, are cooked together as a foundation for candies and icings. In general do not allow the mixture to boil until the sugar is melted, then set to cook over a quick fire and let boil rapidly until the cooking is completed. When chocolate is to be used, add it just before the syrup is taken from the fire, as chocolate calls for no cooking.

CARAMEL SYRUP

Put one cup of sugar into a small saucepan, set over a quick fire and *stir constantly* while the sugar melts and changes to a light brown liquid. Lift the pan occasionally from the fire, that the sugar may not become burned at any one place. The caramel is cooked enough when it has become a bright golden brown color; it will darken a little more before it is changed to syrup, and so should not be kept over the fire too long, or when finished the color will be too dark and the flavor impaired. Add one cup of hot water and return the saucepan to the fire; let the syrup boil about five minutes, then it is ready to use, or it may be stored in a jar for future use. When the water is poured upon the caramel, considerable commotion will take place and care must be taken to keep the hand out of the steam.

DEGREES IN BOILING SUGAR

When the sugar (for the caramel syrup) was cooked to the caramel degree, if water had not been added to it, on cooling it would have snapped and broken like glass. The sugar is caramel when it is melted and cooked to an amber color, or to 345° F. by a sugar thermometer. As the cooking is continued the caramel becomes darker in color, and, if the cooking be continued until the sugar reaches a density of 354° F. the sugar will burn or become carbon.

By setting the sugar to cook with water or other liquid, we may use it (for various purposes, as frostings for cake, candy, etc.) before it reaches the glass-like condition of caramel. A very little cooking changes the density of the syrup, and the sugar passes from one degree of concentration to another very rapidly; thus it must be watched very closely or it will be boiled too little or too much for the desired purpose. A sugar thermometer is very useful in this connection. In making frosting for cake, the sugar, with cold water enough to melt it, is cooked to the " soft ball " degree, or from 236° to 242° F. Without a thermometer, test the syrup by dropping a little of it into cold water; if it may be gathered together into a soft ball (in the water), or if, when the syrup drops from the spoon, a hair-like thread, two or three inches in length, appears, the right degree is reached. In candy-making we often cook the sugar to a higher degree. At about 248° F. the hard ball degree is reached; at this degree a little of the syrup may be gathered together in cold water to form a hard ball. When the syrup, tested in water, forms a ball that clings but does not stick to the teeth, the soft, crack degree (about 290° F.) is reached. At about 310° F. the hard crack degree is reached. At this point in the cooking the candy, pressed between the teeth, leaves them clean and free.

As in sugar boiling, the process is restricted entirely to driving off the water in composition, or that which has been added to the sugar, so a bright, clear day, rather than one in which the atmosphere is saturated with moisture, is desirable. In many frostings and candies a smooth texture is sought; in others a fine-grained texture is admissible.

When smoothness is demanded, the syrup must not be stirred during the cooking, and great pains must be taken to avoid any jarring of the syrup. When a grainy texture is admissible, the mixture may be stirred. The addition of acid in some form " breaks the grain " of the sugar and reduces its liability to granulate. Thus in candies or icings we may use cream of tartar, acetic acid (made from vinegar), lemon juice, glucose or molasses, any one of which will affect the resultant product in greater or less degree. We will look first at candies in which a slight grain is not objectionable.

FRUIT FUDGE

2 cups of granulated sugar
¼ cup of glucose or corn syrup
1½ cups of cream
½ cup of French fruit, cut fine
1 teaspoonful of vanilla

Stir the sugar, glucose and cream until the sugar is dissolved, then cook to the soft ball degree, or

236° F. In cold weather let the thermometer stand in a warm place a few moments before setting it into the saucepan. Stir the mixture occasionally, but very gently. In stirring lift the thermometer to stir underneath it. When the syrup is cooked enough, remove the saucepan to a cake cooler or wire coffee-stand, that a current of air may pass below it. Let stand until it is quite cool, then add the fruit and the vanilla and beat the mixture until it thickens and grains a little, then turn into a bread pan, neatly lined with waxed paper. When set (in about fifteen minutes) turn from the pan, peel off the paper and cut in cubes. In making chocolate fudge, add one or two squares or ounces of chocolate just as the pan is taken from the fire. Fudge in which glucose is used has to be beaten a little longer before it thickens and grains than fudge in which it is not used; if properly handled the fudge will, however, be softer and finer grained.

OTHER VARIETIES OF FUDGE

An almost endless variety of Fudge may be made. Figs, cut in pieces, or nuts, broken in pieces, may be added. Brown sugar or maple sugar may replace all or a part of the white sugar. Part of the fudge may be turned into a saucepan with an ounce of melted chocolate and, when both dishes of candy are cold and beaten, they may be put into a pan to make marbled fudge. Or chocolate may be added to all of the mixture, then part of the mixture may be cooled in ice water and the other half be allowed to cool more slowly. After the half, first ready, has been poured into the pan, it may be covered with marshmallows, split in halves, and then the other half, beaten in the usual manner, be poured over it. Or, when the candy is taken from the fire, half a pound or more of marshmallows may be gradually beaten into it; these cool the candy so that it may be at once turned into the pans.

DIVINITY FUDGE OR SPANISH NOUGAT

1½ cups of brown sugar
½ cup of glucose or corn syrup
½ cup of water
The white of 1 egg
1 teaspoonful of vanilla
1 cup of nut meats, chopped fine

This candy on account of the glucose used may be stirred gently during cooking without its becoming grainy; the stirring should not be continuous. Cook the sugar, glucose and water to the soft ball degree (about 238° F.), then pour in a fine stream onto the white of egg, beaten dry, beating constantly meanwhile; return one-half of the syrup to the fire and cook to the crack degree, nearly 290° F., then pour onto the egg mixture, beating constantly meanwhile; add the vanilla and nuts and turn into a bread pan lined with waxed paper. When nearly cold remove from the tin and cut in cubes. The cubes are often wrapped in waxed paper. This candy, cut in narrow oblong strips and dipped in melted chocolate, is known as nougatines. Almonds are the nuts usually selected for nougatines. This candy is often cooked to a lower degree, both before and after it is first stirred into the white of egg; thus cooked it is not easily handled until after it has stood a day or two.

BEST CARAMELS

1¼ cups of sugar	2 tablespoonfuls of butter
½ cup of glucose	3 tablespoonfuls of flour
1 pint of cream	1 teaspoonful of vanilla
1 yolk of egg	

Put the sugar, glucose and one cup of the cream over the fire to cook. Beat the yolk of egg; add the rest of the cream and very gradually (do not allow the mixture to stop boiling) stir this into the boiling candy; then let cook to the soft ball degree, 236° F., stirring occasionally. Beat the butter to a cream; gradually beat in the flour, then gradually stir this into the candy and let cook to 240 or 245° F., according to the season or the hardness desired in the candy. Add the vanilla and pour into two buttered bread-pans. When cold cut in cubes.

MAPLE CARAMELS

Use maple sugar instead of granulated sugar, or use two cups and one-third of maple syrup and one cup and a fourth of white sugar, keeping the other ingredients the same as in " Best Caramels." For chocolate caramels add three or four squares of chocolate at the same time as the vanilla. For nut caramels add one cup or one cup and a half of nuts just before turning the candy into the pans.

GOOD WALNUT CARAMELS

2½ cups of sugar
¾ cup of glucose
½ cup of butter
⅛ teaspoonful of cream of tartar
2½ cups of whole milk (unskimmed)
1 teaspoonful of vanilla
1 cup of English walnut meats

Put the first four ingredients and one cup of the milk over the fire to cook; stir constantly and, after the mixture has boiled a few moments, gradually stir in the rest of the milk; add only a little at a time, as thus added the milk is less liable to curdle. Stir often and cook to the hard ball degree or about 248° F.; add the nuts and vanilla and turn into two pans. Cut in cubes when nearly cold. Wrap the cubes in waxed paper.

CHOICE CARAMELS

1 pound of sugar (2 cups)
1 pound of glucose (¾ cup)
½ pound of butter (1 cup)
1 pint of cream

Put the sugar, glucose, butter and half of the cream over the fire and stir until the mass boils throughout. Then stir in gradually — so as not to stop the boiling — a second cup of cream. Put in the sugar thermometer, and let the mixture boil, stirring every three or four minutes, until the thermometer registers 250° F. Then stir in a teaspoonful of vanilla, and turn the candy into two brick-shaped bread-pans, nicely buttered, or onto an oiled marble between steel bars, to make a sheet three-fourths an inch thick. When nearly cold, cut in cubes. Roll these at once in waxed paper or let stand twenty-four hours to dry off. Without a thermometer boil the mass to a pretty firm hard ball. No better caramels can be made. The time of boiling varies, but often an hour is required. In summer the caramels will hold their shape better if boiled from two to four degrees higher.

PECAN PRALINES

3 cups of granulated sugar
1 cup of cream
1 cup of sugar cooked to the caramel degree
3 cups of pecan nut meats

Stir the sugar and cream over the fire until the sugar is melted, then let boil to the soft ball degree or to 235° F. Have ready the cup of sugar, cooked to the caramel degree, and pour the first mixture onto the caramel; let boil up once, then remove from the fire and beat until it begins to thicken. Add the nuts and drop by spoonfuls onto marble or waxed paper.

ORANGE-FLAVORED TURKISH PASTE

3 level tablespoonfuls of granulated gelatine
⅔ cup of orange juice
2 cups of granulated sugar
½ cup of cold water
2 tablespoonfuls of lemon juice
4 tablespoonfuls of Curacoa
½ cup of candied cherries, chopped fine

Let the gelatine stand in the orange juice until it has absorbed the liquid. Stir the sugar and water over a slack fire until the sugar is dissolved, then add the softened gelatine and heat to the boiling point; let boil twenty minutes after boiling begins; remove from the fire and let cool a little, then add the lemon juice, wine and fruit, and turn into an unbuttered bread-pan. Let stand in a cool place overnight. To unmold sift XXXX, or confectioner's, sugar over the top of the paste; with a sharp-pointed knife, loosen the candy at the edge, where it adheres to the pan, then gently and slowly pull the paste, in a compact sheet, from the pan and dispose on a board dredged with confectioner's sugar. Cut the paste into strips and then in cubes with a sharp knife. This may be done easily, if sugar be kept between the knife and the paste. Roll each piece in the sugar. This candy is at its best after a few days. Grated rind of orange may be used in place of the wine.

TURKISH PASTE, RASPBERRY FLAVORED

3 level tablespoonfuls of granulated gelatine
½ cup of raspberry juice
2 cups of sugar
⅔ cup of raspberry juice
2 tablespoonfuls of lemon juice

Prepare in the same manner as the orange-flavored paste.

TURKISH PASTE, MINT FLAVORED

½ cup of cold water
3 tablespoonfuls of granulated gelatine
2 cups of granulated sugar
½ cup of cold water
2 tablespoonfuls of lemon juice
4 tablespoonfuls of crème-de-menthe cordial
Green color-paste to tint very delicately

Prepare as the orange-flavored paste. These candies may be stirred gently, if it seems necessary.

FONDANT: CANDY OF SMOOTH TEXTURE

4 cups of granulated sugar
1½ cups of cold water
3 drops of acetic acid or
½ teaspoonful of vinegar or
½ teaspoonful of cornstarch

Stir the sugar and water in a saucepan, set on a comparatively cool part of the range, until the sugar is melted; then draw the saucepan to a hotter place and continue stirring until the syrup boils; remove the spoon and, with a cloth or the fingers wet in cold water, wash down the sides of the saucepan, to remove grains of sugar that may have been thrown there in the cooking; now add the acid, vinegar or cornstarch, and cover the dish; the steam will melt grains of sugar, if there be any on the saucepan. After three or four minutes remove the cover and, if a thermometer is to be used, set it into the syrup. Let the syrup boil to 240° F. In the meantime wet the hand in cold water and with it dampen a marble slab or a large platter, then, without jarring the syrup, turn it onto the receptacle prepared for it. Do not scrape out the saucepan or allow the last of the syrup to drip from it (use the saucepan in making a dish of apple or other sauce), as sugary portions will cause the fondant to be " grainy." When the syrup is cold, with a scraper (such as is used in removing wall paper) or a wooden spatula, turn the edges of the mass towards the center; continue this until it begins to thicken and grow white, then work it up into a ball, scraping the marble clean. When all is collected and worked into a compact mass, lay over it a damp cloth, tucking it in closely; let stand in this way for an hour or more to ripen. Now cut into pieces and pack these closely in an earthen bowl; cover the top of the bowl with a damp cloth and then with heavy paper; *the cloth must not touch the fondant.* This may be used at once or may be kept, in cold weather, several weeks, if the cloth be wrung out of cold water and returned about once a week. It may be used as a frosting for small cakes, for " centers " of bonbons or for coating centers.

COFFEE BONBONS

Roll small pieces of fondant into balls. If the fondant is too soft to handle, add a little XXXX or confectioner's sugar. Let the balls stand until dry on the outside. Put a cup or more of the fondant in a double boiler over warm, but not boiling water, add a few drops of coffee extract and a tablespoonful or more of caramel syrup, also a little water (perhaps a teaspoonful) if needed and stir until melted; drop in a center, then with a dipping fork (made of wire) push it under the coating; when covered, lift out, draw the fork across the edge of the dish to remove superfluous coating, then turn the fork and drop the candy onto waxed paper or oil cloth. In lifting the fork from the bonbon a design may be made.

OTHER BONBONS

Candied fruit, particularly cherries, cut in bits, nuts, broken in pieces or chopped, pieces of fig, dates or ginger may be mixed with fondant for centers. These centers may be dipped in plain white fondant, flavored to harmonize with the center, or, the fondant may be tinted green, pink, etc., with color paste, or brown with chocolate. Black coffee, much reduced by boiling, may be used instead of coffee extract.

PISTACHIO BONBONS

Blanch a few pistachio nuts; split a few and leave these half meats to set on the top of the bonbons. Chop the rest of the nuts; mix with fondant and roll into oblong shapes. Coat these with fondant, tinted light green and flavored with almond and vanilla. If a teaspoonful of vanilla be used for flavoring, add only one-fourth a teaspoonful of almond. Set the half nut in place the instant the center is coated, as the coating stiffens very quickly. To make the coating a little heavier or hold its shape a little better, beat in a few drops of glycerine. Put the rounding side of the nut down.

FONDANT WITH GLUCOSE

2½ cups of sugar
⅓ cup of glucose (any pure corn syrup)
1 cup of water

Put the sugar, glucose and water over the fire, and stir until boiling; wipe down the sides of the saucepan, cover and cook as in the first recipe for fondant. Cook to 238° F. This fondant, on account of the glucose, is less liable to grain than the one previously given. Begin to cream *before* the syrup becomes cold. When the fondant begins to stiffen, scrape it into a bowl and cover with a damp cloth. Use at once or after a time. This fondant, on account of the glucose, as also fondant to which almond paste or chocolate is added, or fondant made with part maple sugar, will not " cream " as quickly as the ordinary fondant. It is " sticky " and can not be easily shaped by hand into centers. It is used almost exclusively for centers that are molded in starch.

TO MOLD CENTERS IN STARCH

Buy a cheap grade of cornstarch and keep it for this purpose. Sift the starch into a biscuit pan, filling it to the top. Smooth the starch with a flat stick long enough to rest on two sides of the pan. The impressions may be made, one at a time, with a thimble, a cork, glass stopper to a bottle or similar articles, but the easiest way is with small plaster moulds glued to a thin strip of wood. The stick should be of such length that the ends may rest on the sides of the pan. Lift up the molds and make a second row of impressions; also make other rows, if it can be done without injuring the shape of the impressions already made. Melt the fondant over hot water, stirring it meanwhile; tint with color paste, if desired (a little on the point of a wooden skewer will tint

Choice Caramels Wrapped in Paper — *Page 226*

Chocolate Bon Bons — *Page 243*

Dipping Oysterettes, Nuts, &c in "Dot" Chocolate — *Pages 243, 244.*

Fruit Fudge — *Page 232.*

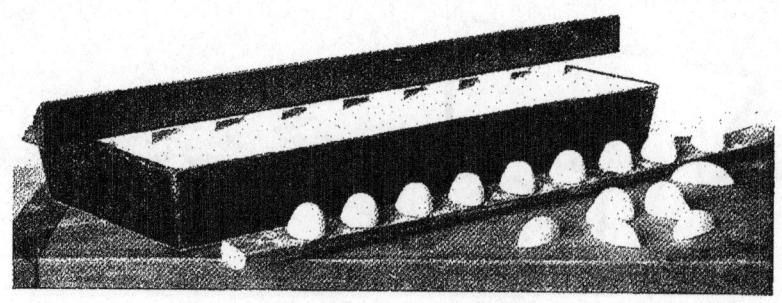

Making Impressions in Starch to Mold Fondant — *Page 242.*

a large quantity), and flavor according to the color. Use rose extract for pink candies and vanilla and almond for light green. Coffee extract will give both tint and flavor. Keep the fondant hot and thin and with a teaspoon drop it into the starch impressions, filling each level with the top of the starch. When cold pick out the candies and brush off the starch. They are now ready for coating with chocolate.

CHOCOLATE DIPPED BONBONS

Slightly sweetened chocolate suitable for dipping candy may be bought in cakes like those sold for cooking purposes and at the same price. As depth of chocolate is needed and all chocolate left over may be used again and again, at least half a pound should be taken, no matter how little dipping is to be done. Break the chocolate in very small pieces, put into a small agate cup and set into warm (not hot) water. If a tiny double boiler be available, so much the better. Stir the chocolate occasionally while it is melting, being careful that no drop of water gets into the chocolate. When the chocolate is cooled to about 70° F., or a little below lukewarm, it is ready for use. Drop in a center, with a dipping fork push it below the chocolate, lift, and when drained a little drop onto a piece of oilcloth or waxed paper. If the candy is to be smooth on top, draw the fork across the edge of the chocolate dish (to remove superfluous chocolate), then slide the candy onto the oilcloth. If there is to be a design on top, let the top of the candy be downward in the chocolate; turn the candy upside down from the fork and draw the fork over the top. Remove to a cool place, to "set" the chocolate.

CHOCOLATE DIPPED NUTS, GINGER ROOT, OYSTERETTES, ETC.

Almonds, unblanched, are dipped with a design on top. Peanuts, with skin discarded, are dipped and dropped in clusters. Drop two or three nuts, dipped one by one, side by side, then drop others above; the chocolate runs together and forms a neat looking and dainty confection. Strips of preserved ginger root are particularly good, dipped in chocolate. Fine-chopped peanuts or almonds, or figs, dates or ginger root may be added to the chocolate; in this oysters may be dipped, to produce a very agreeable confection for Sunday Night tea, etc.

ALMOND NOUGATINES

Prepare the recipe for "Divinity Fudge" or "Spanish Nougat"; when cold cut in oblong pieces about three-eighths of an inch wide and an inch and a half long, and dip in chocolate, making a design on the upper side.

CANDIES COOKED TO A HIGH DEGREE

In cooking candies to a high degree the stirring must be constant during the last part of the cooking.

Cooking for Two 245

PEANUT BRITTLE

For this candy put over the fire one cup and a half of sugar, half a cup of glucose and two-thirds a cup of water; stir till the sugar is dissolved and wash down the sides of the saucepan as in making fondant; cover and let cook three or four minutes, then uncover and let cook without stirring to 275° F. (or until when a little is cooled and chewed it clings but does not stick to the teeth); add two level tablespoonfuls of butter and half a pound of small, raw, shelled peanuts, from which the skins have been taken, and stir constantly until the peanuts are well browned; add a teaspoonful of vanilla extract and a level teaspoonful of soda, dissolved in a tablespoonful of cold water, and stir vigorously. When the mixture is done foaming turn it onto a warm, oiled marble or platter and, as soon as it can be handled, pull it out as thin as possible. With a spatula loosen it from the marble in the center and turn the sheet upside down and pull again as thin as possible. Break into pieces. To remove the skin from the peanuts, cover the shelled nuts with boiling water, let boil once, drain, cover with cold water, and push off the skins. The small *unroasted* Spanish peanuts give the best result.

POP CORN BALLS

1½ cups of sugar
⅓ cup of glucose
⅔ cup of water
½ cup of dark molasses

2 tablespoonfuls of butter
½ teaspoonful of salt
About 5 quarts of hot popped corn

Put the sugar, glucose and water over the fire and stir till the sugar melts; wash down the sides of the pan, cover and let steam five minutes, then uncover and cook without stirring to 280° F. Or test in the same way as peanut brittle. Add the other ingredients and cook until very brittle when tried in cold water. Stir occasionally at first, then constantly. Have the corn in a hot dish; stir while pouring the candy over it. Mix thoroughly, then roll into balls. Do not press the corn together too compactly. Remove all hard kernels of corn before adding the candy.

MOLASSES TAFFY

2 cups of sugar
⅓ cup of glucose
⅔ cup of water
1 cup of molasses

2 tablespoonfuls of butter
1 tablespoonful of vanilla extract

Cook sugar, glucose and water as in Pop Corn Balls, but to 245° F. (hard ball when tested in cold water); add the molasses and butter and cook to 260° F. Pour on oiled slab or platter; while cooling turn the edges towards the center, and when cool enough pull in the hands or over a hook until very light-colored and cold. Flavor while pulling, adding the extract a little at a time. Finally pull out into strips and cut in short lengths.

GLACÉ GRAPES (MALAGA OR TOKAY), CHERRIES, MARSHMALLOWS, ETC.

2 cups of granulated sugar
1 tablespoonful of glucose

1 cup of water

Dissolve the sugar in the water and glucose, stir until the sugar is melted and proceed exactly as in making fondant. Cook to about 295° F. or until the syrup begins to show a slight tendency to an amber color, then remove at once from the fire to a saucepan of boiling water. Only sound grapes can be used, for if juice oozes from the fruit the effect of the candy is spoiled. If marshmallows are of large size, cut them in halves. English walnuts or almonds may also be used. Drop the article to be candied, *gently,* into the syrup, then with dipping fork lift out and set on the bottom of an inverted tin pan. Candied articles do not stick to tin. After a time, even with great care, the syrup will become cloudy. Discontinue the dipping and if necessary prepare another dish of syrup. The cloudy syrup may be used in cooking apples, etc. — but it is not suitable for candied articles.

BOILED FROSTING

¾ cup of fine granulated sugar
⅓ cup of water
2 or 3 drops of acetic acid
White of 1 egg
Grating of lemon rind or
½ teaspoonful vanilla extract

With the sugar and water a syrup is to be made that does not grain; thus the syrup is to be cooked in the same manner as fondant; *i. e.,* stir the sugar and water until the sugar is melted and becomes hot, wash down the sides of the saucepan, cover and let boil three or four minutes, to dissolve any grains of sugar that remain; add two or three drops of acetic acid and let boil undisturbed to about 238° F., or until when the syrup is turned from the spoon a fine thread two inches in length clings from the spoon. Turn the syrup in a fine stream onto the white of egg, beaten dry, beating constantly meanwhile. Continue the beating, occasionally, until the frosting is cold. If the frosting be cooked too much, add a little lemon juice; if when cold it runs from the cake, the syrup was not cooked long enough. To remedy, put the frosting over the fire in a dish of water at just about the boiling point and beat constantly until the frosting thickens.

BOILED CHOCOLATE FROSTING

1½ cups of fine granulated sugar
¾ cup of sweet milk
2 ounces of chocolate, melted
Whites of 2 eggs, beaten dry
1 teaspoonful of vanilla extract

Cook the sugar and milk to 238° F. (soft ball) in the same manner as the sugar and water were cooked in the boiled frosting; add the melted chocolate and, without stirring, pour together onto the whites of eggs. Flavor when cold. This frosting, if it be a little undercooked, will harden upon the outside in time. If it runs from the cake and is returned when cooler, it will not have its original gloss.

NUT CARAMEL FROSTING

½ cup of granulated sugar cooked to caramel
½ cup of boiling water
1 cup of granulated sugar
2 tablespoonfuls of caramel syrup
¼ cup of water
White of 1 egg, beaten dry
½ cup of pecan nut meats

Add the half cup of boiling water to the caramel and let simmer to a thick syrup. Turn this into a bottle for use as required. Boil the sugar, syrup and water to 238° F. or until the syrup dripping from the spoon spins a thread two inches in length. Pour onto the white of egg, beating with an egg beater meanwhile. When all the syrup has been added to the egg, take out the beater, set the dish of frosting over the fire in a dish of boiling water, and beat until the frosting thickens and begins to sugar a little on the sides of the dish; beat in the nuts and spread at once upon a cake, leaving the surface uniformly rough, or with the spoon fashion waves through the frosting. When this is cooked just right, it cuts without crumbling.

DIVINITY FROSTING

2 cups of sugar (granulated brown or maple)
½ cup of Karo Corn syrup
½ cup of water
Whites of 2 eggs, beaten dry
1 cup of pecan nut meats
¼ teaspoonful of salt
4 cooked figs, cut in slices
1 teaspoonful of vanilla extract

Boil the sugar, syrup and water to about 236° F. (the beginning of the soft ball stage). Pour in the usual manner onto the whites of the eggs and return to the fire to cook over hot water until the mixture sugars slightly on the edge; add the nuts, salt, fruit and flavoring and spread upon the cake.

CARAMEL MARSHMALLOW FROSTING

1½ cups of brown sugar
½ cup of cream
1 teaspoonful of butter
½ pound of marshmallows

Cook the sugar, cream and butter forty minutes, counting the time after boiling actually begins. Remove from the fire and beat in the marshmallows. Continue beating until the frosting is of a consistency to spread.

CONFECTIONER'S CHOCOLATE FROSTING

¼ cup of granulated sugar
¼ cup of boiling water
1 ounce of chocolate
Confectioner's sugar to make a paste
1 teaspoonful of vanilla

Cook the granulated sugar and water about five minutes; add the chocolate and let stand till melted, then stir in the sugar and extract. Use while hot. If any be "left over," set aside, covered. When ready to use, add a little hot water and confectioner's sugar if necessary, and it is ready to use.

CONFECTIONER'S CARAMEL FROSTING

4 tablespoonfuls caramel syrup
5 ounces (about one cup) of
sifted confectioner's sugar
1 teaspoonful of vanilla

Heat the syrup, then stir in the sugar and vanilla. If too stiff to spread, add a little boiling water; if too thin, a little more sugar is needed.

FROSTING WITH GELATINE

1 level teaspoonful of gelatine
1 tablespoonful of cold water
2 tablespoonfuls of boiling water
¾ cup of confectioner's sugar, sifted
½ teaspoonful of vanilla extract

Soften the gelatine in the cold water and dissolve in the boiling water; stir in the sugar and flavoring and beat until of the proper consistency. This frosting may be used with pastry bag and tube. If it does not flow freely, set the bag in a warm (not hot) place for a few minutes.

MARSHMALLOW ICING

1 cup of granulated sugar
¼ cup of water
The whites of 2 eggs
¼ pound of marshmallows
½ teaspoonful of vanilla extract

Boil the sugar and water (as in making fondant) to 240° F. Pour in a fine stream upon the egg whites, beaten dry, beating constantly meanwhile. Beat occasionally until cool; add the marshmallows cut in four pieces, each, and the vanilla. This makes a light, fluffy icing that will not run from a cake.

CHAPTER XV

PRESERVATION OF FRUIT AND VEGETABLES BY CANNING, ETC.

IN cities and large towns fresh fruit may be obtained throughout the year and the necessity for "putting up" a large quantity of fruits no longer exists. But if one is distant from markets and, especially, if one has more of any variety of fruit or vegetable than can be made use of while fresh, the surplus should be made available for future use.

Micro-organisms exist everywhere, and under favorable conditions for growth, as when moisture, warmth and proper food are present, they multiply. These organisms grow rapidly in food stuffs containing nitrogen, as meat, fish, eggs, milk and beans, but they do not find so suitable matter for growth in fruits containing much acid and little nitrogen. Lemons, cranberries and rhubarb contain so much acid that they are rarely attacked by micro-organisms. In preserving vegetables and fruit the micro-organisms on the article or the utensils with which the articles must come in contact during the process of preservation must be destroyed, then the product must be sealed to exclude germs from without. But there are many kinds of micro-organisms; some produce spores which (like the dried seeds of plants) may retain their vitality for a long time, even under conditions that destroy the parent germ. Thus while the parent organism might be destroyed if the food product were exposed ten or fifteen minutes to the temperature of boiling water, the spores would require for their destruction exposure to heat at 212° F. for an hour or more. We have no means of knowing just what micro-organisms may be present in the articles we wish to preserve, but it has been found that, usually, the germs that thrive in fruits and fruit juices can be destroyed by cooking ten or fifteen minutes at a temperature of 212° F. To sterilize the utensils put the spoons, jars, covers and such other articles as are to be used over the fire in cold water, let heat gradually to the boiling point, and then boil ten or fifteen minutes. Take the jars from the water, one at a time, and fill at once with the hot material. It is well to let the can set on a cloth, saturated with boiling water, while it is being filled; fill to overflow, leaving no space for germ laden air. Adjust the rubber, take the cover from the boiling water, set in place and close securely. The covers of Mason jars need to be screwed down more tightly when the cans are cold. Never use a rubber twice; purchase a new supply each season. Jars holding a pint or a half pint are the best size for a family of two.

PREPARATION OF FRUIT FOR CANNING

Articles preserved by sterilization, or the destruction of all germ life, are said to be canned. The addition of sugar, as in the canning of fruit, has nothing to do with the success of the process. The fruit will keep just as well, if no sugar be used. If the fruit is to be served with bread and butter, sugar may be added to make it palatable. If fruit juice be put up for use in frozen desserts, omit the sugar. Fruit for canning may be cooked in an open kettle and transferred to the can, or it may be cooked in the jar in which it is to be stored. Prepare the syrup, add the fruit, peeled and stoned as necessary, then cook the required time and seal as directed. Rhubarb, cranberries and green gooseberries, on account of the large quantity of acid in their composition, may be successfully canned without sterilization by cooking. It were safer, perhaps, to sterilize the jars and covers, though, if bacteria were present, they might not attack these foods.

CRANBERRIES CANNED FOR SUMMER USE

Heat fruit jars gradually, then rinse jars and covers in boiling water. Put as many cranberries as possible into each jar, then pour in cold water to fill the jars to overflow; adjust the rubbers and covers and set the jars aside in a cool place. *Green* gooseberries may be canned in the same way.

CANNED RHUBARB

Sterilize jars and covers. Cut the peeled stalks of rhubarb of a length to come nearly to the top of the jar and fill to overflow with fresh-drawn, cold water; adjust rubbers and covers and store in a cool, dark place.

GRAPE JUICE

Wash the grapes and pick them from the stems. Set them in a preserving kettle over the fire, crush with a pestle and let them slowly heat to the boiling point. Let cook until the skins are tender (about fifteen minutes), then strain through two folds of cheese cloth, pressing out all the juice possible. Heat the juice to the boiling point and turn into sterilized jars, filling them to overflow; put on rubbers and sterilized covers; or store in sterile bottles with sterile corks and sealing wax. For ices it is preferable to put up fruit juices without sugar. For other use sugar may be added. Use half a cup of sugar to a quart of juice.

BERRY AND CURRANT JUICES

The juice of berries and currants may be canned in the same manner as grape juice. Such juice may be made into jelly at any time. Raspberry and strawberry juice are particularly good for sherbets, punches and the like, and for these uses they should be put up without sugar. When using sugar take a cup for each quart of juice, except currant juice. On account of the acidity of currants take a pint of sugar for each quart of juice.

CANNED STRAWBERRIES OR RASPBERRIES

Hull and weigh the berries. For each pound of choice berries allow ten ounces of sugar and one-fourth a cup of water or an equal quantity of juice pressed from inferior berries. Cook the sugar and liquid to a thick syrup and let cool a little. Put the berries, washed and drained, into fruit jars and pour the syrup over the berries in the jars, filling them to overflow; adjust the rubbers and covers. Surround with water at about the temperature of the jars and let boil ten minutes after boiling begins. Tighten the covers. Store in a dark, dry and cool place.

CANNED PEACHES OR PEARS

Cut the fruit in halves (this can be done more easily before the skin is removed) and remove stones, or core and skin. Put into jars. For each quart jar allow two cups of sugar and a cup of water; make a syrup of the sugar and water, skim carefully and use to fill the sterilized jars to overflow. Add half a dozen kernels taken from the peach stones, before adding the syrup. Adjust the rubbers and covers loosely and let cook about ten minutes after boiling begins. Tighten the covers and let cool in the boiler, or remove one at a time to a pan of hot water and fill to overflow with boiling syrup, then adjust the rubbers and the covers.

CANNED PINEAPPLE

Remove the outer skin, then cut in slices, pick from the core with a silver fork or grate according to the use to which the canned product is to be put. Grated pineapple, for omelets, sherbets, Bavarian creams, etc., should be canned without sugar; also pineapple, picked from the core to be used in salads or cocktails, is in better condition if canned without sugar. Can slices of pineapple in the same manner as peaches or pears.

JELLY MAKING AND JELLIES

All varieties of fruit when about ripe contain pectin. If the juice be withdrawn from the fruit, the pectin is withdrawn with it. Boil the juice with the proper proportion of sugar and the pectin will cause the mass to jelly. Pectin is not fully developed until the fruit is nearly ripe; long keeping changes the character of the pectin as does, also, too long cooking of the juice with sugar. Then for success in jelly making let the fruit be not over ripe, and let it be freshly gathered. Also avoid cooking the juice and sugar too much.

Acid fruits make the best jelly. No jelly is better than that made of currants. Large, firm fruit, as apples, crab apples and quinces, must be boiled in water until soft. Avoid stirring the fruit during cooking as it is thought to make the jelly cloudy. The flavoring matter and pectin will become dissolved in the water. No water should be added to juicy fruits, as grapes, currants and berries. The water added to firm fruits must be evaporated by cooking before the addition of sugar. By this cooking the fresh flavor of the fruit is diminished somewhat.

The juice may be extracted from juicy fruits by heating them very slowly, either on the back of the range or in a double boiler. Juice may be extracted from currants without heat, by simply squeezing the fruit in a bag with the hands, then letting drip from the bag.

A flannel bag is thought to give the clearest jelly, but a bag made of new cotton of close texture answers admirably.

The quantity of sugar needed varies somewhat with the season, more being required in a cold wet season than in a season of much sunshine. Usually a cup of sugar to each cup of juice is the right proportion, though many successful jelly makers use but three-fourths a cup of sugar to a cup of juice; the latter proportion is taken especially when the juice of firm fruits is used and the water is evaporated by cooking before the addition of the sugar.

For jellies made with firm fruit cook the juice rapidly fifteen or twenty minutes; have the sugar made hot in the oven, add it, and let the mixture boil about two minutes. Try a little on a cold saucer; as soon as it jellies on the saucer it is ready to pour into the glasses. When the juice is put over the fire, set the jelly glasses on a towel in a pan, pour lukewarm water in and around the glasses and let it gradually heat nearly to the boiling point. To make the sugar hot in the oven, spread it on tin or agate plates; do not have the oven too hot and stir the sugar occasionally. Let juice from juicy fruits boil about five minutes before adding the sugar.

COVERING JELLIES

Bacteria and yeasts, the micro-organisms with which we have to deal in canning, do not thrive in a heavy sugar syrup, thus jellies and "pound for pound" preserves need not be sealed hermetically, but other organisms, molds, grow freely on moist sugary substances exposed to the air. To protect jelly from molds cover with a towel as soon as cold and as soon as possible cover more securely. The simplest and most satisfactory cover is white paper. Cut out pieces of paper the size of the glass at the top of the jelly and a second set of papers about an inch in diameter larger than the first. Brush over one side of the smaller papers with alcohol or brandy and press upon the jelly. Brush the edge of the second pieces with beaten white of egg or mucilage and press down, over the top of the glass and upon the sides of the glass, to which it will closely adhere. Store in a cool dry place.

CURRANT, APPLE AND CRAB APPLE JELLIES

Follow the directions given under jelly making and jellies.

BLACKBERRY-AND-APPLE JELLY

3 pounds of blackberries
1½ pounds of apples
1 cup of water
2½ pounds of sugar

Core the apples, and cut in small pieces, without removing the skins. Mash the berries with a wooden pestle; add the water and apple and let simmer ten minutes, mashing the fruit occasionally. Strain through two folds of fine cheesecloth; let the juice boil, then add the sugar and cook gently half an hour, stirring occasionally. Store in jelly glasses. The apple gives a firmer jelly than the berries alone will give.

APPLE-AND-RASPBERRY JELLY

½ peck of apples
1 pint of raspberry juice or juice of 4 lemons
Sugar as needed or ¾ cup to each cup of juice

Cut the apples in quarters, removing imperfections; pour on boiling water until it can be seen through the pieces, cover and let cook until soft throughout. Let drain in a bag. When cold enough to handle press out the last of the juice with the hands. Do not add this to the juice secured by draining, but cook by itself. To the drained juice add the raspberry juice (fresh or canned) and let boil fifteen minutes. Have the sugar made hot in

Fruit Cooked in the Jars — *Pages 254, 256.*

Apple and Raspberry Jelly — *Page 260*

Pop-Overs — *Page 277*

Baking Powder Biscuit — *Page 280*

Fruit and Nut Rolls — *Page*

the oven; add the sugar and let boil till the mixture jellies slightly on a cold dish. Jelly containing apple grows firm on keeping.

APPLE-AND-MINT JELLY

2 pounds of "Greenings"
2 bunches of garden mint
Juice of 1 lemon
Green color-paste
¾ cup of sugar to each cup of juice

After the apples are cooked and drained, there should be about a pint of juice by draining and a pint by pressing the bag. Keep these portions separate.

Wash, dry and chop fine the mint leaves stripped from the stalks. Add these to the apples when they are partly cooked. Add the lemon juice and color-paste a short time before the jelly is to be poured into the glasses. This gives a very delicate flavor of mint; much of the flavor seems to be dissipated during cooking. Crême de menthe cordial made at home, or purchased, will give a more pronounced flavor to the jelly.

GRAPEFRUIT MARMALADE

Take six grapefruit and four lemons; cut each fruit in quarters and slice the quarters through pulp and rind as thin as possible, discarding all seeds. Weigh the prepared fruit, and to each pound add three pints of cold water. Set aside for twenty-four hours. Let boil gently until the rind is perfectly tender, then set aside until the next day. Weigh the material and to each pound add one pound of sugar. Let cook until it thickens slightly on a cold dish. The mixture will thicken still more on cooling and care must be taken not to cook it too much. Stir occasionally, while cooking, to avoid burning. Store as jelly. With a small, hard-wood board upon which to rest the fruit, and a thin, sharp knife, the slicing is quickly done. Use all the water designated.

ORANGE MARMALADE

Substitute one dozen oranges for the grapefruit and follow the recipe for grapefruit marmalade.

APPLE MARMALADE

Pare, quarter and core the apples and put over the fire with just enough water to keep the fruit from burning; cover closely and let cook until soft; press through a colander. Measure the pulp and allow three-fourths a cup of sugar to each cup of pulp. Stir and cook until when tested on a cold saucer the mixture does not separate. Often a lemon or an orange is used to each one or two pounds of apple. Slice as for orange marmalade, discarding the seeds; let cook in water to cover until the peel is tender, then add to the apple pulp.

PEACH MARMALADE

Prepare in the same manner as apple marmalade.

Cooking for Two

APPLE BUTTER

½ peck of sour apples
1 quart of sliced sweet apples
Cider, fresh or boiled
Spices to taste

Pare, quarter, core and slice the sour apples; add the sweet apples. Weigh the apples and take sugar equal to half the weight of the apples. Add cider until it comes nearly to the top of the apples and let cook, stirring occasionally with a perforated paddle that comes for the purpose or with a slitted wooden spoon. When the apples are soft and well broken up, add the sugar and spice in quantity as desired and stir constantly until of the consistency of marmalade. Water may take the place of the cider. Cinnamon, mace, nutmeg and cloves one or more are the spices usually selected. Peach or plum butter is made in the same way.

TOMATO MARMALADE

4 quarts of ripe tomatoes
6 lemons
1 cup of raisins
4 pounds of granulated sugar

Remove the skins from the tomatoes and slice the lemons very thin, discarding the seeds. Seed the raisins. Put the ingredients into a preserving kettle in layers. Heat slowly to the boiling point, then let simmer until quite thick. Seal in jars while hot. The recipe makes about three pints.

ORIENTAL PRESERVE

5 pounds of green tomatoes
6 lemons
1 pound of sugar
2 cups of water
1 medium jar of preserved ginger

Dissolve the sugar in the water and add the tomatoes, lemons and ginger root cut in thin slices, also the syrup from the ginger jar. Let simmer until the tomatoes are shriveled. Seal in glass jars. Keep three or four weeks before using.

BLACKBERRY JAM

Put the berries in a preserving kettle, cover closely and let become hot, then with a wooden pestle press through a sieve fine enough to keep back the seeds. Measure the pulp and for each two cups take one cup of sugar. Heat slowly to the boiling point, stirring often. Let cook nearly half an hour, stirring almost constantly. Store as canned fruit, or cook an hour or more and store as jelly. This makes a particularly good sauce for cornstarch puddings and the like.

SUNSHINE STRAWBERRIES

Put into the preserving kettle, in layers, as many pounds of sugar as of hulled, washed and drained strawberries. When the juice is drawn out a little, set over the fire to cook twenty minutes after boiling commences. Turn the berries into agate pans or earthen plates, cover with panes of glass and set in the sun. Let stand two days, stirring two or three times each day. Store without reheating in jars or glasses. The time of cooking may be cut down to ten minutes, if the fruit be left in the sun a day or two longer.

GINGERED PEARS

4 pounds of pared-and-sliced pears
3 small lemons
¼ pound of ginger root
1 cup of water
3 pounds of sugar

Cut the ginger root as small as possible; add water to cover well and let simmer to make a strong decoction. Strain off the water, of which there should be one cup, add to it the lemons, cut in thin slices (discard the seeds), and let cook until the peel is tender; add the sugar and when dissolved the sliced pears and cook slowly until the pears are tender.

BAR-LE-DUC CURRANTS AND GOOSEBERRIES

Take selected gooseberries or currants of large size, one by one, and with tiny embroidery scissors carefully cut the skin on one side, making a slit of perhaps one-fourth an inch. Through this, with a sharp needle, remove the seeds, one at a time, to preserve the shape of the fruit. Take the weight of the fruit in strained honey, and, when hot, add the prepared fruit. Let simmer three or four minutes. Carefully skim out the fruit. Reduce the syrup, at a gentle simmer, to the desired consistency. Pour over the fruit. Then store as jelly.

CANNING VEGETABLES

To can vegetables successfully, one needs have access to a garden, and take the vegetables before the sugar in composition has changed to starch. Only tiny peas, lima beans, string beans, and corn "in the milk" can be put up without fear of failure. The time of cooking will vary a little from year to year, according to the season and condition of the ground; but these things modify the time of cooking less than does the manner in which the canning is done. In certain canners the cooking is done under a heavy pressure of steam. In some of the steam cookers, while the steam pressure makes an appreciable difference in the time needed for canning, longer cooking is demanded than in the best canners. In others, the pressure of the steam corresponds to that obtained in an ordinary kettle, closely covered, or in a wash boiler. The time given in the following recipes is for canning when an ordinary kettle or a wash boiler is fitted up for the purpose with a rack, upon which the jars may stand. This rack or trivet is to insure the circulation of water below the jars. A tin sheet filled with holes resting on baking-powder box covers or a rack made by fastening narrow strips of wood upon two lengthwise strips of wood answers all purposes. Of course, the sheet or rack needs be of a size to let down easily into the kettle or boiler.

CANNED CORN

Pack the corn (see above), cut from the cobs, into jars, pressing it down tight and filling the jars nearly to the top. Lay a folded cloth on the rack. On this set the jars. Pour into the kettle lukewarm water to one-third the height of the jars. Put on the jar covers. Cover the kettle, and let cook three hours after boiling begins. If the jars are not now full, use one or more jars to fill the others to overflow. Adjust the rubbers and covers, return to the fire, and cook one hour and a half. Then adjust the covers, and let cool in the kettle. If Mason jars be used, tighten the covers again when the jars are cold.

CANNING PEAS

Select the peas while young and tender. Shell and look them over, wash in cold water, then scald by pouring over boiling water and draining immediately. Pack in glass jars, shaking down well. Fill to the brim with cold water. Adjust the rubbers, and screw on covers loose. Put a cloth or plate in a kettle with a flat bottom, to prevent contact, then put in the cans, separating them from each other with a folded cloth. Fill kettle not quite to cover of cans with cold water. Bring to boiling-point, and boil one hour, adding boiling water as that in the kettle evaporates. The kettle should be covered from the first. At the end of an hour add boiling water to fill the jars to overflow, fasten the covers and cook half an hour.

CANNED STRING BEANS

Cut the young tender green beans into pieces, lengthwise; cut butter beans into three or four pieces crosswise. Put these into cold water as cut. Drain and put into jars. Set into the kettle as above.

When thoroughly heated fill the jars with boiling water, cover and let cook one hour. Add half a teaspoonful of salt to each pint jar, also, if needed, boiling water to fill to overflow. Adjust the rubbers and covers and let cook twenty minutes. Fasten down the covers.

CANNED TOMATOES

Peel small ripe tomatoes and cut out the hard part round the stem end. Put, whole, into the sterilized jar as many as the jar will hold without crushing. In the meantime cook enough pared-and-sliced tomatoes as are needed to make about a pint; pour this, while hot, around the tomatoes in the jar and shake the jar to fill all the open spaces. Put on the cover and let cook set on a folded cloth on a rack in a saucepan or steam cooker half an hour. Have ready hot tomato; fill the jar to overflow and cover as usual.

CANNED ASPARAGUS

The asparagus should be fresh-cut. Use only the tender portion of the stalks. Wash and drain this and put it in the cans with the heads up; cook without water one hour; put a teaspoonful of salt into a quart of boiling water and use to fill the jars to overflow. Adjust the rubbers and covers and let cook nearly an hour longer.

A NEW WAY OF CANNING FRUIT AND VEGETABLES

A new way has been discovered by which fruits can be canned without boiling. By this method the fruits retain their natural shape, color, and flavor, and remain plump and attractive in appearance. It is called the intermittent Pasteurizing method.

Clean fruit or vegetables are placed in clean cans, and water that has been boiled to sterilize it is poured over it, completely filling the cans. The covers are then put on light, but not screwed down, after which the cans are set in a boiler of water up to the cover. The water in the boiler is then heated until the temperature in the center of the cans records 165° F. The cans are held at this temperature for fifteen minutes. They are then removed, and the tops screwed down firm. After standing from twenty-four to forty-eight hours, the cans are again heated to the same temperature for the same length of time. A day or two later they are heated for the third time, after which the contents of the cans are sterile, and will keep perfectly.

The principles involved in this method of canning are as follows: The fermentation and molds on canned goods are caused by the growth in the fruit and juice of microscopic plants. These plants are propagated by spores which correspond to the seed of higher plants. These spores are produced by the million. They are blown about by the wind, and are everywhere present, being especially abundant on the fruit itself.

With moisture and a summer temperature, these spores grow very rapidly, resulting in fermented and putrefactive products. By heating them to a temperature of 165° F., every spore that has started to grow will be killed. The spores that have not started to grow will not be killed by the first heating, but by waiting twenty-four to forty-eight hours almost all will germinate. The second heating kills all these, and, if any spores are still left, they germinate and are killed by the third heating. Fruits and vegetables thus sterilized in the cans keep practically in their natural condition, and represent the perfection of canned goods.

Corn and *peas* cannot be preserved successfully by this method, but all of the fruits and such vegetables as tomatoes, green beans, wax beans, cauliflower, asparagus, etc., when thus treated, keep perfectly, retaining their natural color, flavor, and texture.

PICKLES

Micro-organisms do not thrive in strong acids, thus with proper care fruit and vegetables may be kept in vinegar for some time.

SMALL GHERKINS

1 quart of small cucumbers
¼ cup of table salt
Cold water

Vinegar *scalding hot*
2 or 3 chilli peppers
1 tablespoonful of mixed spices

As soon as the cucumbers are picked, scrub them without breaking the skin and throw into cold water, in which the salt has been dissolved. Let stand overnight, pour off the water, add fresh water and drain, then pack the cucumbers, peppers and spices in a sterilized jar; adjust the cover, pour in vinegar to overflow, tighten the jar and store in a dry cool place. After the jar is opened, if the vinegar scums over, pour it off and replace with a new supply, scalding hot. The pickles should thus keep in good condition even if the jar be opened daily.

PICCALILLI

1 quart of green tomatoes
1 pint of red tomatoes
1 head of celery
2 red sweet peppers
1 green sweet pepper
1 large mild onion
½ small head of cabbage

1 ripe cucumber
½ cup of salt
3 cups of vinegar
1 pound of brown sugar
½ teaspoonful of mustard
½ teaspoonful of pepper

Chop the vegetables, cover with the salt and let stand overnight. Drain and press in a cloth, to remove all the liquid possible; add the vinegar, sugar and spices and let cook until clear (nearly an hour). Store hot in sterilized jars as canned fruit.

CHAPTER XVI

FLOUR MIXTURES: QUICK BREADS

THE cooking of grains, as mush or porridge, is of comparatively recent date, but the grinding of grains into meal or flour and mixing the product with water and baking it is a custom as old as written history. The most delicate and feathery cake that is made to-day is a direct and lineal descendant from the cake of stone-ground meal and water, baked on stones made hot in the blazing campfire of primitive man.

In flour mixtures the essentials are flour, salt, wetting and leaven, or something to make the mixture light and porous. The leaven may be either carbon dioxide, evolved in various ways, air beaten or folded into the mixture (sponge cake), or the expansion of a cold liquid when heated. Usually all three agents are present and at work in a flour mixture.

In quick breads (time is a necessity, when carbon dioxide is evolved by the growth of a microscopic plant — yeast — introduced into the dough); the carbon dioxide is usually generated by the use of bicarbonate of soda (an alkali) and an acid, as cream of tartar, sour milk, molasses, etc.

Keep in mind that the proportion of flour to liquid

determines the consistency of the mixture, and that the quantity of liquid used determines the size of the finished product. Different names are given to mixtures, according to the proportion existing between the flour and the water. As, when one measure of liquid is used to one or two measures of flour, the mixture is called a *batter;* and when one measure of liquid is used to three or four measures of flour, the resulting mixture is a *dough*.

BATTER AND DOUGH

When a batter is made of equal measures or parts of flour and liquid, it may be poured from the dish in a continuous stream, and it is known as a thin or pour batter.

When a batter is made of one measure of liquid to two measures of flour, it breaks while being turned from a dish and is known as a thick or drop batter.

SOFT OR STIFF DOUGH

When one measure of liquid is used to three measures of flour, a *soft* dough is formed — to four measures of flour, a *stiff* dough results. A soft dough sticks to the sides of the bowl; a stiff dough while being mixed gathers to itself all the material on the sides of the bowl, and the bowl is clean, when the dough is mixed. In practice there are gradations between these mixtures. The mixture for fine baking-powder biscuit is neither a soft nor a stiff dough, but intermediate between the two. All doughs are mixtures of a consistency to be kneaded with the hands.

PROPORTIONS OF SALT AND FLOUR. One-fourth a teaspoonful of salt is needed to each cup of flour, except when shortening that has been previously salted is used, when a little less is required.

PROPORTIONS OF BAKING POWDER AND FLOUR. Two level teaspoonfuls of baking powder to each cup of flour is needed, except in mixtures where eggs or much beating introduces air into the mixture (heated air expands, continued heat hardens the cell walls, and the finished product is lightened to a certain degree). In the beating of butter and sugar " to a cream " air is beaten into the mixture, but the greatest quantity of air is incorporated, when the whites and yolks of eggs are separated and air is beaten in to their full capacity of retention.

PROPORTIONS OF SODA AND CREAM OF TARTAR. Half a level teaspoonful of soda and a level teaspoonful and one-fourth of cream of tartar furnish, in the effect produced, a very close equivalent to two level teaspoonfuls of baking powder.

LIQUID USED WITH BAKING POWDER, SODA AND CREAM OF TARTAR MIXTURES. When bicarbonate of soda (an alkali) and cream of tartar (an acid) are used in making baking powder (and the same should be true when we measure these ingredients ourselves), they are so carefully weighed that one exactly neutralizes the other, leaving in the dough in which they are used no excess of either acid or alkali; thus no free acid, such as would exist in sour milk, lemon juice or molasses, can be added to the mixture, unless enough alkali to neutralize the acidity be, also, added.

GENERAL RULE FOR BAKING POWDER, SODA AND CREAM OF TARTAR MIXTURES. Avoid the use of acids, as sour milk, molasses or lemon juice, in mixtures lightened with baking powder or bicarbonate of soda and cream of tartar.

OCCASIONAL USE OF BAKING POWDER WITH SOUR MILK OR MOLASSES. Sometimes sour milk or cream is more readily available than sweet milk; soda may be added to this, to correct the acidity, and the milk then can be used with baking powder as in case it were sweet milk, if allowance be made for the carbon dioxide resultant from the combination of the soda and sour milk. In using molasses the acidity must be neutralized with soda; then baking powder may be used to lighten the mixture.

PROPORTIONS OF SODA AND BAKING POWDER TO BE USED WITH SOUR MILK AND MOLASSES. Use half a level teaspoonful of soda for each cup of molasses or thick sour milk or cream. Cut down the quantity of baking powder to one level teaspoonful to each cup of flour, or if eggs are used the quantity of baking powder may be cut down still more.

METHOD OF COMBINING FLOUR MIXTURES. An article over-porous on one side and heavy on the other, or with streaks of heaviness here and there, is neither wholesome nor attractive in appearance. Again, when soda or baking powder is stirred into a liquid, especially if it be a hot or an acid liquid, bubbles of gas begin to appear at once and are lost before the mixture can be stirred into the dough; accordingly, then, to secure a mixture of even lightness throughout, it is necessary that the dry leavening agents be sifted with the flour two or three times, and salt, and sometimes sugar, is sifted with these. Now stir the liquid into the dry ingredients and bake as soon as possible.

How to Add Shortening. When a small quantity of shortening, as one, two or three tablespoonfuls, is to be added to a mixture, it may be melted and beaten in at the last. When a larger quantity is to be used, it may be beaten until creamy, and the sugar beaten into it, as in cake making; or it may be cut into the flour with a knife or the fingers, as in making biscuits, or partly cut in and partly folded in, as in making pastry.

How to Add Eggs. If a hollow cake, like popovers, is to be produced, add the egg, beaten without separating the white from the yolk, to the milk and beat the two together into the dry mixture. When a spongy texture is desired, beat the whites and yolks separately, then add the yolks with the milk and, at the last, beat in the whites.

How to Bake Quick Breads. Quick breads are steamed, baked in the oven, in individual portions, also in loaves or sheets, and on a griddle on the top of the stove. Breads containing sugar and butter, one or both, burn more easily than do those without such ingredients. Eggs are cooked at a low temperature, and thus mixtures containing many eggs should be cooked more slowly than those with no eggs.

POP OVERS

1 egg, beaten light
1 cup of milk
1 cup of sifted pastry flour
¼ teaspoonful of salt
6 teaspoonfuls of butter

Do not separate the white from the yolk of the egg; beat light, add the milk and continue to use the beater while the flour and salt are gradually beaten into the liquid. Butter six cups of an iron gem pan; half fill the other six with boiling water, put a teaspoonful of butter into each of the buttered cups and pour the mixture into them. Bake on the floor of a moderate oven about thirty-five minutes. Muffin or pop over pans with only six compartments are not often found, but the pan with a dozen cups can be used successfully by half filling the unused cups with water.

RYE MEAL MUFFINS
(Sample Recipe)

½ cup of rye *meal*
½ cup of wheat flour
2 tablespoonfuls of sugar
½ teaspoonful of salt
2 level teaspoonfuls of baking powder
1 egg
⅓ to ½ cup of milk
2 tablespoonfuls of melted butter

Sift together, three times, all the dry ingredients. Beat the egg, add the milk and stir into the dry ingredients. Lastly, beat in the butter. Bake in six well-buttered muffin cups in a moderate oven about twenty-five minutes. Half fill the other six cups with boiling water. The egg may be omitted, or the white may be used to clarify the coffee for two or three mornings and the yolk be used in the muffins. Heat the pan before filling.

CORN MEAL, ARLINGTON MEAL, OR GRAHAM FLOUR MUFFINS

Prepare as Rye Meal Muffins, substituting one of the above ingredients for the rye meal. With corn meal, either white or yellow, a third of a cup of sugar is often approved.

SALLY LUNN

2 cups of pastry flour
¼ teaspoonful of salt
3 tablespoonfuls of granulated sugar
½ teaspoonful of soda
1½ level teaspoonfuls of cream of tartar
1 egg with yolk or white of another
½ cup of milk
3 tablespoonfuls of melted butter

Sift together the dry ingredients. Add the milk to the beaten eggs and stir into the dry ingredients, stir in the butter; turn into a buttered shallow pan and let bake about twenty minutes. Cut in squares and serve hot or cold. This mixture may be baked in a muffin pan.

OLIVE SANDWICHES — *Page 307*

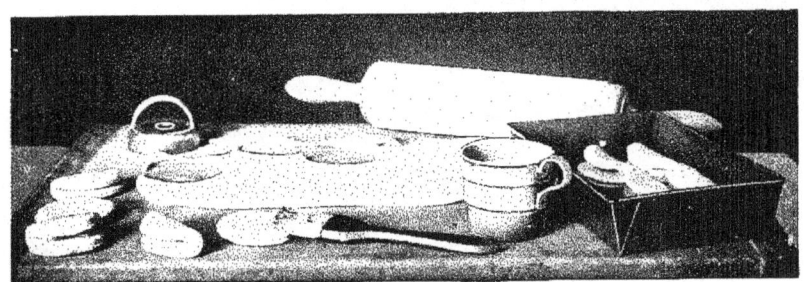

SHAPING PARKER HOUSE ROLLS — *Page 297*

Bread and Coffee Cake made with One Yeast Cake — *Page 302.*

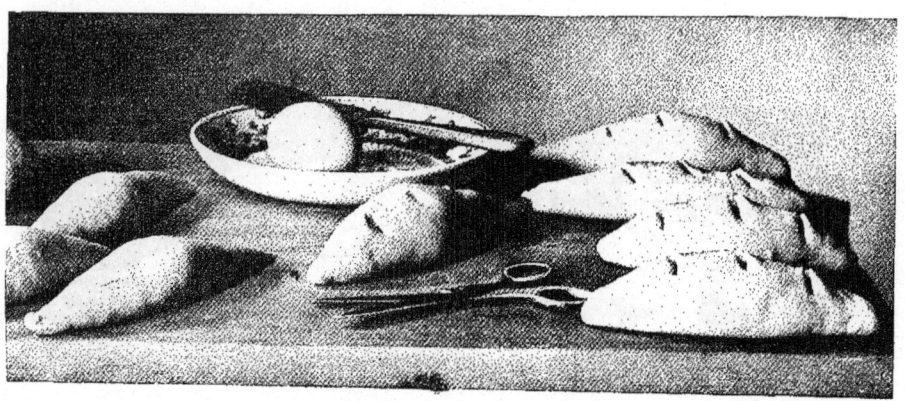

Shaping Lady Finger Rolls — *Page 294*

Ready to Make Bread — *Page 290.*

DELICATE CORN MEAL MUFFINS

½ cup of corn meal
½ cup of boiling water
2 tablespoonfuls of butter
½ cup of pastry flour
½ teaspoonful of salt

2 teaspoonfuls of baking powder
2 tablespoonfuls of sugar
1 egg, beaten light
½ cup of milk

Pour the boiling water over the corn meal, add the butter and mix thoroughly; cover and let stand an hour or longer; add the flour, salt, sugar and baking powder sifted together; add the egg and milk and mix all together thoroughly. The mixture is quite thin. Bake in a hot, well-buttered muffin pan about twenty-five minutes. The recipe will make one dozen small muffins.

SOFT CORN BREAD
(Miss Scott)

1 pint of sweet milk
½ cup of white corn meal
½ teaspoonful of salt

1 tablespoonful of butter
1 egg, beaten light
1 level tablespoonful of baking powder

Scald the milk in a double boiler, stir in the meal and let cook three hours, then beat in the other ingredients. Note that it is a tablespoonful and not a teaspoonful of baking powder. Turn into a buttered baking dish suitable for the table. Bake about forty minutes. Serve hot from the dish. This is often called Spoon corn bread.

BAKING POWDER BISCUIT

2 cups of sifted pastry flour
4 level teaspoonfuls of baking powder
½ teaspoonful of salt
2 to 4 tablespoonfuls shortening
½ to ⅔ cup of milk or water

Pass together through a sieve, three times, the flour salt and baking powder. With a knife or the tips of the fingers work in the shortening; add the liquid a little at a time, mixing it with a knife meanwhile to a soft dough, but one that can be handled. Turn the dough on to a floured board, turn it with the knife until lightly floured, then knead with the hands slightly, to get it into a smooth mass; pat with the rolling pin and roll into a sheet about three-fourths an inch thick; cut into rounds; set these close together in a buttered pan and bake from fifteen to twenty minutes. White flour, or half white and half entire wheat or Graham flour or rye meal, may be used. The recipe makes from twelve to sixteen biscuits, according to size.

FRUIT-AND-NUT ROLLS

2 cups of sifted pastry flour
½ teaspoonful of salt
4 level teaspoonfuls of baking powder
¼ cup of shortening
About ½ cup of milk
1 egg, if desired
1 tablespoonful of softened butter
¼ cup of cleaned currants or Sultana raisins
¼ cup of filberts, cut in 3 or 4 pieces
2 tablespoonfuls of sugar, if desired

Sift the dry ingredients together, three times, and work in the shortening with a knife or the tips of the fingers. Beat the egg — this may be omitted, it simply makes the rolls more nutritious — add part of the milk and mix to a dough. Knead the dough (on the board) slightly, then roll into a rectangular sheet about one-third an inch thick. Brush the sheet of dough with the softened butter, then sprinkle with the nuts and fruit (also the sugar if it is used). Roll the dough over and over compactly, then cut the roll in pieces an inch long. Set these on end close together in a buttered baking pan. Bake about twenty-five minutes.

BLACKBERRY ROLY POLY

1 pint of blackberries
¼ cup of water
¾ cup of sugar
1½ cups of pastry flour
3 level teaspoonfuls of baking powder
½ teaspoonful (scant) of salt
¼ cup of shortening
Yolk of 1 egg
Milk or water
White of 1 egg, beaten slightly
Granulated sugar

Cook the berries with the water in a covered saucepan until softened and strain through a sieve fine enough to keep back the seeds; add the sugar and let cook until quite thick, stirring occasionally. Sift together the flour, baking powder and salt, work in the shortening and mix to a dough with the yolk of egg and a little milk or water. Turn the dough onto a floured board and knead, to get it in shape, then roll out into a rectangular sheet one-fourth an inch thick; cut this into four pieces longer than wide.

Spread each piece with the blackberry mixture, roll up like a jelly roll and set into a baking pan. Brush the top of each roll with white of egg, then dredge with sugar. Bake about twenty-five minutes. Serve hot with the rest of the blackberry, kept hot in boiling water, as a sauce.

STRAWBERRY SHORT CAKE

1¼ cups of pastry flour
¼ cup of potato flour or cornstarch
4 level teaspoonfuls of baking powder
½ teaspoonful of salt
¼ cup of shortening
Milk as needed
Butter to spread the cake
1 basket of strawberries
1 cup of granulated sugar

Hull and wash the berries, cut them in halves and mix with the sugar; let stand in a warm but not hot place while the cake is baking. Prepare the ingredients as baking powder biscuit mixture, leaving it a little softer. Turn dough into a buttered pie plate, spread it evenly, drawing it away from the center somewhat. Let bake about twenty minutes. With a sharp pointed knife, cut the crust all around midway between the top and bottom, then gently pull it apart. Set one piece on a plate, spread with butter, pour on part of the prepared berries, set the other half of the crust above the berries, spread it with butter and then with the rest of the berries. Serve either with or without cream.

Cooking for Two

HOT APPLE TRIANGLES

2 cups of flour
¼ cup of sugar
3 level teaspoonfuls of baking powder
¼ teaspoonful of salt
¼ cup of butter
2 tart apples in small pieces
1 egg

⅓ cup of sweet milk
1 apple, pared and cut in eighths
1 or 2 tablespoonfuls sugar
1 teaspoonful of cinnamon
1 tablespoonful of cleaned currants

Sift together the flour, sugar, baking powder and salt; with the tips of the fingers work in the butter and add the pieces of apple. Beat the egg; add the milk and use to mix the dry ingredients to a dough. A little more milk may be needed. Spread the dough, with a spoon, in a round pan. Press the eighths of apple into the dough at equal distances apart, dredge the top with the sugar and cinnamon and sprinkle over the currants. Bake in a hot oven. Serve, cut in triangles, with butter for luncheon or supper.

BLUEBERRY TEA CAKE OR MUFFINS

2 cups of sifted pastry flour
4 level teaspoonfuls of baking powder
1 cup of sugar
½ teaspoonful of salt
1 egg, beaten light

½ cup of milk
2 tablespoonfuls of melted butter
1 cup of blueberries dredged with a little flour

Sift together the dry ingredients and mix with the egg and milk; beat in the butter and the berries. Bake in a sheet or in a muffin pan. This recipe may be easily halved. Use either the white or the yolk of the egg.

CEREAL GRIDDLE CAKES

½ cup of ready-to-eat cereal, as Egg-O-See, Granose flakes, etc.
½ cup of thick sour cream
⅛ teaspoonful of soda
Yolk of 1 egg, beaten
¼ teaspoonful of salt
¼ cup of sweet milk
½ cup of sifted flour
1 level teaspoonful of baking powder
White of 1 egg
Slice of salt pork, to oil the griddle

Mash and sift the soda before measuring and stir it into the cream; pour the cream over the cereal and add the yolk, salt, sweet milk and the flour sifted with the baking powder. Mix all together thoroughly, then beat in the white of egg, beaten light. Drop from the spoon in small cakes upon a hot well-oiled griddle. When the cakes are well filled with bubbles, they should be brown underneath and ready to turn, to brown the other side. A heavy iron frying pan answers nicely for a griddle.

CORN MEAL GRIDDLE CAKES

½ cup of corn meal
⅔ cup of flour
2½ level teaspoonfuls of baking powder
¼ teaspoonful of salt
1 tablespoonful of sugar
1 egg, beaten light
1 cup of sweet milk
1 tablespoonful of melted butter

At night scald the milk, pour it over the corn meal, mix, cover closely and let stand till morning. Add the other ingredients and bake as above.

Cooking for Two

BREAD GRIDDLE CAKES

Soak stale bread, from which the crust has been taken, in cold water. When the bread is soft, turn it into a piece of cheese cloth and wring out the water. Take:

1 cup of softened bread
1 egg, beaten light
2 level teaspoonfuls of sugar
½ teaspoonful of salt
¾ cup of pastry flour

1½ level teaspoonfuls of baking powder
About ½ cup of milk
Bake as previously directed

GREEN OR CANNED CORN GRIDDLE CAKES

1 cup of corn pulp
1 egg, beaten light
½ teaspoonful of salt
⅓ cup of sweet milk

1 tablespoonful of melted butter
½ cup of sifted flour
1 level teaspoonful of baking powder

These griddle cakes are good with creamed chicken, or with the remnants of stewed chicken (much sauce and little chicken). For use with chicken add one-fourth a teaspoonful of black pepper and a slice of green or red pepper, chopped fine.

PLAIN GRIDDLE CAKES

1 cup of sifted flour
¼ teaspoonful of salt
½ teaspoonful of baking powder

½ teaspoonful of bicarbonate of soda
1 cup of thick, sour milk
1 or 2 tablespoonfuls of melted butter

Sift together the flour salt and baking powder, stir the soda into the sour milk and use to mix the dry ingredients to a batter; mix in the butter and bake as usual. This recipe will make about eight cakes. A cup of sweet milk and a level teaspoonful of baking powder may be substituted for the sour milk and soda.

CHAPTER XVII

FLOUR MIXTURES CONTINUED: BREAD AND OTHER YEAST MIXTURES

THE INGREDIENTS FOR BREAD MAKING

THE ingredients required for making yeast bread are: flour, yeast, salt and liquid. Sugar is sometimes used.

PROPORTIONS OF THE INGREDIENTS

The quantity of liquid used determines the size of the finished loaf. One cup of liquid with one-fourth a cup of liquid yeast (or compressed or dry yeast diluted with one-fourth a cup of liquid) will make one loaf of bread of a size to bake in what is known as a "brick-loaf pan"; or it will make about one and three-fourths pounds of bread dough. The quantity of flour used, together with the manipulation of the ingredients, has much to do with the texture of the bread. For a firm, fine-grained loaf from three to four and more measures of flour to one of liquid are needed. For bread of more open texture from two and one-half to three measures of flour to one of liquid will suffice. Take half a teaspoonful of salt for each loaf of bread. A tablespoonful of butter or other shortening to each cup of liquid will make the bread more tender. The quantity of yeast to be used will depend upon the time given to the process and the temperature at which the dough is kept. For bread mixed at night, to be baked in the morning, one-third a cake of compressed yeast will be required for each pint of liquid. A larger proportion, accordingly, of yeast, as one-fourth a cake is necessary when but one loaf is made.

YEAST

Floating everywhere around us in the air are microscopic organisms that more nearly resemble plant than animal life. To certain of these organisms the name yeast is applied. These organisms, in a suitable environment, feed on sweet and nitrogenous bodies, or substances, and grow and multiply very rapidly. Chemical change (fermentation) is the result of this growth. The conditions essential to the growth of these minute plant organisms are warmth, moisture, air and something sweet and nitrogenous to feed upon. All these conditions may be secured when the plants are mixed in moistened flour and left in a temperature between 75° to 95° F. As the plants feed upon the sweet substances in the flour a rearrangement of the molecules of flour takes place, the sugar in composition is broken up and alcohol and carbon dioxide are formed. The carbon dioxide lightens the dough.

In any variety of yeast used we have a collection

of yeast plants massed together in such a manner that the life of the plants may be preserved for a time.

Dry, home-made and compressed yeast, all will give good results, but as compressed yeast can now be purchased almost everywhere, the recipes will be written for this form of yeast. In using home-made yeast allow half a cup to each pint of liquid to be used in making bread. Compressed yeast may be kept for several days or a week; dry yeast for a much longer time, but eventually the plants will die.

EFFECT OF HEAT AND COLD ON YEAST PLANTS

In working with yeast mixtures we must keep in mind that we are dealing with plant life and treat the mixtures accordingly. If you pour boiling water over a sprouting seed or a young plant, you would not expect it to continue to grow. Yeast plants are of the same nature, and if you pour boiling water or scalding hot milk over a yeast cake to soften it, you need not expect the plants to grow and multiply and thus lighten the mixture into which you stir them. When the properly treated plants have done their work and you have no longer use for them, then the heat of the oven is needed to drive off the alcohol and carbon dioxide and to set the glutinous cell walls, to keep the dough light.

Yeast plants bear cold much better than heat; life is kept in a dormant state at about 30° F. Thus yeast cakes may be kept in good condition some days in a refrigerator. In a refrigerator bread and rolls about ready for the oven may be kept in that condition some hours or over night, and be ready for baking at any moment.

In practice, when set into the refrigerator, bread should not be quite as light as rolls or bread in individual portions, for some time must elapse before the cold penetrates entirely through the loaf, and during this time the loaf will be growing lighter or more porous.

THE KIND OF FLOUR FOR BREAD MAKING

A bread flour is one that takes up a large quantity of liquid; a pastry flour, one that takes up but little liquid. Then less in quantity of bread flour than of pastry flour would be needed with one cup of liquid, the measure for a loaf of bread. With a little experience one may easily learn to distinguish these flours. Bread flour is granular and goes through the sieve easily. Pastry flour is more solid, is oily and keeps its shape when pressed in the hand. As to variety, rye, graham, whole wheat (brown in color) and corn flour, as also rye and oat meal, may be used in bread, but for the best results white flour should be combined with these. The proportion of white flour may be varied from time to time, but it should never be less than one-fourth of the full amount taken.

UTENSILS FOR BREAD MAKING

A knife is the proper utensil for mixing dough. An earthen bowl is easily cleaned, and for evident reasons is to be desired when mixing is to be done with a knife. A close-fitting tin cover, with three or four tiny holes in the top, through which gases may escape, with a brick-loaf tin for baking, complete the list of necessary utensils. For cutting biscuit and Parker House rolls a round cutter with sharp edge is desirable, but the cover of a baking powder box, in which a few holes have been made with a nail and a hammer, will answer the purpose. Many rolls are shaped with the hands. That measuring cups and spoons are needful ought to be a foregone conclusion, understood by the time one essays her first loaf of bread.

MIXING THE DOUGH

In making bread with compressed yeast it is customary to add all the flour to the liquid, that is, the mixing of the bread is completed at once. In making biscuit or rolls, in which shortening, sugar, etc., are used, a " sponge " is first made, and when fermentation is assured, the shortening, sugar and rest of the flour are added and the mixture is again set to rise. Thus bread dough rises twice, once after mixing and again after it is set in the baking pan, while biscuit dough rises three and sometimes four times. The repetition of the fermenting process affects the flavor of the finished product, and thus gives an opportunity to diversify the flavor of yeast mixtures. This fact should receive due attention, for bread is a very important staple in our food supply.

In the recipes two varieties of " sponge " will be

noted. As salt, sugar and fat retard the growth of the yeast plants, none of these are added until the "sponge" is light. Sometimes we take all the liquid that is to be used in making the bread or rolls, and into this stir and beat the softened yeast and enough flour to make a batter. Cover the batter and let it stand until puffy and well filled with bubbles. As there is only a small quantity of flour for the plants to feed upon, the sponge is soon ready for use. After the rest of the flour has been added, the mixture will soon double in bulk, which is the sign that a dough is ready to be cut down and made ready for the oven. Another way of making a "sponge" is to soften the yeast in the quantity of water required (one-fourth a cup for one loaf of bread), and into this stir flour to make a stiff dough; knead this, then set it into the warm liquid of which the bread is to be made; when the little ball of dough floats on the liquid, a light and puffy "sponge," add the rest of the ingredients and mix the whole to a dough.

KNEADING THE DOUGH

Learn to knead dough without pushing the fingers into it or scattering flour, etc., over the table and floor. Keep the crust that forms on the surface of the dough, while it is in motion, intact. Keep the dough moving, bring it forward, by turning it at the back with the tips of the fingers, press down upon it with the hand just above the wrist, push it back, then repeat; bring forward, press down and push back, occasionally turning halfway round, until the surface is filled with tiny blisters and the mass is round and smooth. Then return to the bowl, cover closely and set aside out of all drafts, until the mass has doubled in bulk.

SHAPING BREAD DOUGH

Divide the dough made with one cup of milk into two pieces; knead each, one at a time, into a smooth, round ball; take up in the hands, and with the fingers work out the creases on the under side as much as possible. The perfect loaf shows no creases when baked. Set the balls of dough, side by side, in a buttered pan, cover with a cloth and when nearly doubled in bulk the dough is ready to bake. The dough may be shaped in one oval piece, but the slices will be of more uniform size, if it be shaped in two pieces.

SHAPING BISCUIT-AND-ROLL DOUGH

When round biscuit are desired, the dough may be carefully turned from the bowl, upside down, upon a board lightly floured. With the rolling pin press the dough into a sheet half or three-fourths an inch thick, then cut it into rounds. Set these in buttered pans, close together or some distance apart, according as a soft or crusty exterior is desired. If the rounds are set close together, lightly brush the edges that will come in contact with a brush dipped in melted butter, that the biscuit may be easily separated after baking. Or, pieces weighing about two ounces each may be pulled from the dough; knead these into round balls and set them into the buttered pans as before. The first way is employed, when Parker House rolls are to be made, the second, when salad, lady fingers and other fancy-shaped rolls are to be shaped.

BAKING BREAD AND ROLLS

Bread to be baked in individual portions requires a hotter oven than full-sized loaves. The general directions are the same for both bread and biscuit. Divide the time of baking into quarters; in the first quarter the dough should spring, or grow light, a little, and should color in spots and cease to rise. By the end of the second quarter the bread should be of a delicate brown; during the next quarter the baking is practically finished; the heat should be lowered during the last quarter. Loaves of bread of the size indicated should bake in about one hour, biscuits and rolls in about half an hour.

GLAZING BREAD AND ROLLS

If a crisp crust is desired, brush over the surface of the bread or rolls, near the close of baking, with white of egg, slightly beaten. If a soft crust is desired, use a cooked paste made of two teaspoonfuls of cornstarch diluted with cold water and cooked ten minutes with a cup of boiling water. The applications of egg or starch may be repeated several times. For buns, German coffee cake and the like use the paste and dredge with sugar, or sugar and cinnamon, after each application of paste.

STORING BREAD

Cool the bread when taken from the oven on a wire rack. When perfectly cold — after several hours — set aside in a stone jar with a cover. If cut slices are kept in the jar with the loaf, do not toss them from the bread tray into the jar, lay them in carefully, to avoid crumbs. Wash, scald and air the jar once a week in cold weather, two or three times a week in summer.

ONE LOAF OF WHITE BREAD
(Mixed at night)

1 cup of liquid (milk or water or part of each)	¼ cake of compressed yeast With ¼ cup of liquid
1 tablespoonful of shortening	About 4 cups of white bread flour
1 tablespoonful of sugar	
½ teaspoonful of salt	

If milk be used, scald it, then let cool to a lukewarm temperature. Let boil and cool the water. Add the butter, salt and sugar to the hot liquid. Mix the piece of yeast cake with the quantity of liquid designated. Add this to the other liquid ingredients, when all are at the proper temperature. Then stir in about four cups of white flour. When all the ingredients are thoroughly mixed together and the sides of the bowl are free from dough, turn the mass onto a board lightly dredged with flour; knead until the dough is elastic and tiny white blisters are seen on the surface, then return to the bowl, cover closely, to avoid the formation of a crust, and let stand out of a draft until morning. The temperature for the first two or three hours should be about 70° F. After this time, fermentation (growth and reproduction of the yeast plants) being well established, the temperature may be lowered to 40° or 50° F. without disturbance to the process. In the morning the dough should have "doubled in bulk." If so, repeatedly cut through and turn it over with a knife, to let out the gas. The dough may be covered again and left until it is again doubled in bulk, or it may be shaped into a loaf at once.

ONE LOAF OF WHITE BREAD
(Mixed in the morning)

1 cup of liquid milk or water, or part of each
1 tablespoonful of shortening
½ teaspoonful of salt
1 tablespoonful of sugar
1 cake of compressed yeast mixed with ¼ cup of liquid
About 4 cups of flour

ENTIRE WHEAT BREAD

Follow one of the preceding recipes, using white and entire wheat flour, two cups of each, or one cup of white and three of entire wheat.

ONE LOAF OF BREAD AND OF ROLLS MADE WITH ONE YEAST CAKE.
Page 297

GRAHAM BREAD MADE WITHOUT KNEADING — Page 299.

ONE LOAF OF BREAD AND PARKER HOUSE ROLLS, BAKED — Page 297

Bread Sticks tied with Yellow Ribbon — *Page 306*

Lady Finger Rolls — *Page 305*

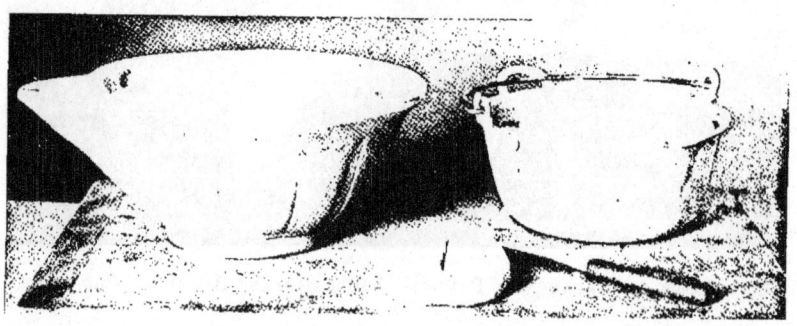

NOISETTE BREAD

1 cake of compressed yeast
¼ cup of lukewarm water
1 cup of scalded-and-cooled milk
1 tablespoonful of shortening
2 tablespoonfuls of molasses

1 cup of noisette or filbert meats
½ cup of entire wheat flour
White flour as needed for dough

Prepare as ordinary bread, adding the nut meats, whole, to the liquid.

PARKER HOUSE ROLLS

Sponge
1 cup of milk, scalded and cooled to lukewarm temperature
1 cake of compressed yeast
¼ cup of scalded-and-cooled milk

2 cups of bread flour
When sponge is light add
½ teaspoonful of salt
1 tablespoonful of sugar
¼ cup of melted shortening
1¾ to 2 cups of bread flour

Soften the yeast in the fourth cup of milk; add to the cup of milk, stir in the flour with a spoon, then beat the mixture until very smooth. Cover it with a plate and let stand in a temperature of about 70° F. until light and puffy, then add the salt, sugar, shortening and flour and mix to a smooth dough. Turn on to a floured board and knead until elastic and the surface shows tiny blisters; cover closely and let stand until doubled in bulk. Turn on to a lightly-floured board, crust or upper side down, roll into a half-inch thick sheet with the rolling pin, cut into rounds, brush over one-half of each round with melted butter and fold the other half over the buttered half. Set close together in a buttered pan. When again doubled in bulk bake about half an hour; glaze during the last of the baking. One-fourth a cake of compressed yeast may be used at night for a loaf of bread, and in the morning the rest of the cake for these rolls.

RYE BREAD
(One loaf)

1 cup of scalded-and-cooled milk	⅓ to 1 whole cake of compressed yeast
½ teaspoonful of salt	¼ cup of lukewarm water
2 tablespoonfuls of sugar	2 cups of sifted rye flour
2 tablespoonfuls of butter	About 2 cups of wheat flour

Knead ten minutes; use white flour in kneading. Bake about three-fourths of an hour.

GLAZED CURRANT BUNS

1 cake of compressed yeast	½ teaspoonful of salt
¼ cup of scalded-and-cooled milk	1 egg
1 cup of scalded-and-cooled milk	½ cup of cleaned currants
1¾ cups of bread flour	About 2 cups of flour
¼ cup of sugar	2 level teaspoonfuls cornstarch
¼ cup of melted shortening	¾ cup of boiling water
	Granulated sugar
	Cinnamon if desired

Soften the yeast in the quarter cup of liquid, add to the rest of the liquid and beat in the first quantity of flour. Beat until the sponge is very smooth, then cover and set to rise. When light add the sugar, salt, shortening, egg, currants and flour and mix to a soft dough. Knead until elastic, cover and set to rise. When doubled in bulk turn upside down on a board, roll into a sheet about half an inch thick and cut into rounds. Set these in a baking pan close together or a little distance apart, according as to whether a soft or crusty exterior is desired. When doubled in bulk bake about twenty-five minutes. Dilute the cornstarch with a little cold water, pour on the boiling water and let simmer ten minutes. When the buns are nearly baked, brush over the top with the starch and dredge thickly with sugar or sugar and cinnamon mixed and return to the oven. Repeat the application of paste and sugar if needed.

GRAHAM BREAD

⅓ cake of compressed yeast
½ cup of lukewarm water
1¼ cups scalded-and-cooled milk
2 tablespoonfuls of butter
1 teaspoonful of salt
¼ cup of molasses
2½ cups of graham flour
1½ cups of white bread flour

Soften the yeast cake in the water. Melt the butter in the milk, add the salt, molasses, yeast in the water and stir in the flour. Mix very thoroughly. The dough is not firm enough to knead. Cover and let stand overnight. In the morning cut the dough through and through with a knife, turning it over and over; meanwhile, turn it into two buttered bread pans. Make smooth with a knife, and let stand to become nearly doubled in bulk. Bake about one hour.

DARK COLORED GRAHAM BREAD

Use the recipe given above, increasing the quantity of molasses to *half a cup*. Cut down the quantity of scalded milk to *one cup*.

ENTIRE WHEAT BISCUIT

¼ cake of compressed yeast (to mix at night)
1 cake of compressed yeast (to mix in the morning)
½ cup lukewarm water
½ cup of scalded milk
½ teaspoonful of salt
¼ cup of melted shortening
¼ cup of molasses
1½ cups sifted entire wheat flour
¾ cup of white bread flour

Soften the yeast in the water, add the liquid ingredients, then stir in the flour; cut through the dough again and again, to mix very thoroughly. The dough is too soft to knead. Cover and set aside, to become light, as usual. Melt a little shortening, dip the fingers into it, pull off bits of the dough (about two ounces or one-fourth a cup) and shape them, one by one, into rounds. If the fingers are kept well-buttered, the dough will not stick to them in the least. Dispose the rounds close together in buttered baking pans. Let become very light, bake about fifty minutes. Glaze with starch or starch and sugar.

ZWIEBACK

1 cake of compressed yeast
¼ cup of lukewarm water
1 cup of scalded milk (cooled)
1 egg and yolk of another
¼ cup of melted butter (or less)
½ teaspoonful of salt
¼ cup of sugar (or less)
Flour for a soft dough
1 white of egg for glazing

Soften the yeast cake in the water, add flour and mix to a dough of a consistency to knead; knead the little ball of dough until elastic, then make two cuts across the top, one-fourth an inch deep, one at right angles to the other. Have the milk cooled to a lukewarm temperature; drop in the little ball of dough and let stand until the ball floats on the top of the milk, a light porous mass or " sponge," then add the other ingredients and mix to a soft dough. Knead until smooth and elastic, cover and set aside to double in bulk, then shape in the hands into oval rolls. Set these close together in a bread pan. When nearly doubled in bulk, bake in an oven hotter than for bread. When nearly baked brush the top with beaten white of egg and return to the oven to dry off. When baked and cold, cut in half inch slices and dry in a moderately heated oven; when well dried out increase the heat and let the slices color a little.

SQUASH BISCUIT

⅓ cake of compressed yeast
½ cup of lukewarm water
½ cup of scalded milk
½ cup of cooked squash
¼ cup of brown sugar
½ teaspoonful of salt
¼ cup of melted butter
About 3 cups of bread flour

Soften the yeast in the water, add the other ingredients and mix to a soft dough. Knead nearly ten minutes, using no more flour than is necessary. Cover and let stand over night. In the morning the mixture should have doubled in bulk. Turn upside down on a floured board, then pat and roll into a sheet nearly an inch thick. Dip a cutter in flour and cut into rounds. Set these close together in a baking pan, first brushing the surfaces that will come in contact with melted butter. When very light (double in bulk) bake about half an hour. Glaze with starch and sugar just before removing from the oven.

ONE LOAF OF BREAD AND A SHEET OF COFFEE CAKE MADE WITH ONE YEAST CAKE

ONE LOAF OF BREAD

⅓ cake of compressed yeast
¼ cup of lukewarm water
1 cup of scalded milk
1 tablespoonful of butter or other shortening
½ teaspoonful of salt
1 tablespoonful of sugar
About 4 cups of flour

Mix the bread at night in the usual manner. Let the bowl of dough stand in a temperature of about 68° F. about two hours; if after that time the temperature falls to 50° or even 40° F., no harm will be done. In the morning the dough should be about twice its original size. Cut it in halves, knead these into rounds and set them side by side in a "brick loaf" bread pan. When the pan is rather more than three-fourths full, bake one hour.

SHEET OF COFFEE CAKE

⅔ cake of compressed yeast
¼ cup of lukewarm water
1 cup of scalded milk
¼ cup of butter or other shortening
¼ cup of sugar
½ teaspoonful of salt
1 egg
About three cups of flour
Cornstarch paste
1 dozen blanched almonds
3 tablespoonfuls of sugar
1 teaspoonful of cinnamon

Melt the shortening in the milk, add the sugar and salt, and when lukewarm the yeast, mixed with the lukewarm water and the egg, and stir in the flour. Enough flour should be added to make a thick batter. The mixture should be almost stiff enough to knead. Cut through and turn it over and over with a knife, then cover closely and set aside with the bread dough. In the morning the mixture should be doubled in bulk. Cut through and through it, with a knife, and turn it over and over. Spread it smoothly in a buttered pan (about 10 by 5 inches) and when light (but not quite doubled in bulk) bake about half an hour. Make a cooked paste with a teaspoonful of cornstarch and half a cup of boiling water; spread the top of the cake with the paste, putting it on generously; sprinkle with the almonds, cut in thin slices, and dredge with the sugar, mixed with the cinnamon, and return to the oven grate, to melt the sugar and brown the almonds. With care this may be reheated.

RYE MEAL BISCUIT

1 cup of milk, scalded and cooled
½ or a whole cake of compressed yeast, according as to time of mixing
¼ cup of scalded-and-cooled milk
1½ cups of sifted bread flour
¼ cup (scant measure) of melted shortening
¼ cup of molasses
½ teaspoonful of salt
1¼ cups of sifted rye meal

Make a sponge of the milk, yeast and bread flour. When light add the other ingredients and beat thoroughly for some minutes. When light, with buttered fingers, shape into about fifteen balls; set these close together in a buttered pan; when light and fluffy bake about twenty-five minutes. Glaze with cornstarch paste before removing from the oven.

KAISER SEMMELN

For sponge
1 cake of compressed yeast
¼ cup of lukewarm water
About ¾ cup of flour

2 cups of boiled water
1 teaspoonful of salt
Between 6 and 7 cups of flour
White of 1 egg or less

Soften the yeast in the lukewarm water, mix thoroughly, then stir in the flour; knead the little ball of dough until it is smooth and elastic. Make a deep cut across the dough in both directions (see illustration page 297). Have the boiled water cooled to a lukewarm temperature and into this put the ball of dough. It will sink to the bottom of the dish, but will gradually rise as it becomes light. In about fifteen minutes it will float upon the water, a light, puffy "sponge." Into this water and sponge stir the salt and between six and seven cups of flour. Knead or pound the dough about twenty minutes. Let rise in a temperature of about 70° F., until the mass is doubled in bulk. Divide into pieces weighing about three ounces each (there should be about fourteen pieces). Shape these into balls. When all are shaped, with a sharp knife cut down into each, to make five divisions. Set the balls into buttered tins, some distance apart, brush over the tops generously with melted butter, and set to bake *at once* in a hot oven. Bake twenty or twenty-five minutes. When nearly baked, brush over with the beaten white of an egg, and return to the oven to finish baking. Bake the biscuit as soon as they are cut and brushed with butter. Only by this means can the shape and fine texture of this form of bread be secured. This recipe is said, by those who have eaten the bread in Vienna, to give a near approach to this justly famous Vienna bread. The Hungarian wheat used in Vienna makes a difference in flavor, which cannot be exactly duplicated in this country.

LADY-FINGER ROLLS

For Sponge
¼ cup of scalded-and-cooled milk
1 cake of compressed yeast
¼ cup of scalded-and-cooled milk
About 1½ cups of bread flour
When sponge is light, add

Yolks of 2 eggs
½ teaspoonful of salt
2 or 3 tablespoonfuls of melted butter
1 tablespoonful of sugar
About 2 cups of bread flour
White of 1 egg for glazing

Prepare the sponge in the usual manner, beating it for some minutes. When light and puffy add the other ingredients and knead fifteen or twenty minutes. Cover and set aside to double in bulk. Divide the risen dough into pieces of two ounces each (about half a cup of dough weighs two ounces). Knead these into balls and dispose on a board dredged lightly with flour; cover closely with a board or pan, and leave them to become light. Roll the balls on **the** board under the fingers, to make long rolls pointed at the ends. Using more pressure on the dough at the ends than in the middle will give the desired shape. Set the rolls on a buttered sheet, some distance apart. When light, with a pair of scissors make three transverse cuts in the top of each roll. Bake about twenty minutes. When nearly baked, brush over with white of egg, and return to the oven to dry the egg.

BREAD STICKS

1 cup of scalded-and-cooled milk	½ tablespoonful of sugar
¼ to 1 whole cake of compressed yeast	½ teaspoonful of salt
	1 tablespoonful of melted butter
¼ cup of lukewarm water	1 white of egg, beaten light
About 1½ cups of bread flour	Flour for soft dough

Make a " sponge " with the first four ingredients and when light add the rest of the materials. Knead until elastic. Cover and let rise until the bulk is doubled. Pull off small pieces of dough and knead into balls; cover on a floured board; when light roll under the hands, on the board, into pencil shapes of a length to fit a bread stick pan. Bake when light. Brush over with slightly beaten white of egg and return to the oven to set the glaze.

TOAST

Cut stale bread in slices of uniform thickness (scant half inch), set on a toaster some distance from the source of heat, turn occasionally to dry out the moisture, then set nearer the heat and color first on one side and then on the other. If moist toast is desired, dip the edges of the toast in boiling, salted water, set on a plate and drop on to it bits of butter. For cream toast, dip the slices in cream sauce, then set onto a plate.

SANDWICHES

Cut the bread in uniform slices, less thick than for toast. Trim off the crusts, if desired, then spread with butter or with such preparation as is desired, nearly to the edge of the bread on all sides. Press two pieces together and serve as soon as convenient. If the sandwiches are to stand, cover closely with an earthen bowl.

OLIVE SANDWICHES

Chop a dozen olives; spread bread prepared for sandwiches with mayonnaise dressing or butter and then with the chopped olives. Press together in pairs. If desired a leaf of lettuce or a branch or two of cress may be set between the two parts of the sandwich.

BACON SANDWICHES

If convenient the bacon should be fresh cooked. Set the slices while hot between the buttered bread, prepared as usual. Press together and wrap singly in waxed paper.

NOISETTE SANDWICHES

Prepare "noisette" bread for sandwiches; spread with butter and with orange marmalade and press together in pairs.

CHEESE AND HERRING SANDWICHES

1 Cream cheese	2 Herring Fillets
2 teaspoonfuls of Beef Extract	Brown or white bread

Work the cheese and beef extract to a smooth paste. Any herring may be used, but those put up in oil are preferable. Such herring are usually choice and tender. Cut the fillets into tiny pieces. Spread the bread with the cheese mixture, sprinkle on the bits of herring and press together in pairs.

CHAPTER XVIII

FLOUR MIXTURES CONTINUED: PASTRY AND PIES

MEN, as a rule, are fond of pastry, especially when it takes the form of a pie. Thus a young housekeeper — at least after a time — will be desirous of knowing how to make a pie. Pastry is made of flour, fat, salt and just enough water to hold the ingredients together in rolling out. Fat makes pastry tender, water toughens it; thus fat rather than water should predominate in the mixture. Pastry flour, which takes up but a small quantity of water, should always be used in this branch of cookery.

For puff-paste the weight in butter equals that of the flour called for, but for ordinary paste fat equal in weight to half the weight of the flour will make good pastry. Lard gives a softer crust than does butter, cottolene or suet; but butter is thought to produce the best tasting pastry. Butter, particularly in winter, is not very pliable, and, in the end, time is saved, if the butter be washed in cold water before it is added to the flour. Pastry is lightened by the expansion of the air enclosed during the making. A little baking powder, one-fourth a teaspoonful to a cup of flour, insures the lightness that an inexperienced cook sometimes fails to secure.

WHY PASTRY IS THOUGHT UNHEALTHFUL

No one of the ingredients in pastry is unwholesome, and fat is absolutely necessary to perfect nutrition; but fat with other food-principles in an artificial combination has often proved unhygienic. To be properly digested, starch must be mixed with the digestive fluids of the mouth, but these fluids have no effect upon fat and, unless the mastication be very much prolonged, the starch surrounded by fat will pass on unchanged to the stomach. Then, if pastry be made, let it be tender, friable and well cooked; and let it be masticated thoroughly.

PASTRY FOR ONE PIE

1¼ cups of sifted pastry flour (5 ounces)

¼ teaspoonful of salt (generous measure)

¼ teaspoonful of baking powder, if desired

⅓ cup (2 to 3 ounces) of shortening, and cold water

Sift together the flour, salt and baking powder; with a knife or the tips of the fingers work the shortening into the flour mixture, then adding cold water, a few drops at a time, with a knife stir the mixture to a paste. Add no more water than is needed to form the ingredients into a stiff paste. This paste is now ready for use.

FLAKY PASTRY FOR ONE PIE

1¼ cups of sifted pastry flour (5 ounces)

¼ teaspoonful of salt (generous measure)

¼ teaspoonful of baking powder
Cold water
¼ cup of shortening (lard or cottolene)
2 tablespoonfuls of butter

Scald an earthen bowl and a wooden spoon, then chill them thoroughly; add cold water to the bowl and in it wash the butter, pressing it with the spoon; when the butter may be gathered into a pliable, waxy mass, remove to a cloth, pat a little, to remove the water, then set aside in a cool place until the paste is ready. Use the lard with the other ingredients in making the paste as given above.

Turn the paste onto a board lightly dredged with flour; turn it in the flour, then pat it lightly with the rolling pin and roll into a square sheet; with a knife cut off bits of the prepared butter and press them lightly on the paste until all is used. Set the pieces of butter on the paste so as to distribute them evenly over the paste. Fold the paste to make three layers; pat with the rolling pin gently, then roll into a sheet; roll up the paste like a jelly roll, and it is ready to use; or it may be covered closely (to keep the outside from drying) and set aside in a cool place until the next day. Often pastry may be handled more easily after it has been left in a cool place some hours or over night.

APPLE PIE

Take a little more than one-half of the pastry, made by either of the above recipes. If the first be selected, turn it over on the board dredged with flour, knead slightly to get into a compact mass, then roll into a round to fit the plate; lift the paste to the plate (agate preferred) and trim so as to leave one-fourth an inch of paste beyond the plate. Pare five or six tart apples and slice them into the plate. Use enough apples to round the slices up well. Mix one-fourth a teaspoonful of salt with two-thirds a cup of sugar and sprinkle over the apple; put on one teaspoonful or more of butter, in little bits, here and there, add a grating of nutmeg, then roll out the rest of the crust in the same manner as the first and cut six or eight half-inch slits in the center to form a design; leave the paste on the board while the edge of the pastry on the plate is brushed over with cold water, then put about three tablespoonfuls of cold water over the apple. Lift the pastry from the board and set it over the apple, letting it lie loosely, as it will shrink in baking. Press the edge of the upper piece of paste upon the edge of the lower and trim if needed to make them even. Then brush the two edges together with cold water and bake about half an hour. The oven should not be too hot or the pastry will brown before it is cooked. After the pie has been in the oven six or seven minutes, the paste should have contracted and risen somewhat.

ENGLISH APPLE PIE

Butter a shallow agate dish. Select one that is deeper than a pie plate. Slice apples into the dish to fill it. Sprinkle on about a cup of sugar, half a teaspoonful of salt and a grating of nutmeg or lemon rind. Put on two teaspoonfuls of butter in bits, here and there, add two or three tablespoonfuls cold water, then roll out half of the quantity of paste indicated in the above recipes. Cut slits in the paste and spread it over the apple, pressing it against the dish on the edge. Bake about forty minutes. Serve with or without cream.

APPLE PIE WITH MERINGUE

Bake the crust as for " Cranberry Tart," page 319. Set the cooked pastry in a suitable plate and fill two-thirds full with sifted apple sauce, reduced by cooking till quite thick. Cover with meringue and let bake eight or ten minutes in a very moderate oven.

Meringue

Whites of 2 eggs, beaten dry
4 tablespoonfuls of granulated sugar
½ teaspoonful of vanilla

Beat two tablespoonfuls of the sugar into the whites, beaten dry, then fold in the rest of the sugar and the vanilla. After the meringue is spread, sift granulated sugar over it. The oven must be moderate. The meringue should not color until after eight minutes.

BLUEBERRY PIE

Line the plate as for an apple pie; mix one pint of berries, two tablespoonfuls of flour, half a teaspoonful of salt and three-fourths a cup of sugar and turn into the plate, put on two teaspoonfuls of butter in little bits, then cover with the second crust and finish as the apple pie with two crusts. All pies are less liable to " run out " in the oven, if the paste be put on loosely. Allow plenty of paste, that the plate may be covered when the paste shrinks.

RHUBARB PIE

2 cups of sliced rhubarb
1 egg
1¼ cups of sugar
2 tablespoonfuls of flour
½ teaspoonful of salt
2 teaspoonfuls of butter

Beat the egg; beat in the sugar, flour and salt and turn into the plate lined with pastry; add the butter in bits, here and there, cover and finish as an ordinary apple pie. Rhubarb canned in cold water may be used instead of fresh rhubarb.

RHUBARB PIE
(Red Lion Inn, Stockbridge)

1 cup of sliced rhubarb
1 egg
1 cup of sugar
2 common crackers, rolled fine
¼ teaspoonful of salt
2 teaspoonfuls of butter
A grating of nutmeg

Beat the egg, add the sugar, salt, rolled crackers and rhubarb. Turn into the plate lined with crust. Put in the bits of butter. Cut the pastry rolled for the upper crust into bands three-fourths an inch wide, and brush over the edge of the under crust with cold water; lay the bands across the filling parallel, one to another, then lay bands across the filling at right angles to these, lattice fashion. Cut all at the edge

PEACH TARTS — *Page 319.*

APPLE TARTS — *Page 321.*

PINEAPPLE TARTS — *Page 310.*

CUSTARD PIE — *Page 317.*

STRAWBERRY TARTS, ST. HONORE STYLE — *Page 320*

of the under paste and press them upon it. Bake about half an hour.

RHUBARB PIE, No. 3

Peel the rhubarb and cut it in slices; cover with boiling water, set over the fire and bring quickly to the boiling point. As soon as the rhubarb changes color and before it loses its shape, drain and press out all of the liquid. Over the rhubarb sprinkle a cup of sugar, sifted with three tablespoonfuls of flour and one-fourth a teaspoonful of salt. Add a tablespoonful of lemon juice or a grating of orange rind; mix and turn into a plate lined with pastry; finish with bands of pastry. Bake about half an hour.

MOCK MINCE PIE

2 common crackers, rolled fine
¾ cup of sugar
½ cup of molasses
¼ cup of liquid from sweet pickle jar or
¼ cup of lemon juice

½ cup of raisins, seeded and chopped
¼ cup of butter
¼ teaspoonful of salt
1 egg, well beaten

Mix all the ingredients together and turn into a plate lined with pastry; cover with paste and bake as an apple pie. Spices as cinnamon, cloves, nutmeg and mace may be added if desired. A teaspoonful of mixed spice will suffice.

LEMON PIE

3 tablespoonfuls of cornstarch	½ teaspoonful of salt
4 tablespoonfuls of cold water	1 cup of boiling water
1 cup of sugar	Juice of 1 lemon
2 tablespoonfuls of butter	Grated rind, if desired

Stir the cornstarch and salt with the cold water; pour on the boiling water and stir and cook until the mixture boils; add the sugar, butter and lemon juice, also grated rind, if it is to be used. Let the mixture stand while a plate is lined and the upper crust is rolled out and made ready. Turn the mixture into the lined plate, brush the edge of the paste with cold water, set the upper paste in place, finish and bake as an apple pie. Lemon rind when eaten often produces flatulency; in such case, omit it.

MINCE MEAT FOR ONE PIE

¾ cup chopped beef (roast or steak)	¼ cup of syrup from sweet pickle jar
1 cup of chopped apple	½ teaspoonful salt
¼ cup of chopped suet or 3 tablespoonfuls of butter	½ teaspoonful mace
	Grating of nutmeg
⅔ cup of sugar	⅛ teaspoonful of cloves
½ cup of molasses	¼ teaspoonful of cinnamon
Grated rind and juice of 1 lemon or	⅓ cup of raisins (Sultanas preferred)

Mix all together, turn into a plate lined with pastry and cover as an apple pie. Bake nearly an hour. Less spice may be used, or two or three tablespoonfuls of "left over" jelly may be added.

Cooking for Two

SOUR CREAM PIE

1 cup of chopped apple
1 cup of stoned raisins
1 cup of sugar
½ cup of sour cream
½ cup of sour milk
¼ teaspoonful, each of cinnamon, nutmeg and cloves
½ teaspoonful of salt

Peel the apples before chopping and chop the raisins; add the other ingredients, mix thoroughly and bake between two layers of pastry.

CUSTARD PIE

We have not seen plates of a depth suitable for custard and other similar pies in small size, thus give the proportions for a pie of ordinary size. Take rather more than half of the crust required for one pie; roll it into a round sheet that will come three-fourths of an inch beyond the edge of the plate; lay it upon the plate evenly, then fold the edge over to meet the plate all around the plate. Flute this double fold of paste with the thumb and finger and press each " fluting " down upon the edge of the plate. In putting the crust upon the plate lift it here and there, where needed, to let out the air below. This should be done with all pies, but is particularly necessary with custard pies. Also, with the thumb and forefinger held together, press the paste upon the bottom of the plate throughout the whole extent and, also, around the edge of the plate close to the bottom, that no large bubble of air may be left to expand and displace the custard while it is baking. Turn the filling into the prepared crust and let bake in a moderate oven nearly an hour. An electric oven is by far the best oven in which to bake a custard or squash pie. For the filling beat four eggs; add half a teaspoonful of salt and three-fourths a cup of sugar and beat again, then gradually beat in three cups of milk. When the pie feels firm to the touch at the center, remove from the oven and grate over it a little nutmeg. Chill before serving.

SQUASH PIE

¼ cup of butter
¾ cup of sugar
½ teaspoonful of salt
½ teaspoonful of ground mace
1 egg and yolk of another
1 cup of cooked-and-sifted squash
1 cup of rich milk

Cream the butter and beat in half the sugar; beat the egg and beat in the other half of the sugar, then beat the two mixtures together; add the other ingredients and mix again. Bake in a plate lined as for a custard pie.

SQUASH PIE, DELAWARE STYLE

1 cup of cooked-and-sifted squash
½ teaspoonful of salt
½ teaspoonful of cinnamon
¾ cup of sugar
1 egg, well beaten
¼ cup of cream
¾ cup of breakfast cocoa made with milk

Mix the ingredients and bake until firm in the center in a plate lined with pastry as for a custard pie.

OPEN CRANBERRY PIE OR CRANBERRY TART

Spread the round of paste over an inverted pie plate (agate or tin is preferable), prick the paste with a fork, here and there, over the sides as well as the top. Bake to a dark straw color. Remove the paste from the plate, wash the plate and set the pastry inside. Turn a cooked filling into the pastry shell and set figures, cut from pastry and baked, above the filling.

COOKED CRANBERRY FILLING

Mix together, thoroughly, two level tablespoonfuls of cornstarch, half a teaspoonful of salt, scant measure, and one cup of sugar; pour on one cup of boiling water and stir until boiling, then add one-fourth a cup of molasses, a teaspoonful of butter and two cups of cranberries, chopped fine. Mix together thoroughly, and let simmer ten or fifteen minutes. Apple, peach or pineapple marmalade make good fillings for an open pie. Heat the marmalade and turn at once into the shell.

CANNED PINEAPPLE FILLING

To a pint can of grated pineapple add half a cup of sugar and the juice of half a lemon; let simmer until thick, then use as above.

PEACH TARTS

Cover inverted individual tins with pastry (it will take but a small piece for two tins, a little " left over " will answer). Set the tins on a pie tin to keep the edge of the paste from the oven. Prick the paste all over with a fork and let bake. It will take about eight minutes. Remove the pastry from the tins and set it onto individual plates. Put a canned peach in each piece of pastry. Pipe whipped cream above and sprinkle the cream with fine-chopped pistachio nuts. Or fill the hollow spaces in the center and around the peach with jelly or marmalade and put a blanched almond in the center of the peach. Serve with the syrup from the peaches as a sauce. Halves of apple, cooked in syrup (sugar and water, half a cup of each, cooked six minutes), may replace the peaches.

STRAWBERRY TARTS, ST. HONORÉ STYLE

Bake the pastry over inverted tins as for "peach tarts." Remove from the tin and half fill with St. Honoré cream, then finish filling with strawberries cut in halves and mixed with sugar.

ST. HONORÉ CREAM

½ cup of milk
¼ cup of sugar
3 tablespoonfuls of flour
⅛ teaspoonful of salt
1 egg

Scald the milk over hot water; sift the sugar, salt and flour together and stir into the hot milk; let cook ten minutes, then add the egg, beaten very light. To add the egg dilute it with a little of the hot mixture, then stir into the rest of the mixture.

APPLE TARTS

Make the pastry by the recipe, " Pastry for One Pie," and roll this into a rectangular sheet. Have ready one-fourth a cup of creamed butter. Spread this over the pastry or put it on, here and there, in little bits. Then roll up the pastry as a jelly roll. Pat and roll this into a sheet, and cut out into rounds. With the small end of a pastry tube cut out three small rounds from half the rounds of pastry. Have ready some stewed-and-sifted apples, cooked dry, seasoned with sugar, a little salt and nutmeg, and chilled. Put a teaspoonful of this sauce in the center of the plain rounds, and brush the edge of one after another with cold water; put a round with holes in it over the apple sauce, and press the edges together closely. Brush the edges with cold water and the top with slightly beaten white of egg. Dredge lightly with granulated sugar, and bake until slightly colored.

CHAPTER XIX

FLOUR MIXTURES CONTINUED: CAKE

To do anything well it must be done often. With nothing in the line of cooking is this more true than with cake-making, and especially that part of the process that has to do with the baking.

But cake is a luxury and not a very hygienic one, as it is often another example of concealed fat. Thus, being an article for occasional rather than daily consumption, the opportunity for practice is infrequent, and it were well for the young housekeeper to confine her efforts to a few varieties.

SOME OF THE QUALITIES OF A GOOD CAKE

Good cake is light, velvety in texture, and fine rather than coarse grained. It does not have a sugary, brittle edge. It is of uniform height, and is baked to a uniform color — the shade depending on the variety of cake — on the bottom, top and sides.

HOW CAKES ARE LIGHTENED

Cakes are made light in the same manner as other batters and doughs, *i. e.* (1) by the expansion of air beaten into some of the ingredients, as eggs, butter,

butter and sugar, or into the finished mixture; (2) by carbon dioxide set free during the growth of yeast plants, or from a carbonate by an acid; (3) by the expansion of the air or gas, or both, when heated; (4) by the hardening (by heat) of the cell-walls during cooking.

INGREDIENTS USED IN CAKE-MAKING

Pastry flour, on account of its whiteness and smoothness and the quality of its gluten content, is better adapted to cake-making than are the so-called bread flours. Powdered sugar gives a dry cake and, now that fine granulated sugar can be bought anywhere, it is rarely used. It is not necessary that the butter be made into handsomely stamped cakes as for the table, but in other respects the choicer the butter the better the cake. Eggs a day old are in the best state for beating. Four eggs should fill the measuring cup and weigh half a pound, but often five will be required to secure this weight and fill the cup. Often eggs are the only liquid used in cake. Water can always be substituted for sweet milk that is called for in a recipe, but there will be a difference in the cake; often the cake is more tender and delicate, but it does not look quite as spongy or white. The grated yellow rind of an orange or lemon that contains the rich, characteristic oil of the fruit gives a most delectable flavor to a cake, but the juice of these fruits contains little flavor, and this, as also the volatile flavor of extract of vanilla, are lost during the cooking. Lemon juice, being an acid, if used in a cake made with baking powder or cream of tartar and soda, will materially change the proportions of the leavening ingredients and spoil the cake. When used, soda to correct the acidity must also be used. Caramel gives a pleasing flavor to cake and one that is retained during cooking. In frosted cakes flavor may be added to the frosting just before it is spread upon the cake without danger of loss, and this will suffice to flavor the whole cake.

PROPORTIONS OF INGREDIENTS

Usually a cake batter is of such consistency that it needs to be spread in the pan. Sometimes the heat of the oven will cause it to sink to a level before cooking begins, but as a rule the batter should be spread with a spoon and drawn away from the center of the pan towards the edges. Exact proportions of ingredients that will answer for all cakes can not be given. In general, twice as much flour, by measure, as of liquid is a safe rule. Eggs are considered a liquid, but half a cup of milk could not replace half a cup of eggs. Butter equal to one-third the volume of flour is not often exceeded. From half to two-thirds the volume of flour is the usual proportion of sugar.

MANNER OF MIXING A BUTTER CAKE

Before beginning to combine the ingredients have everything ready, that the mixing may be done quickly. The oven of a coal or wood range must be put into a condition that will insure the proper heat when the cake is ready. If the butter be firm and cold, rinse the mixing bowl with warm water, wipe it dry and put into it the desired quantity of butter; break the butter in pieces and let stand to soften while other things are being made ready. Butter the pans in which butter cakes are to be baked, or, better, line the pans with paper and butter the paper thoroughly. Pans for sponge cake need neither lining nor buttering. To line a pan, turn it upside down; select thin wrapping paper, spread the paper over the bottom of the pan with the edge of the paper on the edge of the pan, then press down upon the paper over the opposite edge to crease the paper; fold and cut in the crease; put the paper in the pan with the ends hanging over a little. The pan is now ready to butter. Break the eggs, the yolks into one bowl, the whites into another, and set the whites aside in a cool place. Measure or weigh out the sugar and sifted flour, also the liquid and the leavening agents. Sift together, three or four times, the flour and baking powder, or cream of tartar and soda, also salt and spices when used. Have fruit and nuts ready to add to the mixture. Now with a perforated wooden spoon work the butter to a cream, then gradually beat in the sugar, keeping the mass light and fluffy. In cold weather warm the liquid a little, to avoid curdling the butter and sugar. If yolks are to be used, beat them till light and thick, then add to the butter and sugar; rinse the bowl with the liquid and add it to the mixture, alternately, with the flour, etc. Lastly add the whites, beaten stiff. Fruit or nuts may now be added, or they may be added to the creamed butter and sugar before the yolks of the eggs. This is the usual method of mixing a cake in which butter is used, but there are many variations from the rule.

METHOD OF MIXING A SPONGE CAKE

Beat the yolks till thick and light-colored; gradually beat in the sugar; add flavoring (grated rind of an orange or lemon) and lemon juice, if used, then beat the whites till dry; fold half of the whites into the yolks and sugar; fold in half of the flour, the other half of the whites and the other half of the flour. In a sponge cake proper the lightness depends entirely upon the air beaten into the eggs, and great care must be exercised to handle the mixture in such a manner that none of the air cells be broken down. Stirring must be avoided. The cake is mixed entirely by beating and folding, and when ready for the pan will be a delicate, fluffy mass. The long beating of the eggs necessary to insure a light cake renders a sponge cake dry; this may be remedied to some extent by using a greater number of yolks than of whites. Cheaper sponge cakes may be made by cutting down the number of eggs and using milk or water as a part of the liquid; with such cakes a leavening agent must be employed.

BAKING CAKE

In baking cake the size of the cake has much to do with the required temperature of the oven; the larger the cake, the longer is the time necessary to heat the mixture and expand the mass. The cake must not crust over (by heat) until it has risen to the proper height. A cake, in layers, will bake in from fifteen to twenty minutes; in a sheet, in about thirty minutes; in a loaf, from forty minutes to two hours, according to its thickness. *The oven should be at a temperature to raise the cake to its full height in one-fourth the time required for baking.* During this time, the cake should not brown. During the second quarter of the time in the oven, the cake should brown in spots. During the third quarter, the browning should be completed. The heat should be gradually reduced, during the last half of the time in the oven. When baked, butter cakes will separate from the sides of the pan. This will be seen in the last quarter, and during this time the cake will also settle a little in the pan. Let stand a few seconds after removal from the oven, then carefully turn from the pan to a wire cake cooler. Often a cake may be lifted from the pan by the paper hanging from the ends of the tin. Sponge cakes, baked in unbuttered tins, may be inverted and cooled, upside down, in a draft of air. When a cake is thus suspended, the air cells are elongated until dry and firm; and if the cake was light when taken from the oven, lightness is assured thereafter. The oven door may be opened at will during the baking, if it be closed at once and *gently*.

ANGEL OR WHITE SPONGE CAKE

Whites of 4 eggs
¼ teaspoonful of cream of tartar
¾ cup of sugar
½ teaspoonful of vanilla
½ cup of sifted pastry flour

Add the cream of tartar to the whites of eggs, beat dry, and fold in the other ingredients. Bake in tube pan or sheet about 25 minutes.

SPONGE CAKE

2 whole eggs
1 yolk of egg
½ cup of granulated sugar
½ cup of flour
Grated rind of ½ lemon
1 tablespoonful of lemon juice

Prepare according to the directions given above for mixing sponge cake. Bake from twenty to thirty minutes. Baked in the regular sponge-cake pan with feet for cooling, this cake will not be very thick. It may be baked in a new bread pan and then inverted to cool by setting something under the ends of the pan. In serving do not cut sponge cake, but break it apart with two silver forks.

BISCUITS D'EPERNAY

The whites of 3 eggs
The yolks of 4 eggs
½ cup of granulated sugar
Grated rind of ½ lemon
1 tablespoonful of fine-chopped almonds
½ cup of sifted pastry flour
2 tablespoonfuls of melted butter

Prepare as sponge cake, adding the almonds to the yolks and sugar and the melted butter last of all. Bake in small, fancy tins, well buttered, or in a sponge cake pan.

CREAM SPONGE CAKE

1½ cups of sifted flour
2 level teaspoonfuls of baking powder
1 cup of granulated sugar
¼ teaspoonful of salt
2 large eggs
Thick sweet cream
Grated rind of 1 lemon or orange

Sift together, three times, the flour, baking powder, sugar and salt. Break the eggs into a half pint cup, fill the cup with cream, add these with the grated rind to the first mixture and beat thoroughly. Bake in a thick sheet about forty minutes.

QUICK SPONGE CAKE

3 eggs
1½ cups of granulated sugar
½ cup of milk or water
2 cups of sifted flour
2 level teaspoonfuls of baking powder
½ teaspoonful of salt

Beat the eggs, without separating the whites and yolks, and beat the sugar in gradually; add the milk and the flour, sifted two or three times with the baking powder and salt. Bake in a sheet about twenty-five minutes. Half of this recipe may be made by using one whole egg and the yolk of another with half of each of the other ingredients.

WHITE LAYER CAKE

½ cup of butter
1 cup of sugar
½ cup of milk
2 cups of sifted flour
3 level teaspoonfuls of baking powder
Whites of 3 eggs, beaten dry

Mix in the usual manner. See "Manner of Mixing a Butter Cake." Bake in two layers about twenty minutes. Put together with boiled chocolate frosting. Decorate with halves of English walnuts if desired. Or, bake in a sheet about thirty-five minutes and when cold cover with Caramel Nut Frosting.

WHITE NUT CAKE

½ cup of butter
1½ cups of granulated sugar
¾ cup of water
2¼ cups of flour
2 level teaspoonfuls of baking powder
¼ teaspoonful salt
The whites of 4 eggs
1 cup of walnut meats broken in pieces

Mix in the usual manner; bake in a sheet. Frost as desired.

BURNT SUGAR CAKE

½ cup of butter
1 cup of sugar
Yolks of 3 eggs
2 cups of sifted flour
2 level teaspoonfuls of baking powder
1 cup of cold water
3 teaspoonfuls of caramel syrup
Whites of 2 eggs
Frosting for Burnt Sugar Cake:
¾ cup of sugar
⅓ cup of water
2 tablespoonfuls of caramel syrup
The white of 1 egg
1 teaspoonful of vanilla extract

Make both cake and frosting in the usual manner.

NUT AND RAISIN CAKE

½ cup of butter
1 cup of sugar
3 eggs, unbeaten
1 cup of nut meats
½ cup of raisins
2 cups of sifted flour
2 level teaspoonfuls of baking powder
¾ cup of milk
Grated rind of 1 lemon
¼ teaspoonful of cinnamon
¼ teaspoonful of mace

Add the eggs, one at a time, to the creamed butter and sugar and beat in thoroughly. Put the nuts and raisins through a food chopper, then rub these through the flour sifted with the baking powder and spices. Bake in a tube pan or in a sheet. Cover with caramel nut frosting.

MOIST CHOCOLATE CAKE

⅓ cup of butter
½ cup of sugar
Yolks of 2 eggs
½ cup of sugar
½ cup of hot mashed potato
1 ounce of chocolate, melted
¼ cup sweet milk
1 cup of sifted flour
1¼ teaspoonfuls of baking powder
½ teaspoonful cinnamon
½ teaspoonful mace or nutmeg
¼ teaspoonful clove
½ cup of walnut meats chopped fine
Whites of 2 eggs, beaten dry

Cream the butter and beat in first half cup of sugar; beat the yolks of eggs, beat in the second half cup of sugar and beat the two mixtures together; add the potato and chocolate and finish in the usual manner. Bake in a sheet or in layers. Finish with any frosting desired.

ROXBURY CAKES

Yolks of 2 eggs
½ cup of sugar
¼ cup of butter, softened
½ cup of molasses
½ cup of sour milk
1½ cups of sifted flour
1 teaspoonful of cinnamon
½ teaspoonful of cloves
Grating of nutmeg
1 teaspoonful of soda
Whites of 2 eggs
½ cup of seeded raisins
½ cup of walnut meats, broken in pieces

Prepare in the usual manner and bake in small tins; frost with boiled icing. The recipe makes 18 cakes. The recipe may be easily divided, but, as the cakes improve on keeping in an earthen jar, it may not be too large.

LITTLE GOLD CAKES

¼ cup of butter
½ cup of sugar
Yolks of 4 eggs
¼ cup of milk
⅞ cup of sifted flour
1 level teaspoonful of baking powder
1 teaspoonful of orange extract or grated rind of 1 orange

Bake in small fancy tins and cover with boiled frosting.

PLAIN GINGER CAKES

½ cup of molasses
1 teaspoonful of soda
¼ cup of butter
¼ cup of boiling water
2 cups of flour
½ teaspoonful of salt
½ tablespoonful of ginger
½ teaspoonful of cinnamon

Stir the soda into the molasses; melt the butter in the boiling water; turn all into a bowl and stir in the flour, sifted with the salt and spices; add more flour if needed, but keep the dough as soft as can be

Loaf of Biscuit d'Épernay, *Page 328.* Tea Pretzels — *Page 333*

Roxbury Cakes, Biscuits d'Épernay, Strawberry Preserves Between *Pages 328, 332*

White Cake, Cut in Diamonds — *Page 330*

Plain Ginger Cakes — *Page 332.*

Tiny Cream Cakes — *Page 339.*

Shaping Tea Pretzels — *Page 333.*

handled. Roll a little of the dough at a time to a sheet about three-eighths of an inch thick and cut into rounds. Press two pecan nut meats into the top of each, and dredge with granulated sugar. Bake in a moderate oven. The recipe will make about twenty cakes.

TEA PRETZELS

Beat one-third a cup of butter to a cream; gradually beat in one-fourth a cup of sugar, then one egg, beaten without separating the white and yolk, and one cup and a half of pastry flour. Cover the dough and let it remain in a cool place for one hour. Break off small pieces of the dough, knead to a smooth mass, then roll under the hands to the shape of a bread stick, about as thick as a round lead pencil; bring the ends towards the middle of the dough, pressing them onto it about an inch apart, forming two rings, then set on a baking tin, one ring overlapping the other. Brush with a beaten egg, diluted with a little milk, and press blanched-and-sliced almonds onto the dough. Bake in a moderate oven.

WAFER JUMBLES

½ cup of butter
⅓ cup of sugar (granulated)
1 egg beaten light (not separated)
Grated yellow rind of 1 lemon
or
1 teaspoonful of vanilla extract
1¼ cups of flour

Cream the butter; gradually beat in the sugar, the egg, flavoring and flour. Drop with a teaspoon onto a buttered baking sheet or, preferably, turn the mixture into a pastry bag with star tube (half inch) attached and dispose on the baking sheets in rings or figures the shape of the letter S; dredge with granulated sugar and bake in a quick oven. These, containing no liquid but egg, are rather rich and are for occasional not daily use.

PEANUT MACAROONS

The whites of 3 eggs
¼ teaspoonful of cream of tartar
1 cup of granulated sugar
1 teaspoonful of flour
1 pint of peanuts (chopped to a powder)

Beat the whites of the eggs until foamy; add the cream of tartar and beat until dry, then gradually beat in half of the sugar and continue beating until the whole is very light; then cut and fold in the other half of the sugar, the flour and the crushed nuts. Drop by teaspoonfuls onto a tin, lined with a buttered paper, making smooth rounds. Sift granulated sugar on the top of each and bake on the floor of a quick oven from five to seven minutes. Meats from English walnuts or other nuts may take the place of the peanuts. A cherry or bit of firm fruit jelly pressed into the center of the top of each round is an improvement.

ALMOND CRISPS

½ cup of butter
1 cup of powdered sugar
2 eggs
2 tablespoonfuls of milk
2 cups of flour
1 teaspoonful of vanilla extract
¼ teaspoonful of almond extract
Blanched almonds, cut in halves

Cream the butter and gradually beat in the sugar. Reserve the white of one egg to glaze the cakes. Beat the yolk of this egg and the other whole egg; add to the creamed ingredients with the milk, flour and flavoring. More flour may be needed. The dough must be stiff enough to hold its shape when baked. Take a little of the dough onto a floured board, turn it in the flour with a knife, then knead slightly and with the rolling pin roll into a thin sheet. With a French patty cutter stamp the dough into rounds and stamp each round with the same cutter again, to divide each into a crescent and an oval shaped cake Set these on buttered baking pans. Press upon each three halves of almonds, then brush over with the white of egg, reserved for the purpose, and sprinkle the whole with granulated sugar. Bake in a quick oven to a pale straw color.

ROLLED OATS, FRUIT-AND-NUT COOKIES

½ cup of butter
½ cup of sugar
1 egg beaten light
3 tablespoonfuls sweet milk

½ cup of raisins
¼ cup of chopped nuts
1 cup of rolled oats
1 cup of flour
½ teaspoonful of soda

Mix in the usual manner. Add more flour if needed to make a firm dough. Roll into a thin sheet and cut into rounds. Bake in a moderate oven. The recipe makes about thirty cookies.

HONEY DROP COOKIES

½ cup of butter
½ cup of granulated sugar
1 cup of honey
Beaten yolks of 2 eggs
Grated rind of 1 lemon
3 tablespoonfuls of lemon juice

The whites of 2 eggs, beaten dry
3 cups of sifted flour
1 teaspoonful of soda
More flour if needed

Mix in the usual manner. Drop the dough by teaspoonfuls onto a buttered baking pan, shape into smooth rounds. Bake in a moderate oven. For change add half a cup or more of cocoanut.

CHOCOLATE CREAM PIE

2 level tablespoonfuls of butter
½ cup of sugar
1 egg
⅓ cup of milk
⅞ cup of sifted flour
1½ teaspoonfuls baking powder
½ teaspoonful of vanilla extract

Filling for Cream Pie:

¾ an ounce of chocolate
¼ cup of sugar
2 tablespoonfuls of boiling water
¾ cup of double cream
½ teaspoonful of vanilla

Cream the butter; add half the sugar gradually. Beat the egg and beat in the other half of the sugar, then combine the two mixtures; add the milk and the flour sifted with the baking powder and salt. Bake in two small tins. Melt the chocolate; add the sugar and water and cook until smooth; let cool, add to the cream with the vanilla and beat until firm. Put between and on top of the layers.

ENGLISH TEA CAKES

1½ cups of flour
½ cup of sugar
½ teaspoonful of salt
2 level teaspoonfuls of baking powder
½ cup of butter
½ cup of dried currants
1 egg
2 tablespoonfuls of milk
Granulated sugar

Sift together the flour, sugar, salt and baking powder; with the tips of the fingers work in the butter; beat the egg, reserving a tablespoonful of the egg to glaze the cakes, add the milk to the egg and use to mix the dry ingredients to a dough. With the hands roll the dough into balls the size of an English walnut. Set the balls in a buttered pan, some distance apart, brush over with the egg, dredge with sugar and bake in a quick oven. The recipe makes about fifteen cakes. They are good and quickly made.

MARSHMALLOW MARGUERITES

Take any variety of thin, unsweetened cracker, spread lightly with butter and set in a baking pan; on the center of each cracker dispose a marshmallow, with a bit of butter above, — the butter may be omitted, — put the pan into a hot oven until the marshmallow is softened and browned a little, then serve at once.

ORANGE COOKIES

½ cup of butter
1 cup of granulated sugar
Grated rind of 1 orange
1 egg, beaten light
¼ cup of orange juice
2 cups or more of flour
4 level teaspoonfuls of baking powder

Mix in the usual manner, but without separating the white and yolk of the egg. Roll into a sheet, cut into cakes, set into baking pan, dredge with granulated sugar and bake in a moderate oven. Bake one cake, then add more flour if needed.

DROP COOKIES WITH SOUR CREAM

½ cup of butter
1 cup of sugar
1 egg, beaten light
½ cup of sour cream
¼ teaspoonful of sifted soda
2½ cups of sifted flour
3½ level teaspoonfuls of baking powder

Mix in the usual manner, stirring the soda into the cream. Mix the whole together very thoroughly; the mixture will be quite stiff. Drop from a spoon onto buttered tins, shaping each portion into a smooth round. Dredge with granulated sugar. Bake in a moderate oven.

OATMEAL MACAROONS

1 egg, beaten light
½ cup of sugar
½ tablespoonful of melted butter
¼ teaspoonful of salt
½ teaspoonful of vanilla
1¼ cups of rolled oats

Beat the sugar into the egg; add the other ingredients and beat all together thoroughly. Drop from a teaspoon onto a buttered baking sheet and shape in symmetrical rounds. Bake in a moderate oven. The recipe makes about eighteen small cakes.

TINY CREAM CAKES

¼ cup, or 2 ounces, of butter   ½ cup of sifted flour
½ cup of boiling water   1 egg and 1 extra yolk

Set the butter and water over the fire and when boiling add the flour and stir and cook until the mixture separates from the sides of the saucepan. Turn into a bowl, break in the whole egg and beat it in thoroughly, then beat in the yolk. With a teaspoon shape the mixture, on a buttered tin, into rounds about an inch and a quarter across. Bake about fifteen minutes, with strongest heat at the bottom. When cold make an opening on one side and fill with English Cream; dip the top of each in melted fondant and sprinkle with tiny candies (hundreds and thousands). Frosting made of syrup and confectioner's sugar may replace the fondant.

ENGLISH CREAM FILLING

1 cup of milk, scalded   ⅓ cup of sugar
¼ cup of sifted flour   ¼ teaspoonful of salt
¼ cup of milk   ½ teaspoonful of vanilla
1 egg or 2 egg yolks, beaten
   well

Stir the quarter cup of milk into the flour and cook in the scalded milk about fifteen minutes, then stir in the egg, sugar and salt, beaten together; let cook to set the egg; let cool and add the vanilla.

CRULLERS

1 yolk of egg, beaten light	1 white of egg, beaten dry
¼ cup of granulated sugar	¼ teaspoonful, each, of mace and salt
1 tablespoonful of melted butter	About 1 cup of flour

Beat the sugar into the beaten yolk; beat in the butter, fold in the white and then beat in the flour sifted with the salt and mace. Add more flour if needed. The dough must be stiff enough to roll into a sheet about one-third an inch thick. Cut into rectangular pieces (two by three inches), make four parallel slits in each equally distant from each other and the edges of the dough on all sides. Carefully lift up the second and fourth strips, to meet in the center, and cook in hot fat to a golden brown. Drain and sprinkle with powdered sugar.

YEAST DOUGHNUTS

¼ cup of lukewarm water	⅓ cup of melted butter
½ cake of compressed yeast	2 eggs
A little bread flour	¾ cup of sugar
1 teaspoonful of salt	½ teaspoonful of mace or nutmeg
1 cup of scalded-and-cooled milk	About 4 cups of bread flour

At about eight o'clock in the evening soften the yeast in the lukewarm water, mix thoroughly, then stir in flour to make a dough that can be kneaded; knead until elastic and cut the little ball of dough across the top in both directions, then put it into a bowl of tepid water, to stand until it floats on the water, light and puffy. With a skimmer remove "the sponge" to the mixing bowl, add the other ingredients and mix to a soft dough. Knead about fifteen minutes. Cover and set aside until morning. The temperature should not go much below 60° F. In the morning turn the light puffy dough upside down and roll into a sheet half an inch thick. Cut into strips half an inch (generous) wide; twist these and bring the ends together. Set to rise, covered, on a floured cloth or tin. When light fry in deep fat, drain on soft paper and roll in powdered sugar. The fat must not be too hot or the cakes will brown before they are cooked through. Turn frequently while cooking. Cakes made with yeast require longer cooking than those made with soda, etc.

CHAPTER XX

OTHER SWEET DISHES

GELATINE, WHIPPED EGG AND WHIPPED CREAM MIXTURES

In the following recipes, unless otherwise specified, when cream is referred to, a cream that will beat firm is intended. What is sold as double cream at about fifteen cents a half pint should become solid after beating a few moments. Thin cream, such as is taken from milk in a " separator," may be beaten solid by the use of viscogen. One-fourth a teaspoonful of viscogen is added to each three-fourths a cup of cream. Viscogen is easily prepared, and, stored in small receptacles from which the air is excluded, it will keep in good condition until used. Small glass-stoppered bottles are the best receptacles for keeping viscogen; fill the bottles full (air darkens the liquid), then put the stopper in above a narrow strip of waxed paper. Without the paper it is often difficult to remove the stopper.

The proper texture of many sweet dishes depends entirely on the manner in which whipped cream or white of egg is combined with the other ingredients. That a light fluffy texture be retained, the ingredients must be folded lightly together. When the whipped ingredient is to be added to a gelatine mixture, the latter must be evenly chilled, and just on the point of "setting," when the combination is made.

CONCERNING COMMERCIAL GELATINE

Gelatine is usually put up in two-ounce packages, though some few brands are in packages that contain but one ounce. Two ounces of gelatine will jelly two quarts of liquid, scant measure; half a package, or one ounce, jellies one quart of liquid; and one-fourth a package, or half an ounce, will jelly one pint of liquid.

HOW TO USE GELATINE

Gelatine, as it comes in the package, cannot be dissolved in a hot liquid; it must first be soaked in cold water, until it is completely hydrated, or until it will take up no more water. Gelatine will take up four times its weight of cold water. Thus two ounces or a full package of gelatine must be set to soak in eight ounces or a full cup of cold water or other liquid. In most of the recipes given for two people one-fourth or one-eighth a package of gelatine is called for, and one-fourth or one-eighth a cup, respectively, of water is needed. If cold milk or broth be used, the quantity must be increased a little. When the gelatine mixture is to be added to whipped mixtures, as in Bavarian creams, parfaits, etc., it must be cooled to about the same consistency as the mixture to which it is added; otherwise the gelatine mixture would settle to the bottom in a firm mass. Do not cook gelatine; if it is to be added to a "boiled custard" mixture, cook the custard, then add the softened gelatine and remove from the fire. Molds, in which gelatine mixtures with whipped cream or white of egg are to be "set," should be lined with narrow strips of tough, waxed paper. By this means the unmolding of the dish in perfect shape is assured.

CARAMEL JELLY

1 tablespoonful of granulated gelatine
¼ cup of cold water
⅓ cup of sugar cooked to caramel
⅓ cup of boiling water
2 cups of thin cream
¼ cup of sugar
¼ teaspoonful of salt

Soak the gelatine in the cold water. Cook the caramel and boiling water to a thick syrup; add the softened gelatine, the sugar, salt and cream and stir until the sugar is dissolved, then strain into molds.

MOLDED RICE

¼ cup of rice
1 cup of milk
½ teaspoonful of salt
⅓ cup of sugar
Grated rind of 1 orange
1 cup of thin cream
½ tablespoonful of gelatine
4 tablespoonfuls of cold water

Put a pint or more of cold water over the rice, let boil five minutes, then drain, rinse in cold water and drain again; add the milk and grated rind and let cook in a double boiler until the grains are tender; add the sugar, salt and cream, and let become hot, then add the gelatine, softened in the cold water, and stir over ice water until the mixture begins to thicken. Turn into a mold. Serve with boiled custard, sugar and cream, currant jelly or strawberry preserves.

RICE DAINTY

½ cup of cooked rice, every grain distinct
½ cup of pieces of pineapple
½ cup of sugar
½ cup of cream, beaten stiff

Mix the rice, sugar and pineapple, fold in the cream. Serve in glasses.

STRAWBERRY-MARSHMALLOW DESSERT

1 cup of strawberries, cut in halves
½ cup of marshmallows, cut in three or four pieces, each
½ or ¾ cup of double cream
2 tablespoonfuls of sugar
½ teaspoonful of vanilla extract

Beat the cream until firm throughout; beat in the sugar and vanilla, then fold in the marshmallows and nearly all the strawberries. Turn into glass cups. Use the remaining berries to garnish the top of the cream.

INDIVIDUAL CHARLOTTE RUSSE

½ cup of double cream
1 cup of thin cream
½ level tablespoonful of granulated gelatine
4 tablespoonfuls of cold water
¼ cup of sugar
1 teaspoonful of vanilla extract
6 or 8 ladyfingers

Line sherbet cups with ladyfingers trimmed to come half an inch above the top of the glass. Soften the gelatine in the cold water and dissolve by setting the dish in hot water; add the sugar, the thin cream and the vanilla, and stir until the sugar is dissolved; set into a dish of ice-water and stir until the mixture begins to thicken, then fold in the double cream, beaten firm. Put a spoonful at the base of each ladyfinger, in the cups, to hold it firmly in place, then fill the cups to the height of the ladyfingers.

CHARLOTTE RUSSE WITHOUT GELATINE

¾ cup of double cream
¼ cup of sugar (scant measure)
1 teaspoonful of vanilla extract or
2 tablespoonfuls of sherry
Ladyfingers
Candied cherries

Beat the cream until firm, then beat in the sugar and flavoring. Line the cups with ladyfingers and fill with the cream mixture. Decorate with the cherries.

RASPBERRY CHARLOTTE RUSSE

Ladyfingers
1 teaspoonful of granulated gelatine
3 tablespoonfuls of cold water
¾ cup of raspberry juice and pulp
⅓ cup of sugar
¾ cup of double cream

Soften the gelatine in the cold water and dissolve by setting the dish in boiling water; add to the raspberry pulp and juice (fresh or canned berries pressed through a sieve) with the sugar. Set the dish into ice-water and stir constantly until the mixture begins to thicken; then fold in the cream, beaten firm. Turn into cups lined with ladyfingers.

GRAPE JUICE CHARLOTTE RUSSE

1 teaspoonful of granulated gelatine	White of 1 egg
¼ cup of grape juice	1 tablespoonful of lemon juice
½ cup of sugar	½ cup of double cream
½ cup of hot grape juice	Candied violets
	Ladyfingers

Soften the gelatine in the fourth a cup of grape juice and dissolve in the hot juice; add the sugar and lemon juice and let become cold. Beat the white of egg dry and gradually beat the grape mixture into it. Continue beating until the mixture will hold its shape (have the mixture in ice-water meanwhile), then turn into the glasses lined with **ladyfingers**. With pastry bag and star tube decorate with the cream, beaten firm, and the candied violets.

ORANGE MARMALADE MOLD

1 tumbler of orange marmalade	¼ cup of cold water
¾ cup of boiling water	1 tablespoonful of lemon juice if convenient
¼ package of gelatine	

Soften the gelatine in the cold water and dissolve in the hot water; add the marmalade and lemon juice. Stir occasionally until the mixture begins to thicken, then turn into mold. Serve with cream. Strawberry and raspberry jam may be used in the same way.

ORANGE MARMALADE BAVARIAN CREAM

¼ package of gelatine (scant measure)
¼ cup of cold water
1 cup of orange marmalade
1 tablespoonful of lemon juice
1 cup of double cream

Soften the gelatine in the cold water and dissolve over hot water; add the marmalade and fold in the cream, beaten firm. Turn into a mold lined with paper. Strawberry preserves may be used in the same way.

GINGER BAVARIAN CREAM

Stem ginger root, cut in slices or figures
½ cup of preserved ginger, chopped and pounded in a mortar with ginger syrup
1 tablespoonful of granulated gelatine
¼ cup of cold water
1 cup of rich milk
Yolks of 2 eggs
⅓ cup of sugar
1 cup of double cream beaten firm

The " stem " ginger root (preserved in earthen jars) is the best. Use the slices or figures to decorate the bottom of the mold. Soak the gelatine in the cold water. Beat the yolks, add the sugar and cook in the milk, scalded over hot water; add the soaked gelatine and the pounded ginger and stir over ice-water until it begins to set, then fold in the cream.

CARAMEL BAVARIAN CREAM

¼ box of gelatine
¼ cup of cold water
⅔ cup of sugar

½ cup of boiling water
½ cup of chopped almonds
1½ cups of double cream

Soak the gelatine in the cold water. Cook the sugar to caramel; add the boiling water and let simmer to a syrup; add the softened gelatine and the nuts; set into ice water and stir until beginning to set; fold in the cream, beaten firm. When the mixture will hold its shape, turn into a mold. For a more elaborate dish, line the mold with ladyfingers. When unmolded decorate with a cup of cream, beaten stiff, and slices of candied cherries. Set the cream in place with pastry bag and star tube.

II

CUSTARDS AND CUSTARD MIXTURES

In custard mixtures (egg, milk or other liquid, sugar, etc.), as in all egg cookery, the temperature at which the cooking is done largely determines the character of the finished dish. When the mixture is not to be stirred during cooking, set to cook on many folds of paper, surround with water at the boiling point, and let cook in the oven, or, covered, on top of the range. Do not allow the water to boil during the cooking, as the custard will be spoiled. The mixture is cooked when firm in the center. One egg to a cup of milk makes a fairly rich custard, but the custard should be eaten from the dish in which it is cooked. By the use of two eggs, or preferably one egg and two yolks (on account of tenderness that the fat in the yolks gives), a custard firm enough to be turned from the dish in perfect shape is assured. Starchy ingredients, as cornstarch, rice, tapioca, bread or cake crumbs, may be used in the place of the second egg. Half an ounce of rice or tapioca (uncooked), or one whole ounce of cake or bread crumbs are needed to each cup of milk. As high temperature or time is essential to the proper cooking of starchy ingredients, rice, tapioca, cornstarch and the like should be cooked before the egg is added. When the hot custard mixture or pudding is to be turned from the mold, the matter is simplified, if the dish be buttered thoroughly and then dredged liberally with sugar. A mold lined with caramel insures perfect unmolding of the custard or pudding and at the same time provides a sauce for the dish. A tin mold of good quality is the best in using a caramel lining. Cook the required quantity of sugar to caramel over a quick fire. At once turn the caramel into the mold and with a towel held in both hands take up the mold (which will be very hot) and turn it round slowly, that the caramel may coat the entire inner surface of the mold. The mold may be used at once or at some future time.

Steamed Custard — *Page 353.*

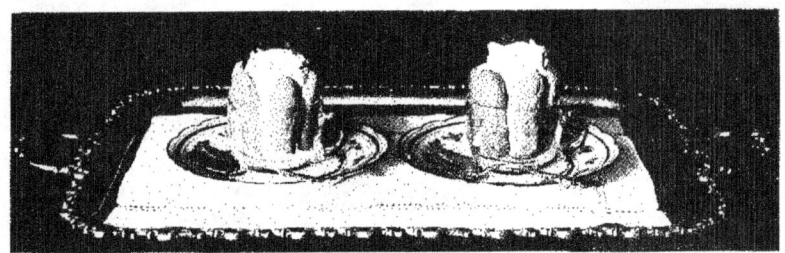

Charlotte Russe for Two — *Page 346*

Chocolate Custard with Whipped Cream — *Page 353*

Custard Renversée with Almonds — *Page 354.*

Orange Marmalade Bavariose. — *Page 348.*

Canned Pear Meringues — *Page 355*

A soft, or "boiled," custard should always be cooked in a double boiler. Whole eggs may be used for this form of custard, but as the yolks give the best results, the whites are usually reserved for some other dish. If the whites are used, beat them dry and fold into the mixture after the yolks and sugar have been cooked in the milk. Have the milk scalded. Beat the yolks, then add the sugar and beat again; add a little of the hot milk, mix all together thoroughly, then pour into the rest of the hot milk. Stir constantly until the mixture coats the spoon; add the whites, if they are to be used, and at once strain into a cold dish, to arrest the cooking.

BOILED CUSTARD NO. 1

1¼ cups of scalded milk, hot
2 yolks of eggs
¼ cup of sugar
¼ teaspoonful of salt
½ teaspoonful of vanilla extract or
Thin yellow rind of ½ orange or lemon

Scald the rind in the milk; add vanilla when the custard is cold. Serve as a pudding sauce, or with blanc mange, caramel jelly, lemon, prune or fig jelly, fig whip, delicate soufflé, etc.

BOILED CUSTARD IN CUPS

1½ cups of scalded milk hot
1 or 2 teaspoonfuls of cornstarch
¼ cup of cold milk
Yolks of 2 eggs
¼ cup of sugar
¼ teaspoonful of salt
½ teaspoonful of vanilla extract or
Thin rind of orange or lemon

Mix the cornstarch with the cold milk and stir and cook in the hot milk until smooth and slightly thickened. Cover and let cook ten or fifteen minutes. Beat the yolks; add the sugar and salt, and beat again, then stir into the hot mixture and continue stirring until the egg looks "set," then remove from the fire; add the vanilla when cold. Cook the fruit rind in the milk.

DELMONICO PUDDING WITH PEACHES OR APRICOTS

Pudding
- 4 to 6 halves of canned apricots or peaches with a little fruit syrup
- ¼ cup of cornstarch
- ¼ cup of cold milk
- 1¾ cups of scalding hot milk
- 1 teaspoonful of butter
- 2 yolks of eggs
- ¼ teaspoonful of salt
- ¼ cup of sugar

Meringue
- 2 whites of eggs
- 4 tablespoonfuls of sugar
- ¼ teaspoonful of vanilla extract

Put the fruit and syrup in a pudding dish; make a thick "boiled custard" of the other ingredients, cooking the starch ten or fifteen minutes in the hot milk before adding the yolks of egg with the sugar. Turn the custard over the fruit. Beat the whites of eggs dry; gradually beat in half the sugar, then fold in the other half and the extract. Spread the meringue over the custard and let stand in a moderate oven about ten minutes. Serve hot or cold.

CORNSTARCH PUDDING

Omit the peaches and meringue from the preceding recipe. Serve hot, from the double boiler, with cream and sugar. An ounce of melted chocolate may be stirred in before the eggs and sugar.

STEAMED CUSTARD

1 egg and 1 extra yolk
3 level tablespoonfuls of sugar
¼ teaspoonful of salt
1 cup of milk

Beat the eggs, add the sugar and salt and beat again; add the milk, mix thoroughly and turn into two custard cups; set in a steamer over boiling water, cover and let cook until firm. The water should not boil during the cooking. A double boiler may replace the steamer or the cups may be set in a pan of water in the oven or on top of the range. Finish while hot by grating a little nutmeg over the top of the custards.

CHOCOLATE CUSTARD, WITH WHIPPED CREAM

½ ounce of chocolate
¼ cup of sugar
2 or 3 tablespoonfuls of cold water
1 cup of milk
2 eggs
¼ teaspoonful, each, of salt and cinnamon

Melt the chocolate over hot water; add two tablespoonfuls of the sugar and the cold water, and stir and cook until smooth; add the milk. Beat the eggs, add the rest of the sugar, the salt and spice and beat again; add the chocolate mixture and turn into charlotte russe molds, buttered and dredged with sugar. Bake as all custards. When cold turn from the molds and fill the open centers with whipped cream. Other molds may be used and the whipped cream be omitted.

CUSTARD RENVERSÉE WITH ALMONDS

½ cup of sugar
¼ cup of blanched almonds
2 whole eggs
2 yolks of eggs
3 tablespoonfuls (level) of sugar
¼ teaspoonful of salt
1½ cups of milk

Cook the half cup of sugar to caramel; add the nuts, cut in slices, cook a moment longer, and use to line a charlotte mold. Beat the eggs; add the sugar and salt and beat again; add the milk, mix thoroughly and turn into the lined mold. Bake in the usual manner. See remarks on custard mixtures at beginning of chapter.

PRUNE WHIP, WITH BOILED CUSTARD

10 prunes
¼ cup of sugar
1 tablespoonful of lemon juice
2 whites of eggs
¼ teaspoonful of salt
Boiled Custard No. 1

Wash the prunes, cover with cold water and let stand overnight. Cook until tender, then press through a sieve. Set to cook in a double boiler with the salt, sugar and lemon juice; beat the whites of eggs dry. When the prune mixture is hot fold the eggs into it; continue to cook and fold until the egg is set. Serve hot or cold with custard No. 1, which should always be served cold.

FIG, PRUNE OR DATE WHIP

4 figs *or*	Scant ¼ cup of sugar
10 prunes *or*	¼ teaspoonful of salt
10 dates	Boiled Custard No. 1, or
The whites of 3 eggs	Cream and sugar

Cook whichever fruit is used and cut it into tiny bits. Beat the whites of eggs dry; gradually beat in half of the sugar, then cut and fold in the rest of the sugar and the fruit. Bake in a buttered-and-sugared dish as any custard. Serve hot with the boiled custard (cold) or with cream and sugar.

CANNED PEAR MERINGUES

From a thin sheet or slices of sponge cake, cut out shapes, rounded at one end and pointed at the other, like the shape of half a pear, but larger. Upon these dispose halves of cooked pears, from which the core has been taken. Fill the core spaces with fine-chopped, preserved ginger and pipe meringue mixture above, to cover the tops of the pieces of pear. Dredge both cake and pear with granulated sugar and set into the oven to cook the meringue. The dish should stand in the oven eight or ten minutes before browning. Serve with the syrup from the pears, or with boiled custard.

MERINGUE FOR PEARS

Beat the whites of two eggs dry; gradually beat in two level tablespoonfuls of sugar, then cut and fold in two tablespoonfuls of sugar.

CUSTARD RICE PUDDING

¼ cup of rice
1 cup of milk
⅓ cup of sugar
¼ cup of raisins or currants
1 egg and 1 yolk
⅓ cup of milk
½ teaspoonful of mace or nutmeg

Blanche the rice, then cook till tender in the cup of milk; add the fruit, the egg, beaten and mixed with the sugar, the spice and half-cup of milk, mix thoroughly and turn into buttered-and-sugared molds. Bake as all custards. Serve, turned from the molds, with wine, orange or currant jelly sauce.

WINE SAUCE

Cook a cup, each, of sugar and water to a thick syrup; add one-third a cup of sherry or claret and if at hand a teaspoonful of lemon juice. A teaspoonful of cornstarch mixed with the sugar improves the sauce for some tastes.

ORANGE SAUCE

Cook a cup, each, of sugar and water with the thin yellow rind of an orange to a thick syrup; strain, add one-third a cup of orange juice and one tablespoonful of lemon juice.

CURRANT JELLY SAUCE

Cook a cup of currant jelly with a cup of water until smooth; add a tablespoonful of lemon juice.

BREAD PUDDING, VIENNOISE

1 cup of fine soft bread crumbs	1 whole egg and yolk of another
½ cup of dried currants	
½ teaspoonful of salt	¼ cup of sugar
½ teaspoonful of cinnamon	¼ cup of sugar cooked to caramel
1½ cups of milk	
	¼ cup of boiling water

Pour the boiling water over the caramel and let boil to a syrup; add the sugar, the milk and the eggs, beaten light. Mix the crumbs, currants, salt and cinnamon and combine the two mixtures. Turn into buttered-and-sugared molds. Let cook in a dish of water as a custard. Serve hot, turned from the molds, with Sabayon or hard sauce.

ORANGE SABAYON SAUCE

Beat one whole egg and one yolk; gradually beat in one-third a cup of sugar. Set the dish over hot water, add the grated rind of an orange, one-third a cup of orange juice and one tablespoonful of lemon juice. Continue beating while the sauce thickens. When thick as a boiled custard, remove to a dish of cold water, to stop the cooking, and serve at once.

CHOCOLATE SOUFFLÉ

2 tablespoonfuls of butter	1½ ounces of melted chocolate
2 tablespoonfuls of flour	¼ cup of sugar
¼ teaspoonful of salt	2 eggs
¾ cup of milk	

Melt the butter and in it cook the flour and salt; add the milk and stir and cook until smooth and thick; add the chocolate, the sugar and the yolks of eggs, beaten light; lastly fold in the whites of the eggs, beaten dry. Bake as a custard. Serve hot, the instant it is done, with whipped cream sweetened and flavored with vanilla, or with frothy or Sabayon sauce.

FROTHY SAUCE

⅓ cup of butter	⅓ cup of boiling water
⅔ cup of sugar	1½ tablespoonfuls of wine or
White of egg, beaten dry	A teaspoonful of vanilla

Cream the butter, beat in the sugar and fold in the white of egg; add the boiling water and flavoring. Mix and serve at once.

III

A FEW SIMPLE HOT PUDDINGS

SCALLOPED RHUBARB WITH MERINGUE

Peel the rhubarb and cut into inch lengths. In a buttered dish put a layer of thin slices of sponge cake, and over this a layer of the rhubarb; sprinkle with sugar, a grating of yellow orange rind and a few grains of salt; continue the layers until the dish is filled. For half a pound of rhubarb use about three-fourths a cup of sugar. Cover the dish and let bake about half an hour. Beat the whites of two eggs dry; gradually beat in two tablespoonfuls of sugar, then fold in two tablespoonfuls of sugar and spread over the pudding. Let bake about twelve minutes in a very moderate oven.

BLUEBERRY BETTY

Remove the crust from slices of stale bread. Put the bread, spread with butter, into a pudding-dish in layers, alternating with blueberries. Sprinkle the blueberries with sugar, a little salt, and, if desired, a grating of nutmeg. Have generous layers of blueberries. Squeeze over the whole the juice of half a lemon, or add two tablespoonfuls of water. Cover the dish, and let bake until the berries are tender. Then remove the cover, to brown the top. Serve with cream and sugar.

STEAMED GRAHAM PUDDING

1 cup of graham or of entire wheat flour
½ cup of white flour
½ teaspoonful of salt
1 teaspoonful of soda
1 teaspoonful of cinnamon mace and cloves, mixed

1 egg
½ cup of molasses
½ cup of milk
4 tablespoonfuls of melted butter
¾ cup of fruit

Sift together the dry ingredients. Beat the egg; add the milk, molasses and butter and stir into the dry ingredients; add the fruit. Use for fruit, raisins, currants, citron, candied peel, chopped figs, dates or prunes, one or a combination of two or more. Steam two and one half hours. Serve with hard sauce.

STEAMED ORANGE PUDDING

¾ cup of scalded milk
½ cup of grated bread crumbs
1 tablespoonful of butter
2 eggs
¼ cup of sugar

Grated rind and juice of half an orange
1 tablespoonful of lemon juice
2 tablespoonfuls of chopped almonds

Pour the milk over the crumbs and butter and let stand an hour. Beat the eggs; add the sugar and beat again; add fruit juice and almonds and mix all together. Steam one hour. Serve with hard sauce.

STEAMED PRUNE PUDDING

⅓ cup of stale bread crumbs
⅓ cup of flour
1 level teaspoonful of baking powder
⅓ cup of fine-chopped suet

⅓ cup of sugar
1 egg, beaten light
⅓ cup of prune purée
¼ teaspoonful of salt
⅓ cup of milk

Mix together the crumbs, flour and baking powder, suet and sugar. To the beaten egg add the purée, salt and milk. Stir the liquid into the dry ingredients. Steam two hours in a buttered, tight-closed mold. An empty baking powder box makes a good mold. Leave plenty of room for the pudding to swell. Serve with hard or liquid sauce.

STEAMED CHOCOLATE PUDDING, SULTANA SAUCE

Pudding

1 cup of sifted pastry flour
1½ teaspoonfuls of baking powder

½ teaspoonful of cinnamon
¼ teaspoonful of salt
1 egg
⅓ cup of sugar

3 tablespoonfuls of melted butter
¼ cup of milk
2 ounces of chocolate

Sauce
¼ cup of sultana raisins
1 cup of boiling water
½ cup of sugar
Flavor to taste

Sift together the flour, baking powder, cinnamon and salt. Beat the yolk of egg light, the white till dry; beat the sugar into the yolk of egg; add the butter and milk and stir into the first mixture; add the chocolate melted over hot water and, lastly, the white of egg. Steam in two or three cups about twenty-five minutes. Cook the raisins tender in the water; add the sugar, let boil five minutes, then flavor and use.

BAKED APPLE DUMPLING

Tart apples
Salt
3 tablespoonfuls of cold water
1½ cups of pastry flour
3 teaspoonfuls of baking powder

¼ teaspoonful of salt
3 tablespoonfuls of butter
1 egg (this may be omitted)
¾ cup of milk (scant measure)

Butter an agate baking dish; into it slice tart apples to fill to the top; add a dash of salt and the cold water. Make a soft biscuit dough of the other ingredients and spread it over the apples. Bake in a quick oven about twenty-five minutes. Invert the dish, so as to have the apples on the top. Serve hot with butter and sugar or syrup.

CANNED PINEAPPLE TOAST

From slices of stale sponge cake cut out as many rounds as there are slices of pineapple to be used. Have the rounds of cake of the same size as the rounds of pineapple or a little larger. Butter the slices of cake, dredge with sugar and set them into the oven to brown and glaze. Cook the syrup from the pineapple with about half a cup of sugar and a tablespoonful of lemon juice; add the slices of pineapple, let boil once, then keep hot until ready to serve. Set a round of pineapple above each round of cake, pour over the sauce, and serve at once.

IV

FROZEN DESSERTS

For freezing desserts at home, the freezing mixture is prepared with ice (or snow) and salt. Often ice may be had by setting a pan of water out of doors overnight. With snow a little water must be used to start the melting process.

In a family of two, when a frozen dish is prepared, especially in cold weather, it is well to make this the sweet dish for both luncheon and dinner, otherwise this form of dessert should be put in the class of dishes reserved for occasional rather than for frequent use.

The ice to be used in a freezer must be made nearly as fine as the salt which is to be used with it;

but for packing a frozen mixture, larger pieces that will not dissolve quickly are preferable. For the same reason very little salt should be mixed with the ice used in packing a frozen dessert that is simply to be kept in this condition.

In many freezers ices may be frozen quickly and at the same time be light and fluffy in texture, but in general the texture of the article is better if it be not frozen too quickly. One measure of salt to three of ice is a fair proportion for mixtures to be frozen in the ordinary freezer. The process will take from five minutes to half an hour, the time depending upon the kind of ingredients used and the make of freezer. Parfaits, being left to freeze without any attention, require to be packed for three or four hours. Use equal measures of ice and salt. Parfaits are at their best when frozen just enough to hold the shape. Too much sugar or wine hinders the freezing process. After the ice has been cracked and the cream beaten, the work of preparing a parfait is very slight. The unmolding of parfaits or any variety of ice once was considered a troublesome matter. If a little air can be let in under the ice, no trouble will be experienced; this may be easily accomplished, if two narrow strips of paper be used to line the mold. Let the end extend out over the edges of the mold. By lifting on these papers air can be let in and the ice easily removed. Any kind of ice packed in a mold made with double covers — the mold being first lined with paper — can be unmolded with ease and without recourse to the water faucet, either hot or cold. With a piece of hard wood of just the size to slip through the mold, the ice may be pressed through upon the serving dish without an instant's delay.

PACKING A MOLD

If ordinary ice cream or sherbet is to be packed in a mold, do not freeze as solid as for serving, lest it prove troublesome to press the mixture closely into the mold, and air spaces be left here and there, which will spoil the shape. Fill the mold to overflow, spread paper over the top and over this press down the cover, tie securely, especially if the mold be made with two covers, and at once bury in the freezing mixture. The mold for parfaits, carefully lined, to avoid salt water, *must* be chilled before use. The flavoring mixture and the whipped cream, which should be of about the same consistency, should be thoroughly chilled, but not combined until the last moment before packing. The recipes given make just enough mixture to fill a quart mold. They may be easily divided and half the mixture frozen in empty baking powder or cocoa cans. Parfaits may be frozen, also, in the can of a freezer and be unmolded in a round like a pie. Or the frozen mixture may be transferred by the spoonful to long-stemmed glasses. In glasses, for special occasion, finish with whipped cream and a cherry. In hot weather the ice in which a parfait is packed will have to be renewed. Ices may be kept, after freezing, for many hours, packed in a fireless cooker.

VANILLA ICE CREAM, PHILADELPHIA STYLE

1 pint of thin cream
½ cup of granulated sugar
½ tablespoonful of vanilla extract

Mix all together and turn into the can of the freezer. Pack with salt and crushed ice in the usual proportion and turn the crank until the mixture is well frozen. At first turn the crank slowly, later turn more quickly. Take out the dasher and scrape the cream from it into the freezer; beat the whole thoroughly, smooth over the top and put on the cover. If the ice floats, turn off the water and repack, using larger pieces of ice and one measure of salt to four or five of ice. Spread burlaps, carpet or newspaper over the top, to keep the ice from melting too fast. The cream may be scalded; in summer this is advisable.

VANILLA ICE CREAM, JUNKET

1 pint of milk
½ cup of double cream
½ cup of sugar
½ tablespoonful of vanilla extract
½ junket tablet,
1 tablespoonful of cold water

Crush the half tablet and let stand in the cold water to dissolve. Heat the milk, cream, sugar and vanilla to about 90° F.; stir in the dissolved tablet, pour into the can of the freezer and let stand in a warm place until the mixture "sets" or jellies. Do not jar the mixture while it is jellying. When cold freeze as in the first recipe. This makes an exceptionally nice ice cream.

CHOCOLATE ICE CREAM

Melt one or two ounces of chocolate over hot water; add three or four tablespoonfuls of sugar and the same quantity of boiling water; stir and cook until smooth, then add to the cream or milk to be used.

CARAMEL ICE CREAM

Allow four extra tablespoonfuls of sugar, to each pint of milk or cream given in the previous recipes. Cook the half cup of sugar, given in the recipes, to caramel, add half a cup of water and let boil to a thick syrup. Add this with the extra sugar to the milk or cream and finish as usual.

FROZEN CUSTARD

2 cups of milk
Yolks of 4 eggs
½ cup of sugar, generous measure
¼ teaspoonful of salt
½ cup of cream
¾ tablespoonfuls of vanilla extract

Use all the ingredients, save the last two, in making a "boiled custard;" when cold add the cream and vanilla and freeze as usual.

STRAWBERRY ICE CREAM

1 pint of milk
½ cup of sugar
2 level tablespoonfuls of cornstarch
½ teaspoonful of salt
1 basket of strawberries
1½ cups of sugar (granulated)
1 pint of cream

Sift together, several times, the sugar, cornstarch and salt, then cook in the milk, scalded over hot water; stir constantly until the mixture thickens and is smooth, then cover and let cook fifteen minutes. Pick over, wash and drain the berries; mix them with the sugar and let stand an hour or more, then press through a fine sieve. Strain the cornstarch mixture into the freezer, and when cold add the cream and begin to freeze the mixture. When half frozen add the strawberries and sugar and finish freezing.

PEACH ICE CREAM

¾ cup of peach pulp
¾ cup of granulated sugar
Juice of ½ lemon
1½ cups of thin cream

Pare and stone choice, ripe peaches and press the pulp through a "ricer;" add the sugar and lemon juice and turn into the can of a freezer, packed in ice and salt; add the cream and freeze as usual.

PEACH CUP

Peach Ice Cream as above
2 peaches, pared and sliced
½ an orange, peeled, seeded and sliced
Sugar to sweeten

Mix the prepared fruit with the sugar; put into chilled cups and dispose peach ice cream above.

PEACH SHERBET

2 cups of water
1 cup of sugar
¾ cup of peach pulp

Juice of 1 orange or equivalent
of peach pulp
Juice of ½ lemon

Boil the sugar and water twenty minutes; let cool, add the fruit juice and freeze. This may be used with slices of fruit for "Peach Cup." Pineapple and peaches make a particularly good combination for "fruit cup."

GRAPEFRUIT SHERBET

2 cups of water
1 cup of sugar
Juice of 1 grapefruit or

1 cup of juice
Juice of 1 lemon
Candied cherries, chopped fine

Boil the sugar and water twenty minutes; let cool, add the fruit juice and freeze. Serve in cups with chopped cherries sprinkled on top.

BLOOD ORANGE SHERBET

2 cups of water
1 cup of sugar
¼ teaspoonful of granulated
  gelatine

1 tablespoonful of cold water
Juice of 3 or 4 "blood"
  oranges
Juice of ½ lemon

Boil the sugar and water twenty minutes; add the gelatine, soaked in the cold water, and when cold add the fruit juice and freeze as usual.

COFFEE PARFAIT

½ tablespoonful of gelatine
⅛ cup of cold water
1 cup of strong coffee

2 yolks of eggs
  cup of sugar
1½ cups of double cream

Vanilla and Strawberry Ice Cream in One Glass — *Page 365*

Ginger Bavarian Cream — *Page 348.*

Peach Ice Cream for Two — *Page 367*

STRAWBERRY-AND-MARSHMALLOW DESSERT — *Page 345.*

GOLDEN PARFAIT, WITH FRUIT — *Page 370*

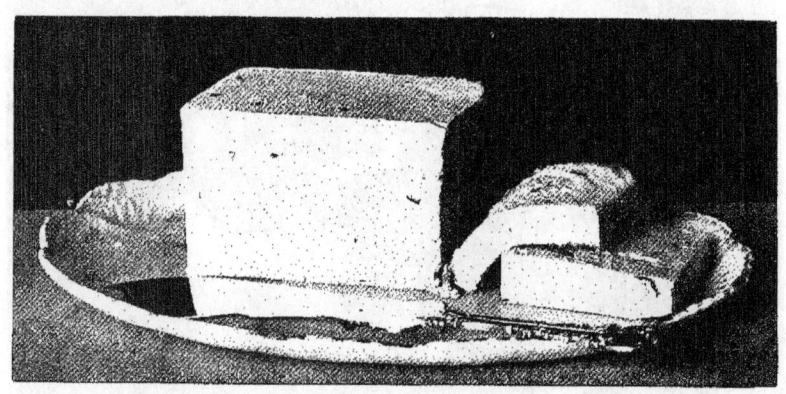

BANANA PARFAIT — *Page 369*

Soak the gelatine in the cold water. Heat the coffee with half the sugar. Beat the yolks, add the rest of the sugar and beat again; cook the yolks in the coffee as boiled custard and when slightly thickened add the gelatine and strain into a cold dish; stir until the mixture thickens a little, fold in the cream, beaten solid, and finish as usual.

BANANA PARFAIT

1¼ cups of banana pulp (about 3 bananas)
¾ cup of sugar
Juice of ½ lemon
1½ cups of double cream
½ cup of candied fruit, cut fine (apricots, pineapple, cherries, etc.)
3 tablespoonfuls of Jamaica rum

Cook the pulp, sugar and lemon juice until scalded throughout. Beat the cream till firm. Soak the fruit several hours or overnight in the rum; a heavy sugar syrup may be used in place of the rum. If the alcohol or syrup be not used, the fruit will freeze too hard to be eaten. Fold the mixture together and finish in the usual manner.

PRUNE PARFAIT

½ pound of prunes
¾ cup of sugar
⅓ cup of prune juice
Juice of ½ lemon
White of 1 egg
1½ cups of double cream

Soak the prunes overnight; cook till tender; remove and discard stones and cut the flesh in bits. Cook the sugar with the lemon and prune juice to soft ball (238° F.), pour in a fine stream upon the white of egg, beaten dry, and beat until cold; add the pieces of prune and fold in the cream. Turn into a quart mold and finish in the usual manner.

CANNED APRICOT PARFAIT

Press enough canned apricots through a sieve to fill a cup. Simmer the pulp with half a cup of sugar until it is quite thick, then set aside to become cold. Beat one cup and a half of double cream until firm; fold into the purée and finish in the usual manner. This parfait, not being very sweet, will freeze in two hours or a little less. Serve with a sauce made by cooking the rest of the syrup in the can with half a cup of sugar. Or, serve the parfait in cups with the sauce poured over and the top sprinkled with fine-chopped pistachio nuts.

GOLDEN PARFAIT, WITH FRENCH FRUIT

⅔ cup of sugar
⅓ cup of water
⅛ teaspoonful of cream-of-tartar

5 yolks of eggs, beaten light
1½ cups double cream
½ cup French fruit
Jamaica rum

Let the fruit soak in rum to cover overnight or for several hours. Cook the sugar, water and cream of tartar to 238° F. (soft ball); pour in a fine stream upon the beaten yolks, beating constantly meanwhile; return to the fire over hot water and beat until the mixture thickens. Beat occasionally until cold. Have the cream beaten solid. Sprinkle some of the fruit into the mold, lined and chilled as usual. Fold the egg and cream mixtures together and turn into the mold, sprinkling in the fruit here and there.

SAUCE FOR VANILLA ICE CREAM

1 cup of sugar
¼ cup of boiling water
⅓ cup of claret or ½ cup of strawberry or raspberry pulp

Cook the sugar and water to a thick syrup. It will take about eight or nine minutes. Cool and add the wine or strained fruit. Serve in cups, pouring the sauce over or around the ice. Sprinkle the top with fine-chopped pistachio nuts.

BANANA PURÉE FOR ICE CREAM

Cook a cup of banana purée (peeled bananas pressed through a sieve) with a cup of sugar and the juice of a lemon until hot throughout; let cool, add a teaspoonful of vanilla and use as a sauce for vanilla ice cream.

VANILLA ICE CREAM WITH MAPLE SYRUP

Put two tablespoonfuls of maple syrup into a chilled sherbet cup; add a spoonful of vanilla ice cream and sprinkle the top of the cream with English walnuts, chopped rather coarse. Caramel syrup as, also, chocolate syrup may be used in the same way.

CHOCOLATE SAUCE FOR ICE CREAM

1 cup of sugar
½ cup of water

1 ounce of chocolate

Cook the sugar to caramel, add the water, let boil to a syrup, add the chocolate and let boil two or three minutes. Strain through a cloth and use cold as the maple syrup.

A SERMONET

"The poetry of life always has a practical side to it, and most practical affairs rightly worked out are full of poetry."—*E. P. Powell, in "The Country Home."*

The women of the home should so arrange their household duties as to allow time for outdoor exercise and some form of healthful recreation."—*"Back to Nature."*

An old adage runs something like this: "A workman is known by his tools." No one expects a carpenter with dull planes or broken saws, and who does not own a glue-pot or a spirit-level, to turn out a finished job. A woman may use a hair or hat pin for a larding-needle and slice bacon or bone a chicken or a fish with a knife that will not take, much less keep, an edge; but she who makes no effort to supply herself with fitting implements of her trade certainly has no great love for her calling, and is not destined to shine therein. The cook who visits the public library to examine dictionaries of cooking, in order to discover what a certain chef uses in Hollandaise sauce to give it an odd and piquant flavor, will never beg for work. Her calling means more to her than the buying power of the money she receives on Saturday night.

Yet, granting that this be true, the old adage needs an amendment or an addition, for the modern workman is known by the disposition he makes of his tools. A kitchen pantry has its uses, but it is turned from its legitimate purpose, when it is made into a storehouse for the utensils needed at the range and sink. Go into your kitchen to get breakfast or dinner, and count the steps you might save, were the various saucepans, frying-pans, forks, dredgers, etc., needed in the actual cooking of the meal, where the hand can be quickly laid upon them. Note the distance between the stove and sink. In two houses lately visited two rooms lay between them. Is the refrigerator conveniently placed in reference to the pantry or the place where food is prepared for cooking? Modern houses, supposedly, are planned aright, but do not go on the supposition that whatever is is right. Do not waste your strength in useless, monotonous walking back and forth in the kitchen. Have things arranged to save steps, and put in the extra time in the open air.

Truly we might spend vastly more time out of doors and at the same time supply our tables with a greater variety of food, if receptacles holding sifted flour of various kinds, well dried out and ready for instant use, were in close proximity to mixing-bowls, egg-beaters, baking-tins, measuring-cups, sugar, butter, eggs, baking-powder, and other commodities.

Make the doing of work as easy as possible by having every utensil or food product as near as possible to the place where it is to be handled. Then do things often, and you will have no consciousness of the motions you go through to secure the result. When dancing the two-step or the waltz, who, save the beginner or the teacher, analyzes the result to find out the postures or positions that go to produce it?

We say of certain housekeepers among our acquaintances, "They have a 'faculty' of turning off work." Possibly this faculty is nothing but the exponent of an unusually active and attentive mind.

In reading the newspaper aloud, there are those whose whole attention is fixed on the words they are speaking. Others, while they are giving to the spoken words the inflection needed to convey the proper meaning of the author, have their eyes at the other end of the line or even at the end of the paragraph, and know what is coming next. Thus, in laying the table and cooking a meal, the woman with "faculty" carries in her mind many things at one and the same time. She is never in danger of forgetting any one item or of not knowing the exact condition of all at a given moment. Such a woman can prepare a meal of three or four courses, properly selected, and made ready to cook beforehand, in the time that another would give to the cooking of a single dish. She would also finish with no more fatigue than if she had stood and watched over the one dish, knife and fork or skimmer in hand, during every moment of the cooking.

Simplify the cooking during the hot months. Complicated dishes, sauces, rich cakes, and pastry are certainly out of season — to say the least. Fruit and berries are always welcome, and, when tired of the old way of serving with cream and sugar, try them with oil and acid. Those who are conservative lose half the joy of life, and the first place where one's conservatism crops out is in respect to food.

Know what you are going to do before you enter the kitchen, then go straight to the mark without dallying. Fuel and precious time are often wasted, while one is trying to make up her mind what she will do. Then, worn out in trying to find something easy to make, calling for nothing tangible in the way of ingredients and little cooking, the matter is given up, and the grocer is telephoned to bring something in the inevitable paper bag. We fail to see any satisfaction in this kind of housekeeping. Housekeeping is a business to be conducted in summer and in winter. To be always equal to it, take a holiday often. Do not stagnate. Initiate new projects in your business. Rejoice in it. Avoid overwork and overheat, but keep up your interest. We love those things upon which we expend our efforts.

UNDER-NUTRITION AND OVER-NUTRITION

The two mistakes into which the new housekeeper is most often led are under-feeding and over-feeding. There are so many things she wishes to have in her new home that the allowance for food is often drawn upon to supply things more highly prized; and the items for food are restricted to whatever is cheap, regardless of its composition. Starch is the principal compound in cheap foods. But there are individuals whose digestive organs are not tolerant of starch, and they are just as intolerant of fat, if it be presented as a steady diet. In the main, the dietary of such individuals needs include plainly cooked fresh meat and fish, with green vegetables, while fancy breads, cereals, and sweets, in the form of pastry, puddings, and cakes, are to be avoided, except on rare occasions.

On the other hand, many new housekeepers think meat, fish, and, possibly, eggs, the only articles having any considerable nutritive value, and, consequently, the only articles to be considered in eating to live. The idea that bulk is needed to insure the best digestive action is undreamed of by them, or, if considered at all, they think it is secured by these same nutritious articles rather than by bread with green and starchy vegetables. The normal stomach can digest a little of any kind of food, and health will be better, if monotony in selection be avoided. But these, and other matters of like import, are easily worked out, provided the desire be present to choose food in accordance with the laws of dietetics.

Do not follow the lead of those misguided butterflies who think that physical exercise that savors of practical utility detracts from health no less than from dignity. To those who can do things is given an added dignity. The women of this century must be able to execute as well as to know. Then, too, any proper physical exercise will tend to set the blood in circulation, deliver the nutritious elements of the food ingested where they are needed, and drive waste matters out through the pores of the skin. Often dish-washing in a well ventilated kitchen will prove a most efficacious remedy for the dull, drowsy sensations just after breakfast. Let active exercise start the perspiration, and cold extremities will become warm, the brain clear, and the day will not be lost.

MENUS FOR A FAMILY OF TWO, A WEEK IN JANUARY

"Everyone knows that money alone cannot make good dishes, however good the raw materials may be."

SUNDAY

BREAKFAST	DINNER	SUPPER
Grapefruit	Broiled Fillet of Beef with Potatoes Anna	Rasped Rolls
Broiled Bacon	Baked Squash	Sliced Apples, Baked in Bean Pot
Hashed Potato in Ramequin	Celery	Fudge
Dry Toast	Canned Raspberry Charlotte Russe	
Coffee	Small Cups of Coffee	

MONDAY

BREAKFAST, 7.30 o'clock	DINNER, 1 o'clock	SUPPER
Cereal, Cream	Lamb Chops (Neck) Casserole	Stewed Lima Beans
Creamed Ham with Poached Eggs	Lettuce Salad	Bread and Butter
Cold Apple Sauce	Chocolate Bread Pudding (Meringue)	Fig Cookies
Doughnuts	Small Cups of Coffee	Canned Pears
Cocoa		Tea

TUESDAY

BREAKFAST	DINNER	SUPPER
Cereal	Ham-and-Macaroni Timbales	Cream Toast
Hot Dates, Thin Cream	Creamed Celery au gratin	Sponge Jelly Roll
Lamb-and-Potato Hash	Apple Dumplings	Cocoa
Muffins	Small Cups of Coffee	
Coffee		

WEDNESDAY

BREAKFAST	DINNER	SUPPER
Cereal, Thin Cream	Beefsteak Pie	Hot Baltimore Samp, Maple Syrup, Cream
Bacon	Baked Potatoes	Fig Cookies
Apple Fritters	Celery-and-Apple Salad	Cocoa
Coffee	Caramel Sponge, Boiled Custard	
	Small Cups of Coffee	

THURSDAY

BREAKFAST	DINNER	SUPPER
Broiled Tripe	Pork Tenderloin, Roasted, Hot Apple Sauce	Hot Rye-meal Muffins
Baked Potatoes	Mashed Potato	Canned Fruit
Canned Corn Griddle Cakes	Boiled Turnip	Cream Cheese
Coffee	Dates in Lemon Jelly	Cocoa
	Small Cups of Coffee	

FRIDAY

BREAKFAST	DINNER	SUPPER
Grapefruit	Broiled Fresh Fish, Maître d'Hôtel Butter	Hominy, Cream
Broiled or Fried Oysters	Mashed Potato	Bread and Butter
Buttered Toast	Boiled Cabbage	Boston Baked Beans
Coffee	Apple Pie	Canned Fruit
	Small Cups of Coffee	Tea

SATURDAY

BREAKFAST	DINNER	SUPPER
Boston Baked Beans, Reheated on Toast	Cold Pork Tenderloin	Canned Corn Custard
Mustard Pickles	Sweet Potatoes Southern Style	Baking-powder Biscuit
Doughnuts	Cabbage Salad	Honey in the Comb
Coffee	Steamed Chocolate Pudding Sultana Sauce	Tea
	Small Cups of Coffee	

MENUS FOR A FAMILY OF TWO, A WEEK IN JANUARY

Formerly, "swooning Angelina, in company, toyed tenderly with a chicken wing (and) later retired to the pantry to stuff herself with jam and pickles."—*Adapted from The Virtue of Gluttony.*

SUNDAY

BREAKFAST	DINNER	SUPPER
Rolls. Marmalade. Coffee	Steamed-and-Baked Fowl Scalloped Potatoes Celery. Fruit Jelly Chocolate Custard	Sardines. Olives Bread and Butter Crackers

MONDAY

BREAKFAST	LUNCHEON	DINNER
Cereal Bacon Broiled in Oven Baking-powder Biscuit Evaporated Peaches, Stewed Coffee	Hot Dates Cream-of-Celery Soup Browned Crackers	Cold Fowl. Baked Potatoes Canned Corn Baked Tapioca Custard Pudding with Raisins

TUESDAY

BREAKFAST	LUNCHEON	DINNER
Cereal, Milk Sardines in Sauce on Toast Corn-meal Muffins Coffee	Zwiebach. Cocoa Stewed Figs	Soufflé of Fowl Canned Corn Fritters Baked Potatoes Cranberry Sauce Lettuce, French Dressing Cheese

WEDNESDAY

BREAKFAST	LUNCHEON	DINNER
Bacon Broiled in Oven Small Baked Potatoes Graham Muffins Baked Bananas Coffee	Tomato Rabbit Crackers Canned Pineapple Cookies	Fresh Codfish, Steamed (2 pounds) Egg Sauce (yolks of 2 eggs) Steamed Potatoes Stewed Tomatoes Pineapple Soufflé (whites of 2 eggs)

THURSDAY

BREAKFAST	LUNCHEON	DINNER
Cereal, Milk Potatoes Warmed in Milk Sausage Broiled in Oven Apple Sauce Toasted Muffins Coffee	Bread-and-Butter Sandwiches Raw Apples	Beef Stew (Slice from Vein) Baking-powder Biscuit Rice Pudding with Raisins

FRIDAY

BREAKFAST	LUNCHEON	DINNER
Cream Toast Fried Mush, Syrup Coffee	Oyster Stew Cole Slaw Cored Apples, Cooked in Syrup Bread and Butter	Creamed Fresh Codfish au Gratin Baked Potatoes Scalloped Tomatoes Prune Whip in Cups

SATURDAY

BREAKFAST	LUNCHEON	DINNER
Cereal with Dates, Milk Crumbed Oysters, Fried Bread and Butter Coffee	Macaroni with Cheese and Tomato Coffee Jelly, Boiled Custard	Lamb Chops, Broiled Canned Peas Stewed Potatoes Hulled Corn, Milk and Syrup Tea

MENUS FOR A FAMILY OF TWO, A WEEK IN FEBRUARY

meal should be taken at leisure, body and mind being, for the time being, given up to it, and to agreeable social intercourse. —Horace Fletcher.

SUNDAY

BREAKFAST
Orange Halves
Eggs, Poached in Broth on Toast
Yeast Rolls, Reheated
Cocoa

DINNER
Veal Balls en Casserole
Lettuce Salad
Half of Prune Pie
Coffee

SUPPER
Peanut Butter Sandwiches
Sliced Oranges
Tea

MONDAY

BREAKFAST
Finnan Haddie, Cooked in Milk
Stewed Potatoes
Fried Mush
Coffee

DINNER AT NOON
Corned Beef, Boiled Potatoes
Boiled Turnip
Stewed Tomatoes
Half of Prune Pie
Cocoa

SUPPER
Cream Toast
Evaporated Peaches, Stewed
Hot Milk Sponge Cake
Tea

TUESDAY

BREAKFAST
Oranges
Cold Corned Beef, Sliced Thin, Mustard
White Hashed Potatoes
Doughnuts
Coffee

DINNER
Slice of Frozen Salmon, Boiled, Egg Sauce
Boiled Potatoes
Canned Peas. Pickles
Apple Tapioca Pudding
Coffee

SUPPER
Creamed Corned Beef au Gratin
Bread and Butter
Baked Apples, Thin Cream
Tea

WEDNESDAY

BREAKFAST
Orange Halves
Broiled Bacon
Omelet with Peas
Buttered Toast
Coffee

DINNER
Corned Beef-and-Potato Hash, with Poached Eggs
Stewed Tomatoes
Bread Pudding
Tea

SUPPER
Salmon Salad
Bread and Butter
Coffee
Oatmeal-and-Fruit Cookies

THURSDAY

BREAKFAST
Sliced Bananas, Thin Cream
Dried Beef, Broiled
Baking-powder Biscuit
Coffee

DINNER
Lamb Chops (neck) en Casserole
Cole Slaw
Apple Pie
Cheese
Tea

SUPPER
Buttered Toast
Stewed Prunes
Cream Cheese
Cookies
Tea

FRIDAY

BREAKFAST
Orange Halves
Canned Corn Griddle Cakes
Dry Toast
Coffee

DINNER
Slices of Fish Baked with Bread Dressing
Philadelphia Relish
Mashed Potatoes
Stewed Onions
Nuts Molded in Lemon Jelly
Coffee

SUPPER
Boiled Rice, Cheese Sauce
Tea
Chocolate Candies

SATURDAY

BREAKFAST
Orange Halves
Creamed Dried Beef
Baked Potato Cakes
Toast
Coffee

DINNER
Slice of Beef Tenderloin, Broiled
Baked Potatoes
Canned Corn (half can) Stewed
Prune Soufflé, Custard Sauce
Tea

SUPPER
Smoked Halibut
Bread and Butter
Apple Sauce
Roxbury Cakes
Tea

SIMPLE MENUS FOR FAMILY OF TWO ADULTS, FEBRUARY

(Man and woman, at work outside the home, noon dinner.)

If a meal is taken when the appetite is at the most healthy point of keenness, and no more is eaten than nature requires, business may be resumed pleasantly and without deranging the digestive powers. — *Thomas Walker*.

SUNDAY

BREAKFAST
Oatmeal. Hot Dates, Cream
Rye-meal Muffins
Coffee

DINNER
Hot Veal Loaf, Tomato Sauce
Lima Beans (Dried), Buttered
Cabbage Salad
Rice Pudding

SUPPER
Bread and Butter
Apple Sauce. Cream Cheese
Cocoa

MONDAY

BREAKFAST
Ralston Breakfast Food
Bananas, Cream
Toasted Muffins (left over)
Coffee

DINNER
Cold Veal Loaf
Sliced Potatoes, Broiled and Buttered
Cold Lima Beans, French Dressing
Rice Pudding (left over)
Cereal Coffee

SUPPER
Hot Stewed Tomatoes
Graham Bread. Bacon
Stewed Prunes
Drop Cakes. Tea

TUESDAY

BREAKFAST
Veal Loaf-and-Potato Hash
White Mountain Rolls
Orange Marmalade
Coffee

DINNER
Small Slice Halibut, Sautéd in Bacon Fat
Plain Boiled Potatoes
Cabbage Boiled Dressing
Sliced Oranges. Wafers
Cereal Coffee

SUPPER
Creamed Macaroni with Cheese
Dried Beef
Stewed Figs
Bread and Butter
Tea

WEDNESDAY

BREAKFAST
Shredded Wheat Biscuit with Poached Eggs
Stewed Prunes
Rolls (Reheated)
Cocoa

DINNER
Beef Tenderloin, Broiled
Potatoes in Milk (Left Over)
Canned Wax Beans
Bromangelon. Coffee

SUPPER
Rice Cooked with Bacon and Tomatoes
Canned Fruit. Toast
Tea

THURSDAY

BREAKFAST
Eggs Baked in Cups, Bits of Toast
Date Muffins
Coffee

DINNER
Half Shoulder of Lamb, Steamed
Small Turnips, Boiled and Buttered
Cold Wax Beans French Dressing
Gelatine Blanc Mange
Fruit Jelly
Cereal Coffee

SUPPER
Hot Succotash (Canned)
Bread and Butter
Canned Fruit
Sweet Wafers
Cocoa

FRIDAY

BREAKFAST
Sardines in Cream Sauce on Toast
Baked Potatoes
Graham Rolls
Coffee

DINNER
Canned Salmon, Hot Egg Sauce
Plain Boiled Potatoes
Canned Beets, French Dressing
Lemon Jell-O Wafers
Cereal Coffee

SUPPER
Oyster Stew, Crackers
Pickled Beets
Bread and Butter
Cranberry Sauce
Coffee

SATURDAY

BREAKFAST
Bacon, Fried Potatoes
Hecker's Buckwheat Cakes
Orange Marmalade
Coffee

DINNER
Cold Shoulder of Lamb
Sautéd Bananas
Hot Oatmeal, Buttered
Stewed Figs, Custard Sauce
Drop Ginger Cakes
Tea

SUPPER
Hot Curried Salmon
Beets, French Dressing
Bread and Butter
Coffee Jelly
Whipped Cream
Tea or Hot Water

MENUS FOR A FAMILY OF TWO, A WEEK IN MARCH

"The man who is proud of his wife should occasionally tell her so."

SUNDAY

BREAKFAST

Grapefruit Cut in Halves
Two Pan-broiled Chops
Creamed Potatoes
Corn-meal Muffins
Cereal Coffee

LUNCHEON FOR ONE

Apple-and-Date Salad
Bread and Butter
Cocoa Macaroons
Hot Cocoa

DINNER

Beef Balls en Casserole
(½ a lb. of beef, half recipe)
Lettuce, French Dressing
Cream Cheese
Browned Crackers
Cherry Jell-O, Whipped Cream
Tea or Black Coffee

MONDAY

BREAKFAST

Grape-nuts, Cream
Milk Toast with Poached
Eggs above
Corn-meal Muffins, Reheated
Cereal Coffee

LUNCHEON FOR ONE

Bread and Butter
Pecan or English Walnut
Meats
Cocoa. An Orange

DINNER

Pound Slice of Halibut
Baked with Bread Dressing
Drawn Butter Sauce
Philadelphia Relish (Half
Recipe)
Mashed Potatoes
Half a Can of String Beans
Baked Caramel Custard

TUESDAY

BREAKFAST

Orange, Cut in Halves
Halibut au Gratin
Mashed Potato Cakes
Dry Toast. Coffee

LUNCHEON FOR ONE

Half-pint of Oysters, Stewed
Bread and Butter
Stewed Prunes. Cheese

DINNER

Slice of Beef Tenderloin
Broiled (¾ a lb.)
Baked Sweet Potatoes
Half Can of String Beans,
French Dressing
Fig Whip (whites of two eggs)
Boiled Custard (yolks of two
eggs)
Black Coffee

WEDNESDAY

BREAKFAST

Boiled Rice, Cream
Broiled Bacon
Cold Sweet Potatoes, Broiled
Rye-meal Muffins
Stewed Prunes
Coffee

LUNCHEON FOR ONE

Muffins Toasted
Orange Marmalade
Cocoa

DINNER

Cream-of-Celery Soup
Rump of Veal (four pounds,
60c.), Roasted
Macaroni Baked with Milk
and Cheese
Spinach (half peck)
Stewed Figs. Cream

THURSDAY

BREAKFAST

An Orange, Cut in Halves
Eggs Shirred with Crumbs
in Cups
Yeast Rolls, Reheated
Coffee

LUNCHEON FOR ONE

Smoked Halibut—Toasted
Over the Fire
Bread and Butter
Apple Sauce
Cup of Coffee

DINNER

Pint of Oysters, Scalloped
Baking-powder Biscuit
Celery Hearts
Philadelphia Relish
Baked Apple Dumpling
(Pint Dish)
Small Cups of Coffee

FRIDAY

BREAKFAST

Malt Breakfast Food, Cream
Smoked Halibut, Creamed
Potatoes, Cut in Quarters
and Boiled
Baking-powder Biscuit, Toasted
Coffee

LUNCHEON FOR ONE

Sliced Banana, Cream
Bread and Butter
Cream Sponge Cake. Cocoa

DINNER

Cold Roast Veal, Sliced Thin
Baked Potatoes, Brown Gravy
Spinach (left over) with
Boiled Egg
Floating Island (sponge
cake, etc.)
Half Cups Coffee

SATURDAY

BREAKFAST

Toasted Corn Flakes, Cream
Poached Eggs on Toast
Coffee

Veal Soufflé, Cream Sauce
Sweet Potatoes
Southern Style

DINNER

Lettuce Salad
Individual Charlotte Russe
Half Cups Coffee

MENUS FOR A FAMILY OF TWO, A WEEK IN MARCH

"The kitchen is a country in which there are always discoveries to be made."
La Reyniere.

SUNDAY

BREAKFAST

Cereal with Dates, Cream
Rye-meal Muffins
Cocoa

DINNER

Tomato Soup
Cold Veal Loaf, Sliced Thin
Mashed Potato
Canned Lima Beans
Sweet Pickles
Baked Caramel Custard
Small Cup of Coffee

SUPPER

Sardines. Lettuce
Bread and Butter
Cereal Coffee

MONDAY

BREAKFAST

Poached Eggs on Toast
Bacon
Toasted Muffins
Fried Cereal, Maple Syrup
Tea

LUNCHEON

Lettuce-and-Lima Bean
Salad
Baking-powder Biscuit
Baked Custards
Oatmeal Macaroons
Cereal Coffee

DINNER

Cream-of-Potato Soup
Veal Loaf
Escalloped Tomatoes
Baked Apple Dumpling
Coffee

TUESDAY

BREAKFAST

Cereal, Cream
Salt Codfish Creamed
Boiled Potatoes
Apple Dumpling (Reheated)
Coffee

LUNCHEON

Turkish Pilaf
Prune-and-Apple Pie (Half)
Tea

DINNER

Stewed Chicken
Baking-powder Biscuits
Baked Squash
Pickles or Cranberry Sauce
Rice Pudding with Raisins
Small Cup of Coffee

WEDNESDAY

BREAKFAST

Molded Cereal, Baked,
Cream
Scrambled Eggs
Potatoes Cooked in Milk
Toasted Biscuit
Cereal Coffee

LUNCHEON

Welsh Rabbit. Pickles
Lemon Fanchonettes
Coffee

DINNER

Chicken Floured and Fried
Baked Sweet Potatoes
Celery Salad
Prune-and-Apple Pie (Half)
Tea

THURSDAY

BREAKFAST

Oranges
Creamed Chicken on Toast
Rice-and-Corn-meal Griddle
Cakes
Coffee

LUNCHEON

Cream-of-Celery Soup
Browned Crackers
Hot Gingerbread. Cheese
Cocoa

DINNER

Hamburg Steak
Mashed Potatoes
Buttered Parsnips
Cole Slaw
Cocoa Junket, Whipped Cream
Oatmeal Macaroons
Tea

FRIDAY

BREAKFAST

Oranges
Eggs Cooked in Shell
Mashed Potato Cakes
Dry Toast. Cocoa

LUNCHEON

Macaroni with Cheese
Cole Slaw
Bread and Butter
Gingerbread. Cereal Coffee

DINNER

Fish Chowder
Lettuce Salad
Canned Fruit. Cream Cheese
Oatmeal Macaroons
Coffee

SATURDAY

BREAKFAST

Cereal, Cream
Bacon, Fried Eggs
(Delicately Cooked)
French Fried Potato
Corn-meal Muffins
Cereal Coffee

LUNCHEON

Fish Chowder (Reheated)
Pickles
Bread and Butter
Orange Marmalade
Tea

DINNER

Veal with Brown Sauce
Buttered Lima Beans
(Dried or Canned)
Lettuce-and-Egg Salad
Queen of Puddings
Coffee

MENUS FOR A FAMILY OF TWO, A WEEK IN APRIL

"How sweet the butter our own hands have churned." — Charles Reade.

SUNDAY

BREAKFAST
Grape Nuts, Cream
Salt Codfish Balls
Radishes
Spider Corn Cake
Coffee

DINNER
Broiled Lamb Chops
Mashed Potatoes
Browned Onions
Lettuce, French Dressing
"Steamed" Custard

SUPPER
Bread and Butter
Baked Rhubarb
Pecan-Nut Wafers
Tea

MONDAY

BREAKFAST
Granose Flakes
French Omelet
Hashed Potatoes
Spider Corn Cake
(Reheated)
Coffee

LUNCHEON FOR ONE
Stewed Lima Beans
Bread and Butter
Lettuce, French Dressing
Toasted Cracker
Cream Cheese. Tea

DINNER
Hamburg Steak
Asparagus on Toast
Drawn Butter Sauce
Steamed Prune Pudding,
Hard Sauce
Half Cups of Coffee

TUESDAY

BREAKFAST
Oranges, Cut in Halves
Half a Salt Mackerel Cooked
in Milk
Stewed Potatoes
Buttered Toast
Coffee

LUNCHEON FOR ONE
Lettuce-and-Lima-Bean
Salad
Bread and Butter
Steamed Prune Pudding
(Reheated)
Tea

DINNER
Fresh Fish Chowder
Buttered Parsnips
Pickles
Baking-powder Biscuit
Custard
Half Cups of Coffee

WEDNESDAY

BREAKFAST
Cereal. Stewed Prunes
Eggs Poached in Broth
(flank ends of Chops)
Entire-Wheat Rolls (Reheated)
Coffee

LUNCHEON FOR ONE
Lettuce, Prune-and-Pecan
Nut Salad
Bread and Butter
Cookies. Cocoa

DINNER
Cream-of-Onion Soup
Veal Cutlets, Breaded,
Horseradish
Tomatoes Cooked with
Bread Crumbs
Baked Rhubarb
Sponge Cake

THURSDAY

BREAKFAST
Broiled Bacon
Eggs in the Shell
Dry Toast. Fried Mush
Coffee

LUNCHEON FOR ONE
Cream Toast
Sponge Cake
Cocoa

DINNER
Round Steak en Casserole
Macaroni with Tomato Sauce
Lettuce, French Dressing
Sliced Banana, Lemon Jelly
Cream

FRIDAY

BREAKFAST
Remnants of Beef en Casserole
Baking-powder Biscuit
Honey in Comb
Coffee

LUNCHEON FOR ONE
Baking-powder Biscuit,
Toasted
Orange Marmalade
Frizzled Dried Beef
Tea

DINNER
Fresh Fish Mousse
(without truffles)
Mashed Potatoes
Spinach Greens
French Toast, Vanilla Sauce

SATURDAY

BREAKFAST
An Orange Cut in Halves
Dried Beef in Cream Sauce
Boiled Potatoes
Rye-meal Muffins
Coffee

LUNCHEON AWAY FROM HOME

DINNER
Cold Veal Loaf, Sliced Thin
White Hashed Potatoes
Spinach-and-Egg Salad
Corn Starch Blanc Mange,
Cream and Sugar
Half Cups of Coffee

MENUS FOR A FAMILY OF TWO, A WEEK IN APRIL

"To cook well requires experience, and that only comes after much practice."

SUNDAY

BREAKFAST

An Orange Cut in Halves
Broiled Bacon
Broiled Potatoes
Radishes
Boston Brown Bread, Toasted
Coffee

DINNER

Tenderloin from 2½ lbs.
Sirloin Steak,
Broiled, Maitre d'Hôtel
Butter
Mashed Potatoes
Stewed Tomatoes (Canned)
Lemon Sherbet. Cookies
Filtered Coffee

SUPPER

Lettuce, Prune-and-Nut Salad
Graham Bread and Butter
Cookies. Tea

MONDAY

BREAKFAST

Grape Nuts, Cream
Scrambled Eggs, Reformed
Style
Mashed Potato Cakes, Fried
Cream Toast
Coffee

LUNCHEON FOR ONE

Hot Buttered Toast
Dried Beef
Stewed Prunes
Cocoa

DINNER

Hamburg Steak, a la Tartare
Scalloped Potatoes
Boiled Onions, Buttered
Bread Pudding, Thanksgiving Style
Coffee

TUESDAY

BREAKFAST

Lamb's Liver, and Bacon
Creamed Potatoes
Buttered Toast,
Marmalade
Coffee

LUNCHEON FOR ONE

Hot Bacon Sandwich
Bread Pudding (left over)
Cocoa

DINNER

Cream-of-Onion Soup, Croutons
Fillets of Halibut(1 lb.),
Baked in Broth
Small Baked Potatoes
Boiled Parsnips (two) Buttered
1 Banana, Sliced with
Lemon Jelly, Cream
Half Cups of Coffee

WEDNESDAY

BREAKFAST

Boiled Potatoes'
Creamed Smoked Beef
Stewed Peaches
Evaporated
Glazed Buns (Yeast)
Coffee

LUNCHEON FOR ONE

Poached Egg on Toast
Glazed Buns
Cocoa

DINNER

Top of Sirloin Steak, Broiled
Mashed Potatoes
Spinach
Baked Macaroni
Baked Bananas, Sultana
Raisin Sauce
Half Cups of Coffee

THURSDAY

BREAKFAST

Boiled Rice, Cream
Parsley Omelet
Potatoes Hashed in Milk
Honey in the Comb
Muffins
Coffee

LUNCHEON FOR ONE

Hot Cheese Crouton
Stewed Peaches (Evaporated)
Ginger Cakes
Cereal Coffee

DINNER

Fricassee of Veal Steak
Boiled Potatoes
Cold Spinach and Egg,
French Dressing
Caramel Junket
Half Cups of Coffee

FRIDAY

BREAKFAST

An Orange Cut in Halves
Salt Codfish Balls
Horseradish
Boston Brown Bread, Toasted
Coffee

LUNCHEON FOR ONE

Veal-and-Potato Hash
Bread and Butter
Fig Cookies
Cocoa

DINNER

Fish Chowder
Cabbage Salad
Steamed or Baked Custards
Fig Cookies
Half Cups of Coffee

SATURDAY

BREAKFAST

Slice of Fresh Fish Broiled
or Brook Trout Fried
Bacon. Lyonnaise Potatoes
Radishes
Rice Griddle Cakes, Maple
Syrup
Coffee

DINNER

Veal Cutlets (hashed raw veal)
Creamed Parsnips au gratin
Lettuce, French Dressing
Caramel Custard Renversée
Half Cups of Coffee

MENUS FOR A FAMILY OF TWO, A WEEK IN MAY

It is not desirable to cut down the expenditure for food to the lowest point at which nutritive food may be obtained, if the income justifies a larger expenditure. — *Norton.*

SUNDAY

BREAKFAST

Grape Nuts, Cream
Eggs Poached in Broth on Toast with Broth Thickened
Zwieback. Coffee

DINNER

Cream-of-Spinach Soup
Cold Veal Loaf, Sliced Thin
Mashed Potatoes
Brown Sauce
Lettuce, French Dressing
Boiled Rice, Maple Syrup

SUPPER

Lettuce-and-Egg Salad
Bread and Butter
Cocoa. Fruit Cookies

MONDAY

BREAKFAST

Fresh Pineapple
Sardines on Toast, Cream Sauce
Rice Griddle Cakes
Coffee

LUNCHEON FOR ONE

Baked Potato
Dried Beef, Frizzled
Rhubarb Baked with Raisins
Fresh Bread, Pulled and Browned

DINNER

Lamb Stew with Vegetables
Hot Asparagus, Buttered
Browned Crackers
Cream Cheese
Pineapple
Coffee

TUESDAY

BREAKFAST

Cold Veal Loaf, Sliced Thin
Stewed Potatoes. Radishes
Baked Rhubarb. Dry Toast
Coffee

LUNCHEON FOR ONE

Stewed Lima Beans (dried), Buttered
Bread and Butter
Caramel Junket, Whipped Cream
Velvet Sponge Cake (half recipe)

DINNER

Breast of Lamb, Steamed and Browned
Steamed Potatoes, Browned
Cold Asparagus, French Dressing
Ginger Bavarian Cream Cake
Coffee, Half Cups

WEDNESDAY

BREAKFAST

Egg-O-See. Cream
Lamb-and-Potato Hash with Green or Red Pepper
Spider Corn Cake
Rhubarb Marmalade
Coffee

LUNCHEON FOR ONE

Lettuce and Lima Beans, French Dressing
Bread and Butter
Stewed Prunes
Tea

DINNER

Fresh Fish, Broiled, Red Pepper Butter
Mashed Potatoes
Cucumbers, Fresh or Pickled
Strawberries. Sponge Cake
Coffee, Half Cups

THURSDAY

BREAKFAST

Fresh Fish Cakes. Bacon
Dry Toast. Stewed Prunes
Coffee

LUNCHEON FOR ONE

Lettuce, Prunes and Nuts, French Dressing
Bread and Butter
Cup Custard

DINNER

Tomato Soup (lamb broth)
Lamb Souffle
Bermuda Potatoes
Asparagus, Drawn Butter
Lemon Pie
Coffee, Half Cups

FRIDAY

BREAKFAST

Malt Breakfast Food, Cream
Sliced Bananas. Eggs in Ramequins
Parker House Rolls, Reheated
Cereal Coffee

LUNCHEON FOR ONE

Creamed Asparagus on Toast
Lemon Pie
Cocoa

DINNER

Half a Blue Fish, Broiled
Scalloped Potatoes
Spinach with an Egg
Baking powder Biscuit
Strawberries
Coffee

SATURDAY

BREAKFAST

Strawberries
Broiled Lamb's Liver and Bacon
Small Potatoes, Baked
Rye-meal Muffins
Cereal Coffee

DINNER

Cream-of-Spinach Soup
Bluefish-and-Egg Salad
Bread and Butter
Floating Island
Coffee

MENUS FOR A FAMILY OF TWO, A WEEK IN JUNE

Plain, simple foods, as direct as possible from fields, orchards and woods, should always be our aim.

SUNDAY

BREAKFAST

Pineapple
Yeast Rolls, Butter
Coffee

DINNER

Hot Hamburg Roast,
Brown Sauce
Baked Potatoes
Stringless Beans, Buttered
Cress, French Dressing
Individual Strawberry Short-
cakes
Half Cups of Coffee

SUPPER

Sardines!
Thin Bread and Butter
Olives
Cheese. Crackers

MONDAY

BREAKFAST

Lemonade
Toasted Corn Flakes, Cream
Scrambled Eggs
Baking-powder Biscuit
Grapefruit Marmalade
Tea

LUNCHEON FOR ONE

Potato-and-Sardine Salad
New Rye-meal Bread and
Butter
A Canned Pear
Cookies. Coffee

DINNER

Cold Hamburg Roast
Old Potatoes, Boiled and
Mashed
Asparagus, Butter Sauce
Strawberries, Cream
Half Cups of Coffee

TUESDAY

BREAKFAST

Salt Codfish Supreme
Potatoes Hashed in Milk
Rye-meal Bread, Toasted
Stewed Rhubarb
Cereal Coffee

LUNCHEON FOR ONE

Beef-and-Potato Hash
Sliced Banana, Top of Milk
Velvet Sponge Cake. Tea

DINNER

Fresh Salmon, Boiled, Egg
Sauce
Boiled Potatoes
Green Peas. Cucumbers
Strawberries
Baking-powder Biscuit
Half Cups of Coffee

WEDNESDAY

BREAKFAST

Green Pea Omelet, Bacon,
Broiled
Twin Mountain Muffins
Honey
Cereal Coffee

LUNCHEON FOR ONE

Lettuce-and-Salmon Salad
Bread and Butter
Coffee
Slice of Pineapple

DINNER

Two Slices from Fillet of
Beef, Broiled
Maitre d'Hôtel Butter
Boiled Asparagus, Hollan-
daise Sauce
New Potatoes
Sugared Pineapple
Half Cups of Coffee

THURSDAY

BREAKFAST

Boiled Rice, Cream
Eggs Poached in Timbale
Molds on Toast,
Cream Sauce
Marmalade. Doughnuts
Coffee

LUNCHEON FOR ONE

Deviled Ham Sandwich
Lettuce, French Dressing
Custard Pie
Tea

DINNER

Rump of Veal, Roasted,
Brown Sauce
Potatoes Cooked with Veal
Green Peas. Lettuce
Strawberries. Custard Pie
Half Cups of Coffee

FRIDAY

BREAKFAST

Cold Veal, Sliced Thin
White Hashed Potatoes
Rice Griddle Cakes,
Syrup
Cereal Coffee

LUNCHEON FOR ONE

White Sauce Thickened with
Cheese on Toast
Lettuce, French Dressing
Doughnuts. Coffee

DINNER

Half a Blue Fish, Broiled
Mashed Potatoes. Peas
Cucumber, French Dressing
Strawberries
Half Cups of Coffee

SATURDAY

BREAKFAST

Grape Nuts, Cream
Broiled Honeycomb Tripe
Lyonnese Potatoes
Radishes
Toast
Coffee

LUNCHEON FOR ONE

Cold Veal, Sliced Thin
Lettuce, French Dressing
Hot Toast
Caramel Junket
Tea

DINNER

Veal Soufflé
White Sauce with Peas
Scalloped Tomatoes (Canned)
Individual Strawberry
Shortcake
Half Cups of Coffee

MENUS FOR A FAMILY OF TWO, A WEEK IN JULY

Wholesome and palatable food is the first step in good morals, and is conducive to ability in business, skill in trade, and healthy tone in literature. — *Richards.*

SUNDAY

BREAKFAST	DINNER	SUPPER
Wild Strawberries Broiled Dried Beef Baking-powder Biscuit Coffee	Sweetbreads, Sauted Green Peas Potatoes Hashed in Milk Lettuce, French Dressing Coffee Jelly, Whipped Cream	Bread. Blueberries. Milk

MONDAY

BREAKFAST	LUNCHEON FOR ONE	DINNER
Grape Nuts, Cream Creamed Sweetbreads on Toast Graham Muffins Coffee	Dried Beef Sandwich Raspberries, Cream Cup of Tea	Broiled Beef Tenderloin New Potatoes Asparagus on Toast Caramel Junket Coffee

TUESDAY

BREAKFAST	PICNIC DINNER	SUPPER
Hot Granose Flakes, Cream Asparagus Omelet Graham Muffins, Toasted Coffee	Cold Boiled Eggs Sardines. New Pickles Bread and Butter Sandwiches Fruit Tarts	Creamed Asparagus on Toast Broiled Dried Beef Cookies Tea

WEDNESDAY

BREAKFAST	LUNCHEON FOR ONE	DINNER
Scrambled Eggs Hot Buttered Toast Berries, Cream Cocoa	Lettuce, Sardine-and-Egg Salad Bread and Butter Cookies. Tea	Salmon Steak, Baked Potato Balls or Whole Potatoes New Peas. Cucumbers or Lettuce-and-Peppergrass Salad Raspberry or Lemon Sherbet

THURSDAY

BREAKFAST	LUNCHEON FOR ONE	DINNER
Boiled Rice Salmon in Curry Sauce Pop Overs Coffee	Sliced Tomatoes French Dressing Hot Buttered Toast Tea	Broiled Lamb Chops Potatoes Mashed with Tomato Stringless Beans Charlotte Russe

FRIDAY

BREAKFAST	LUNCHEON FOR ONE	DINNER
Poached Eggs on Toast, Cream Sauce Pop Overs, Reheated Berries Coffee	Hot Baked Potato, Butter Cold Lamb Chop Yeast Rolls Cup of Cocoa	Fillets of Black Bass (Baked or Fried) Scalloped Potatoes Stringless Bean Salad Sugared Pineapple

SATURDAY

BREAKFAST	DINNER	SUPPER
Shredded Wheat Biscuit Raspberries, Cream Scrambled Eggs Yeast Rolls, Reheated Coffee	Boiled Breast of Lamb, Caper Sauce Soufflé of Remnants, Sunday White Turnips Boiled Potatoes Tomatoes, French Dressing Prune Soufflé Boiled Custard	Thin Slices of Cold Lamb Lettuce, French Dressing Bread and Butter Berries Little Cakes Tea

MENUS FOR A FAMILY OF TWO, A WEEK IN AUGUST

What and how great the virtue and the art
To live on little with a cheerful heart. — Pope.

SUNDAY

BREAKFAST
Muskmelon Cut in Halves
Eggs Poached in Milk
Dry Toast
Coffee

DINNER
Broiled Lamb Chops
Braised Lettuce on Toast
Baked Potatoes
Tomatoes, French Dressing
Peach Ice Cream

SUPPER
Lettuce-and-Egg Salad
Bread and Butter
Sliced Peaches
Tea

MONDAY

BREAKFAST
Gluten Grits, Cream
Broiled Salt Mackerel
Boiled Potatoes
Sliced Tomatoes
Rye Flour Rolls
Coffee

LUNCHEON FOR ONE
Dried Beef, Frizzled
Stewed Tomatoes
Bread and Butter
Sliced Peaches. Cookies

DINNER
Hamburg Steak, Panned
Potatoes Hashed in Milk
Celery
Individual Blackberry Short
cakes
Half Cups of Coffee

TUESDAY

BREAKFAST
Berries
French Omelet
Saratoga Potatoes
Rye Muffins, Toasted
Coffee

LUNCHEON FOR ONE
Hot Bacon Sandwich
Cup of Cereal Coffee
Stewed Pears

DINNER
Slice of Salmon, Baked
Egg Sauce
Baked Potatoes
Cucumbers, French Dressing
Cornstarch Pudding,
Red Raspberry Sauce
Half Cups of Coffee

WEDNESDAY

BREAKFAST
Muskmelon Cut in Halves
Dried Beef in Cream Sauce
White Hashed Potatoes
Parker House Rolls
Coffee

LUNCHEON FOR ONE
Lettuce-and-Salmon Salad
Bread and Butter
Coffee
Sliced Peaches

DINNER
Cold Veal Loaf, Sliced Thin
Boiled Potatoes,
Hot Brown Sauce
Mayonnaise of Lettuce-and-
Celery Hearts
Gelatine Blanc Mange,
Sliced Peaches
Half Cups of Coffee

THURSDAY

BREAKFAST
Bartlett Pears
Cold Veal Loaf
Delmonico Potatoes
Cereal Griddle Cakes
Coffee

LUNCHEON FOR ONE
Poached Egg on Toast
Blanc Mange (left over),
Sugar, Cream

DINNER
Slice of Beef Tenderloin
Broiled
Boiled Corn
Creamed Celery
Tomatoes, French Dressing
Charlotte Russe

FRIDAY

BREAKFAST
Melon
Corned Beef Hash
Green Corn Fritters
Bread and Butter
Coffee

LUNCHEON FOR ONE
Cold Corned Beef
Baked Potato
Sliced Tomato
Bread and Butter
Tea

DINNER
Cream-of-Tomato Soup
Broiled Sword Fish
Boiled Beets
Scalloped Potatoes
Apple Tapioca Pudding,
Cream
Half Cups of Coffee

SATURDAY

BREAKFAST
Broiled Calf's Liver
with Bacon
White Hashed Potatoes
Hot Baked Apple Sauce
Coffee

LUNCHEON FOR ONE
Curried Sword Fish
Yeast Rolls
Butter
Apple-and-Celery Salad
Tea

DINNER
Cream-of-Celery Soup
Braised Calf's Liver
Turnips, Carrots, Potatoes
Lettuce Salad
Apricot Omelet
Half Cups of Coffee

MENUS FOR A FAMILY OF TWO, A WEEK IN SEPTEMBER

I am not one thing and my expenditure another. My expenditure is me. — Emerson.

SUNDAY

BREAKFAST

Grapes
Green Corn Fritters
Toast
Coffee

DINNER (GUESTS)

Tip of Beef Loin, Roasted
Franconia Potatoes
Stewed Cucumbers
Sweet Pickled Pears
Peach Ice Cream
Coffee

SUPPER

Bread and Butter
Sliced Peaches
Tea

MONDAY

BREAKFAST

Boiled Rice, Thin Cream
Broiled Bacon, Broiled
Apples
Small Potatoes, Baked
Toast. Coffee

LUNCHEON FOR ONE

Hot Baked Sweet Apples
Bread and Butter
Cocoa

DINNER

Cream-of-Corn Soup
Cold Roast Beef, Sliced Thin
Mashed Potatoes
Summer Squash
Lettuce, Cheese, Toasted
Crackers
Coffee

TUESDAY

BREAKFAST

Cold Roast Beef in Gravy
Mashed Potato Cakes, Baked
Sliced Tomatoes
Muffins
Coffee

LUNCHEON FOR ONE

Corn on the Cob, Boiled
Bread and Butter
Sliced Peaches

DINNER

Fresh Fish and Oysters in
Casserole
Stewed Tomatoes and Corn
Lettuce Salad
Apple Pie. Coffee

WEDNESDAY

BREAKFAST

Grapes
Broiled Honeycomb Tripe
Stewed Potatoes
Cereal Griddle Cakes
Coffee

LUNCHEON FOR ONE

Lettuce, Date-and-Apple Salad
Bread and Butter
Doughnut. Cocoa

DINNER

Beef Stew (Roast Beef Remnants)
Celery-and-Apple Salad
Sponge Jelly Roll
Steamed Custard
Coffee

THURSDAY

BREAKFAST

Muskmelon
Broiled Bacon
Delmonico Potatoes
Doughnuts. Coffee

LUNCHEON FOR ONE

Stewed Tomatoes
Fresh Graham Bread and
Butter
Slice of Sponge Jelly Roll
Cup of Cocoa

DINNER

Macedoine of Fresh Fruit
Calf's Liver. Hashed
Baked Potatoes
Green Corn Custard
Sliced Tomatoes, French
Dressing
Cheese. Toasted Crackers
Coffee

FRIDAY

BREAKFAST

Salt Codfish, Creamed
Baked Potatoes
op Overs
P Coffee

LUNCHEON FOR ONE

Cheese Toast
Hot Apple Sauce
Rolled-Oats-and-Fruit Cookies
Tea

DINNER

Fillets of Fish Baked with
Dressing
Mashed Potato
Baked Beets, Buttered
Sliced Peaches, Cream
Cake or Cookies
Coffee

SATURDAY

BREAKFAST

Creamed Fish in Shell
Poached Egg above Potato
Border
Cucumbers
Bread and Butter
Coffee

LUNCHEON FOR ONE

Fresh Lima Beans, Stewed
Bread and Butter. Tea
Grapes

DINNER

Oyster Stew. Pickles
Peach Shortcake
Coffee

INEXPENSIVE MENUS FOR TWO, A WEEK IN OCTOBER

"The food supply is not limited by any barrier but ignorance;" — "Ultimately the problem of cheap living controls the existence of the nation as well as of the individual." — *Haig.*

SUNDAY

BREAKFAST
Broiled Bacon
French Omelet
Fried Mush
Dry Toast
Coffee

DINNER
Veal Steak, Breaded
Scalloped Potatoes
Buttered Beets
Squash Pie
Half Cups of Coffee

SUPPER
French Toast
Apple Sauce
Cream Cheese
Cookies. Tea

MONDAY

BREAKFAST
Gluten Grits, Cream
Eggs Shirred in Cream
Rye-meal Muffins
Coffee

LUNCHEON FOR ONE
Cheese Toast
Baked Apple
Squash Pie
Tea

DINNER
Nut Loaf
Tomato Sauce
Celery
Steamed Custard
Cookies
Half Cups of Coffee

TUESDAY

BREAKFAST
Egg-O-See, Cream
Cold Nut Loaf,
Buttered and Broiled
Toasted Muffins
Coffee

LUNCHEON FOR ONE
Ladyfinger Rolls
Cocoa
Grapes

DINNER
Broiled Fresh Fish
Celery-and-Lettuce Salad
Poor Man's Rice Pudding
Tea

WEDNESDAY

BREAKFAST
Honeycomb Tripe
Breaded and Fried
White Hashed Potatoes
Rolls, Reheated
Cereal Coffee

LUNCHEON FOR ONE
Hot Toasted Corn Flakes,
Cream
Doughnuts
Cocoa

DINNER
Hamburg Steak
Baked Sweet Potatoes
Creamed Celery Au Gratin
Apple Tapioca Pudding
Tea

THURSDAY

BREAKFAST
Ralston Health Food, Cream
Eggs Cooked in the Shell
Doughnuts
Stewed Prunes
Coffee

LUNCHEON FOR ONE
Hot Buttered Toast with
Melted Cheese
Apple Sauce
Tea

DINNER
Half a Hot Roast Chicken,
Giblet Sauce
Cranberry Sauce
Mashed Potatoes. Celery
Lima Beans, Buttered
Blanc Mange
Coffee

FRIDAY

BREAKFAST
Smoked Halibut, Creamed
Baked Potatoes
New Pickles
Spider Corn Cake
Coffee

LUNCHEON FOR ONE
Spider Corn Cake, Reheated
Apple Sauce
Cheese
Cocoa

DINNER
Fresh Fish Chowder
Cole Slaw
Mother's Apple Pie, Cream
Coffee

SATURDAY

BREAKFAST
Grape Nuts, Cream
Eggs Shirred with Tomato
Bacon Rolls
French Fried Potatoes
Dry Toast. Cereal Coffee

LUNCHEON FOR ONE
Yeast Muffins, Toasted
Apple or Orange Marmalade
Cocoa

DINNER
Half of Cold Roast Chicken
Candied Sweet Potatoes
Tomato Salad
Bread Pudding

MENUS FOR A FAMILY OF TWO, A WEEK IN NOVEMBER

The first requisite for strength and power of endurance is a satisfactory and sufficient supply of albumens. — *Haig.*

SUNDAY

BREAKFAST

Hot Granose Flakes
Hot Baked Apples, Cream
Small Baked Potatoes
Broiled Bacon
Boston Brown Bread, Toasted
Coffee

DINNER

Fricassée of Chicken (Half Chicken)
Sweet Pickles
Baking-powder Biscuits
Squash. Celery
Cottage Pudding
Hard Sauce with Fruit Purée
Half Cups of Coffee

SUPPER

Cream Toast
Honey Cookies
Cocoa

MONDAY

BREAKFAST

Grape Nuts, Cream
Hashed Chicken on Toast
(Baking-powder Biscuits)
Apple Marmalade
Bread and Butter
Coffee

LUNCHEON FOR ONE

Lettuce-and-Egg Salad
Boston Brown Bread and Butter
New Figs
Tea

DINNER

Hashed Round Steak, Mother's Style
Boiled Potatoes
Stewed Tomatoes
Rice Pudding with Raisins
Tea

TUESDAY

BREAKFAST

Oatmeal, Cream
Fried Honeycomb Tripe
Lyonnaise Potatoes
Rye-meal Muffins
Coffee

LUNCHEON FOR ONE

Fresh English Muffins, Toasted
Apple Marmalade. Cocoa
Salted Pecan Nuts. Dates

DINNER

Half Chicken, Baked, Cranberry Sauce
Scalloped Potatoes
Baked Squash. Lettuce Salad
Prune Jelly, Whipped Cream
Half Cups of Coffee

WEDNESDAY

BREAKFAST

Smoked Halibut, Creamed
Small Potatoes, Baked
Toasted Muffins (English)
Coffee

LUNCHEON FOR ONE

Creamed Halibut (reheated) on Toast
Apple-and-Date Salad
Bread and Butter
Tea

DINNER

Breaded Lamb Chops, Fried
Tomato Sauce
White Hashed Potatoes
Celery
Baked Bananas, Sultana Sauce
Half Cups of Coffee

THURSDAY

BREAKFAST

Hominy, Cream
Broiled Bacon
Fried Potatoes
Hot Apple Sauce Toast
Cereal Coffee

LUNCHEON FOR ONE

Cheese Melted on Bread
Apple Sauce
Little Nut Cakes. Coffee

DINNER

Roast Loin of Lamb (boned)
(Chops for Wednesday, removed)
Franconia Potatoes. Squash
Banana Fritters, Jelly Sauce
Bread Pudding, Meringue
Half Cups of Coffee

FRIDAY

BREAKFAST

Grapes
Salt Codfish Balls
Home Made Pickles
Fried Hominy, Caramel Syrup
Cereal Coffee

LUNCHEON FOR ONE

Egg Poached in Broth on Toast
Celery
Little Nut Cakes. Tea

DINNER

Cream-of-Celery Soup
Fried Pickerel, Tomato Sauce
Mashed Potatoes
French Turnips
Eclairs. Half Cups of Coffee

SATURDAY

BREAKFAST

Egg-O-See, Cream
Fried Oysters
Home Made Pickles
Baking-powder Biscuit
Doughnuts. Coffee

LUNCHEON FOR ONE

Celery-and-Nut Salad
Baking-powder Biscuit Reheated
Grapes

DINNER

Cold Roast Loin of Lamb
Broiled Apples
Mashed Potatoes. Spinach
Caramel Junket
Little Nut Cakes
Half Cups of Coffee

MENUS FOR A FAMILY OF TWO, A WEEK IN DECEMBER

"Permanent improvements in the standard of life depend rather upon wise spending than upon large earnings."

SUNDAY

BREAKFAST

Baltimore Samp, Cream
Cold Boiled Ham
White Hashed Potatoes
Hot Buttered Toast. Coffee

DINNER

Chicken Breast en Casserole
Fruit Jelly
Sweet Potatoes, Southern Style
Boiled Onions Celery Hearts
Chestnut Parfait
Oatmeal Fruit Cookies
Small Cups of Coffee

SUPPER

Toasted Crackers, Buttered
Oatmeal Fruit Cookies
Cocoa
Toasted Marshmallows

MONDAY

BREAKFAST

Cold Boiled Ham, Mustard
Sweet Potatoes, Reheated
Corn Meal Muffins
Coffee

LUNCHEON FOR ONE

Hot Baltimore Samp
Maple Syrup, Cream
Piece of Cranberry Pie
Tea

DINNER

Slice of Halibut, Boiled
Drawn Butter Sauce
Boiled Potatoes
Lettuce. French Dressing
Cranberry Pie
Small Cups of Coffee

TUESDAY

BREAKFAST

Cereal, Cream
Sliced Ham Fritters
Hot Apple Sauce
Doughnuts
Coffee

LUNCHEON FOR ONE

Creamed Halibut au gratin
Baked Potato
Yeast Rolls

DINNER

Chicken Pie
Cranberry Sauce
Creamed Celery
Rice Pudding
Half Cups of Coffee

WEDNESDAY

BREAKFAST

Chopped Ham
Scrambled with Eggs
Sliced Potatoes, Cooked in Milk
Yeast Rolls, Reheated
Cereal Coffee

LUNCHEON FOR ONE

Remnants of Chicken Pie, Reheated
Cold Rice Pudding
Tea

DINNER

Cream-of-Celery Soup
Boston Baked Beans, with Pork
Spinach
Cottage Pudding, Sultana Sauce
Half Cups of Coffee

THURSDAY

BREAKFAST

Cereal, Cream
Ham Timbales, Cream Sauce
Small Baked Potatoes
Buttered Toast Coffee

LUNCHEON FOR ONE

Baked Bean Salad
Bread and Butter
Coffee
Grapes

DINNER

Chicken Legs and Wings, Sautéd
Mashed Potato
Spinach-and-Egg Salad
Apples Pralinée. Cream Cookies
Half Cups of Coffee

FRIDAY

BREAKFAST

Cereal, Cream
Baked Beans, Reheated
Baking Powder Biscuit
Coffee

LUNCHEON FOR ONE

Date, Apple and Lettuce Salad
Entire Wheat Bread with Butter
Cheese
Doughnuts
Cereal Coffee

DINNER

Fried Oysters, Cole Slaw
Baking Powder Biscuit, Reheated
Date Whip, Boiled Custard
Half Cups of Coffee

SATURDAY

BREAKFAST

Cereal, Cream
Broiled Honeycomb Tripe
Small Potatoes, Baked
Rye-meal Muffins
Apple Ginger. Coffee

LUNCHEON FOR ONE

Rye-meal Muffins, Toasted
Orange Marmalade
Cream Cheese
Doughnuts
Cocoa

DINNER

Boiled Lamb, Caper Sauce
Boiled Turnips
Boiled Potatoes
Apple Pie, Cream
Half Cups of Coffee

THANKSGIVING DINNER

I
Roast Chicken, Bread Stuffing
Stewed Cranberries
Oysters-and-Celery au gratin in Shells
Sweet Potatoes en Casserole
Lettuce Salad
Hot Apple Turnovers (Reheated)
Plain Charlotte Russe
Nuts. Raisins. Coffee

II
Chicken-and-Tomato Bouillon
Roast Duck, Potato-and-Pecan Nut Dressing. Onions
Apples Cooked Whole in Syrup
Bits of Currant Jelly Above
Celery Salad
Golden Parfait with French Fruit
Lady Apples. Maple Fondant Bonbons
Half Cups of Coffee

CHRISTMAS DINNER

I
Oyster Soup, Gherkins
Roast Duck
Apple-and-Celery Salad
Potatoes, Scalloped, with Grated Onion   Squash
Plum Pudding, Hard Sauce
Liquid Sauce
Tangerine Oranges.   Grapes
Coffee

II
Grapefruit Cocktail
Tip of Beef Sirloin, Roasted
Parboiled Potatoes Cooked with the Meat
Baked Bananas, Sultana Sauce
Cress or Endive, French Dressing
Caramel Almond Bavariose
Fondant Peppermints
Half Cups of Coffee

SUNDAY DINNER (Winter)

Delicate Celery Soup
Roast Tenderloin of Beef
Tomato Sauce
Potatoes Anna
Baked Squash
Canned Stringless Beans
French Dressing with Onion Juice
Mock Mince Pie or Sliced Figs in Jelly
Coffee

SUNDAY DINNER (Summer)

Broiled Lamb Chops
Melting Potatoes
Spinach Greens
Caramel Ice Cream (Junket)
Strawberries
Sponge Cake

SUNDAY NIGHT TEA
(Winter, Guests)
Creamed Oysters (chafing dish)
Olives. Salted Peanuts
German Apple Cup
White Cake, Caramel Nut Frosting
Coffee

SUNDAY NIGHT TEA

(Summer, Guests)
Chicken, Green Pea-and-Cucumber Salad
Bread-and-Olive Sandwiches or Bread and Butter Sandwiches
Raspberry Sherbet
Tea

SUNDAY DINNER
(Spring Guests)

Lamb and Tomato Soup
Broiled Sweetbreads
Maitre d'Hôtel Butter
Asparagus Cooked as Peas
Lettuce, French Dressing
Parker House Rolls, (Reheated)
Vanilla Ice Cream
Maple Syrup
Half Cups of Coffee

SUNDAY DINNER
(Autumn Guests)

Muskmelons
Chicken en Casserole
Sweet Pickle Jelly
Kaiser Rolls
Tomatoes Stuffed with Mayonnaise of Celery
Sliced Peaches, Sugar, Cream
Wafer Jumbles

Index

Air, 3
Almond Crisps, 334
  Nougatines, 244
Almonds, Custard Renversée with, 354
Apple Butter, 263
  Cup, German, 209
  Dumpling, Baked, 361
  Jelly, 260
    with Blackberries, 260
      Mint, 261
      Raspberries, 260
  Marmalade, 261
  Pie, 311
    English, 312
    with Meringue, 313
  Sauce, Quick, 219
    Strained, 219
  Tarts, 321
  Triangles, Hot 283
Apples, Baked with Dates 221
  Broiled with Ham, 125
  Pralinée, 221
Apricot Parfait, 370
Arlington Meal Muffins, 278
Asparagus, 174
  Canned, 268
  as Peas, 174
  with Poached Eggs, 71
  Salad, 202

Bacon, Broiled, 99
  Fried in Deep Fat, 127
  Sandwiches, 307
  with String Beans, 172
Baking Powder Biscuit, 280
  with Sour Milk, etc., 275

Banana Parfait, 369
  Purée for Ice Cream, 371
  Whip, 225
Bananas, Baked, Sultana Sauce, 225
Bar-le-duc Currants, etc, 265
Bass, Fillets of, 81, 83
Batter and Dough, 273
Bavarian Cream, Caramel 349
  Ginger, 348
  Marmalade, 348
Beans, Boston Baked, 181
  Reheated, 127
  Sandwich, 183
  Dried Lima, 181
  Green Shell, 171
  Lima, Baked, 182
  String, 172
    with Bacon, 172
Beef Balls with Spaghetti, 119
  Broth, Standard, 139
  Cakes, Broiled, 96
    Pan-broiled, 97
  Corned, Boiled, 112
  Hash, 123
  Tea, 36
    Recipe for, 37
  Tenderloin, Roast, 106
Beets, 176
  Pickled, 176
Biscuit, Baking Powder, 280
  Entire Wheat, 300
  Rye Meal, 303
  Squash, 301
  and Roll Dough, Shaping, 293

Index

Biscuits D'Epernay, 328
Black Bass, Fillets of, etc., 81
  Rolled, 83
Blackberry Roly Poly, 281
Blanquette of Veal, 119
Blueberry Betty, 359
  Pie, 313
  Tea Cakes, 283
Bonbons, Chocolate Dipped, 243
  Coffee, 240
  Molding in Starch, 242
  Other, 241
  Pistachio, 241
Bouillon, Chicken and Tomato, 138
Bread, Entire Wheat, 296
  Graham, 299
  Griddle Cakes, 285
  One Loaf, 295-296
  Pulled, 149
  Rye, 298
  Soft Corn, 279
  Sticks, 306
  Storing, 295
  Stuffing for Roast Chicken, 118
    Fish, etc., 82
Bread Dough, Kneading, 292
  Mixing, 291
  Shaping, 293
Bread Making, Ingredients for, 286
  Kinds of Flour for, 290
  Utensils for, 290
Bread Pudding, Viennoise, 357
Bread and Rolls, Baking, 294
  Glazing, 294
Breads, Quick, 272
  Baking Powder with Sour Milk, etc., 275
  General Rule for, 275
  How to Bake, 276
    Add Eggs, 276
      Shortening, 276
  Liquid Used in, 274
  Method of Combining Materials in, 275
  Proportions of Baking Powder and Flour, 274
  Salt and Flour, 274
  Soda and Cream of Tartar, 274
Breakfast Dish, Late Summer, 71
Breast of Fowl en Casserole, 114
Brook Trout, Sautéd, 78
Broth, Fish, for Soup, etc., 140
Broth, Standard Beef, 139
Brown Sauce, 147
Buns, Glazed Currant, 298
Butter, 195
  Maître D'Hôtel, 196
  Red Pepper, 86
Butter Sauce, Drawn, 145

Cabbage Salad, 201
Cake, Angel, 328
  Baking, 327
  Burnt Sugar, 330
  Coffee, 302
  Cream Sponge, 329
  How Lightened, 322
  Ingredients Used in, 323
  Mixing of Butter, 324
  Mixing of Sponge, 326
  Moist Chocolate, 331
  Nut and Raisin, 331
  Proportions of Ingredients 324
  Qualities of Good, 322
  Quick Sponge, 329
  White Layer, 330
  White Nut, 330
  Sponge, 328
Cakes, Cereal Griddle, 284
  Corn Meal Griddle, 284
  Green Corn, 285
  Little Gold, 332
  Plain Ginger, 332
  Roxbury, 332
  Tiny Cream, 339
Calf's Liver, Hashed, 114
Candies Cooked to High Degree, 245

Index

Canned Asparagus, 268
  Berry and Currant Juices, 255
  Corn, 266
  Cranberries, 254
  Grape Juice, 255
  Peaches or Pears, 256
  Peas, 267
  Pineapple, 257
  Rhubarb, 255
  Strawberries or Raspberries, 256
  String Beans, 267
  Tomatoes, 268
  Vegetables, 265
    New Way, 269
Caper Sauce, 146
Caramel Junket, 44
  Syrup, 230
Caramels, Best, 235
  Choice, 236
  Good Walnut, 236
  Maple, 235
Carbon, 3
Carbon Dioxide, 3
Carbohydrates, 9
Casserole, Breast of Fowl en, 114
  Fresh Fish en, 88
  Sirloin Steak en, 101
  Spanish Veal Balls en, 113
Celery, Creamed, 170
  Hollandaise Style, 169
  Soup, Delicate, 151
Cellulose, 10
Cereal Griddle Cakes, 284
  with Cheese, 51
Cereals, Breakfast, 164
  Method of Cooking, 165
Charlotte Russe, Grape Juice, 347
  Individual, 346
  Raspberry, 346
Cheese, 45
  with Cereal, 51
    Creamed Macaroni, 52
  Macaroni Baked with, 51
  Omelet, 47
  Ramequins, 50

  with Rice and Tomato, 53
  Sandwiches (hot), 50
  and Herring Sandwiches, 308
  Savory, 47
  Sticks, 47
  Timbales, 48
  Toast with Bacon, 49
  with Toasted Wafers, 46
Chicken Bechamel in Cases, 126
  Breast in Jelly, 134
  Broiled, 99
  Broth, 133
  Chopped, in Jelly, 135
  Creamed, 125
  Pie, 116
  Roast, 117
Chicken and Tomato Bouillon, 138
Chicken and Tomato Soup, 137
Chocolate and Cocoa, 35
Chocolate Cream Pie, 336
  Custard with Cream, 353
  Dipped Bonbons, 243
    Nuts, etc., 244
  Frosting, Boiled, 248
    Confectioners, 250
  Ice Cream, 366
  Junket, 44
  Pudding, Steamed, 360
  Sauce for Ice Cream, 372
  Soufflé, 357
  Two Cups of, 36
Chops, Lamb, Broiled, 96
  Planked, 101
  Mutton, Pan-broiled, 97
Chowder, Fresh Fish, 92
Cocoa and Chocolate, 35
Codfish, Broiled, Fresh, 85
  Creamed, Salt, 89
Coffee, 32
  Boiled, 34
  Bonbons, 240
  Cake, 302
  Filtered, 34
  Jelly, 136
  Making, 32

Index

Parfait, 368
Combustion, 3
Cookies, Honey Drop, 336
    Oat, Fruit and Nut, 335
    Orange, 337
    Sour Cream, 338
Cooking, List of Supplies Needed, 24
    Milk, 40
    Preparation of Fish for, 73
    Meat for, 95
    Principal Methods, 20
    Puffy Omelet on Gas Range, 70
    Tender Meat, 95
    Less Tender Meat, 109
Corn, Boiled, 177
    Bread, Soft, 279
    Chowder, 180
    Canned, 266
    Creamed, etc., 177
    Creole Style, 178
    Custard, 178, 179
    Fritters, 179
    Green, 177
    (Green) Griddle Cakes 285
    Soup, Cream of, 150
Corn meal Griddle Cakes, 284
    Muffins, 278
    Delicate, 279
Corned Beef, Boiled, 112
    Hash, 123
Cornstarch Pudding, 352
Cottage Pie, 127
Crackers, Toasted, 149
Cranberries, Canned, 254
Cranberry Filling, 319
    Pie, 319
Cream, 194
    Eggs Poached in, 65
    Filling, English, 339
    Fish Baked in, 84
    Pie, Sour, 317
    Soups, 148
    St. Honore, 320
    to Thicken Thin, 195
Cream Cheese with Wafers, 46
Creamed Chicken, 125

Codfish, Salt, 89
    Ham with Eggs, 124
    Fish in Shells, 85
    Macaroni with Cheese, 52
Creole Spaghetti, 48
    Hash, 123
Crisps, Almond, 334
Croquettes, Macaroni, 54
    Thick Sauce for, 147
Croutons for Soup, 149
Crullers, 340
Cucumbers to Serve with Fish, 82
Currant Jelly, 265
    Sauce, 356
Currants, Bar-le-duc, 265
Custard, Boiled, No. 1, 351
    in Cups, 351
    Chocolate, etc., 353
    Frozen, 366
    Green Corn, 178, 179
    Pie, 317
    Renversée, 354
    Rice Pudding, 356
    Steamed, 355
Custards, etc., 349

Date Whip, 355
Dates, 218
    Baked in Apples, 221
Delmonico Pudding with Peaches, etc., 352
Desserts, Frozen, 362
Dextrin, 10
Digestibility of Fats and Oils, 188
    Fruit, 213
Digestion of Fats, 187
    Pastry, etc., 188
Dough, Soft or Stiff, 273
Doughnuts, Yeast, 340
Drawn Butter Sauce, 145
Dressing, Cooked Salad, 198
    French, 197
    Mayonnaise, 198
Duck, Wild, Roasted, 108
Dumpling, Baked Apple, 361
Dumplings, Baked with Pot Pie, 121

Index 401

Egg, How to tell the Age of an, 60
Egg Sauce, 146
Eggs, 56
  Beating, 62
  Cooking, 63
  Cooked in Shell, 63
  Composition of, 59
  How to Break, 61
    Separate, 61
  Poached with Asparagus, 71
    in Cream, 65
    with Creamed Ham, 124
    in Fat or Fried, 65
    on Toast, 64
    with Broiled Tomatoes, etc., 71
    with Spinach Purée, 72
  Scrambled, Reformed Style, 66
    with Variations, 67
Emergency Soup, 136
English Cream Filling, 339
  Tea Cakes, 337
Extractives, 8

Fat, Care of, 193
  How to Test for Frying, 190
  Testing for Frying, 76
Fats, 12
  Digestion of, 187
  Effect of Heat on, 189
  Forms of, Used as Food, 187
  Trying out and Clarifying, 192
  Use of in Body, 186
Fats and Oils, Digestibility of, 188
  as Preservatives, 193
Fig Whip, 355
Figs, Dried, 220
Fillets of Black Bass Rolled, 83
  Black Bass, Stuffed, 81
  Fish, Fried, 76
Finnan Haddie, Boiled, 87

Delmonico Style, 87
Fish, 73
  Baked in Cream or milk, 84
  Black Bass, Fillets of, 81 83
  Bluefish, Broiled, 74
  Broiled, 74
  Brook Trout, Sautéd, 78
  en Casserole, 88
  Chowder, Fresh, 92
  Cod, Broiled, 85
    Creamed, 89
  Creamed, in Shells, etc., 85
  Fried in Batter, 77
  Fried Fillets of, 76
  Halibut, etc., Broiled, 75
  Pickerel, Fried, 80
  Preparation for Cooking, 73
  Salmon, Baked, 86
  Boiled, 79
  Sautéd, 77
Fish Balls, Fresh, 89
Fondant, 239
  with Glucose, 241
Food, A Talk on, 1
  Elements Found in, 5
  Experience First Teacher, 2
  Forms of Fat Used as, 187
  Principles, 5
Fowl en Casserole, Breast of, 114
  Sautéd, 115
French Dressing, 197
  Omelet, 67
Fritters, Parsnip, 184
Frosting, Boiled, 247
  Boiled Chocolate, 248
  Caramel Marshmallow, 249
  Confectioner's Caramel, 250
  Confectioner's Chocolate 250
  Divinity, 249
  with Gelatine, 250
  Marshmallow, 257
  Nut Caramel, 248
Frozen Desserts, 362
  Packing a Mold with, 364
Fruit, 212
  Composition and Food Value, 212

Index

Digestibility of, 213
Effect of Cooking, 215
Flavor and Food, 214
Fudge, 232
Glacé, 246
Preparation for Canning, 254
Preparation for Serving, 216
Dates, 218
Grapefruit with Bar-le-duc, 217
  and Oranges, 216
Midwinter Macedoine, 218
Peaches, Sliced, 217
Pineapple, 217
Fruit and Nut Rolls, 280
Frying, Preparation of Food for, 191
Testing Fat for, 76
Fudge, Divinity, 234
Fruit, 232
Other Varieties, 233

Gas Meter, To Read, 17
Gas Range for Baking, 17
To Light, 16
To Manage, 15
Parts of, 14
To Use Economically, 16
Gelatine, Commercial, 343
How to Use, 343
Gelatinoids, 8
Giblet Sauce, 118
Glacé Fruits, etc., 246
Glazed Currant Buns, 298
Glucose, Fondant with, 241
Glycogen, 10
Graham Bread, 299
  Dark Colored, 300
  Muffins, 278
  Pudding, Steamed, 359
Grapefruit Jelly, 226
  Marmalade, 261
  Serving, 216, 217
  Sherbet, 368
Grape Juice, Canned, 255
Griddle Cakes, Bread, 285
  Cereal, 284

Corn Meal, 284
Green Corn, 285
Plain, 285

Halibut, Broiled, 75
Sautéd, 77
Ham, Creamed, with Eggs, 124
Rechaufée, with Broiled Apples, 125
Ham and Macaroni Timbales, 124
Hamburg Roast, 107
Hamburg Steak, Plain, 98
à la Tartare, 97
Hash, Corned Beef, 123
Creole Style, 123
Hashed Calf's Liver, 114
Lamb with Rice, etc., 123
Herring and Cheese Sandwiches, 308
Hollandaise Sauce, Mock, 146
Honeycomb Tripe, Broiled, 104
Honey Drop Cookies, 336
How to Stir, Beat, Fold Ingredients, 61

Ice Cream, Caramel, 366
Chocolate, 366
with Chocolate Sauce, 372
Frozen Custard, 366
with Maple Syrup, 371
Peach, 367
Peach Cup, 367
Strawberry, 367
Vanilla, Junket, 365
Philadelphia, 365

Jam, Blackberry, 264
Jelly, Apple, Currant, etc., 260
Apple and Blackberry, 260
Mint, 261
Raspberry, 260
Caramel, 344
Chicken Breast in, 134
Chopped Chicken in, 135
Coffee, 136
Covering, 259

Index

Cranberry, 220
Figs in Sherry Wine, 227
Grapefruit, 226
Lemon, 222
Making, 257
Orange, 222
Orange Sections in, 223
Prune, 223
Sweet Pickle, 227
Sauce, Currant, 356
Jumbles, Wafer, 333
Junket, 43
  Caramel, 44
  Chocolate, 44
  Ice Cream, 365
  Plain with Whipped Cream, 43

Kaiser Semmeln, 304

Lady-Finger Rolls, 305
Lamb, Boiled, 113
  Chops, Broiled, 96
  Chops, Planked, 101
  Hashed with Rice, etc., 123
  Neck and Shoulder of, 112
Rechaufée, Creole, 128
Lamb-and-Tomato Soup, 138
Lemon Jelly, 222
  Pie, 316
Lettuce Salad, 200
List of Supplies Needed in Cooking, 24
  Utensils and Furnishings for Dining Room, 23
  Kitchen and Pantry, 20
Liver, Calf's, Hashed, 114

Macaroons, Oatmeal, 338
  Peanut, 334
Macaroni, 167
  Baked with Cheese, 51
  (or Spaghetti) with Beef Balls, 119
  Creamed and Au Gratin, 52
  Croquettes, 54
  Italian Style, 53
Macaroni-and-Ham Timbales, 124

Macedoine of Midwinter Fruit, 218
Mackerel, Salt, Cooked in Milk, 89
Maître d'Hôtel Butter, 196
Marmalade, Apple, 262
  Grapefruit, 261
  Orange, 262
  Peach, 262
  Tomato, 263
Marshmallow Icing, 251
  Marguerites, 337
  Strawberry Dessert, 345
Mayonnaise Dressing, 198
Measures, Table of, 19
Measures and Weights, Comparisons of, 19
Measurements, 19
Meat, 93
  Cooking Tender, 95
  Less Tender, Cooking, 109
  Less Tender, Cuts of, 110
  for One Mince Pie, 316
  to Prepare for Cooking, 95
Meats, Broiling Cooked, 103
  Roast, 104
Meringue, 313
Meringues, Canned Pear, 355
Milk, Care of, 42
  Cooking, 40
  Sour, 43
Mineral Matter, 13
Mock Mince Pie, 315
Molasses Taffy, 246
Mold, Orange Marmalade, 347
Mousse, Fish, 90
Muffins, Blueberry, 283
  Corn Meal, 278
  Delicate Corn Meal, 279
  Rye Meal, 277
Mutton Chops, Pan Broiled, 97

Neck and Shoulder of Lamb, 112
Nitrogen, 4
Noisette Sandwiches, 308
Nougat, Spanish, 234

Index

Nougatines, Almond, 244
Nut Caramel Frosting, 248
Nut-and-Fruit Rolls, 280
Nut, Fruit-and-Oat Cookies, 325
Nuts, 214
  Almond Nougatines, 244
  Chocolate Dipped, 244
  Peanut Brittle, 245
Nutrient Ratio, 13
Nutrition, Under and Over, 376

Oatmeal Macaroons, 338
Oil, Olive, Use of, 197
Olive Sandwiches, 307
Omelet, Cheese, 47
  French, 67
  General Varieties of, 67
  Puffy, 68
  Puffy, Cooking on Gas Range, 70
  with Left Overs, 69
Omelets, 58
Onions, 185
Orange Cookies, 337
  Jelly, 222
  Marmalade, 262
    Bavarian Cream 348
    Mold, 347
  Pudding, Steamed, 360
  Sauce, 356
  Sabayon Sauce, 357
  Sections in Jelly, 223
  Sherbet, Blood, 368
Oranges, Sliced, 218
Oriental Preserve, 263
Oyster Soup, Cream of, 152
  Stew, 153

Packing a Mold, 364
Pan-Broiled Beef Cakes, 97
  Mutton Chops, 97
Parfait, Banana, 369
  Canned Apricot, 370
  Coffee, 368
  Golden, with Fruit, 370
  Prune, 369
Parker House Rolls, 297

Parsnip Fritters, 184
Parsnips, Boiled, 183
  Boiled and Sautéd, 183
Pastry for One Pie, 310
  Flaky, 310
  Why Unhealthful, 310
Peach Cup, 367
  Ice Cream, 367
  Marmalade, 262
  Sherbet, 368
  Tarts, 319
Peaches, Evaporated, 220
Peaches or Pears Canned, 256
Peanut Brittle, 245
  Macaroons, 334
Pear Meringues, 355
Pears, Gingered, 265
Peas, Canned, 267
  Creamed, 173
  Green, 173
Pecan Pralines, 236
Pepper and Onion Salad, 201
Philadelphia Relish, 83
Piccalilli, 271
Pickerel, Fried, 80
Pickles, 270
  Small Gherkin, 270
Pie, Apple, 311
  English Apple, 312
  Apple with Meringue, 313
  Blueberry, 313
  Chicken for Two, 116
  Chocolate Cream, 336
  Cottage, 127
  Cranberry, Open, 319
  Custard, 317
  Lemon, 316
  Mince Meat for One, 316
  Mock Mince, 316
  Pineapple, Canned, 319
  Rhubarb, 314, 315
  Sour Cream, 317
  Squash, 318
  Squash, Delaware, 318
  Veal Pot, 121
Pineapple, Canned, 257
  Toast, Canned, 362
Planked Lamb Chops, 101
Popcorn Balls, 245

Index 405

Pop Overs, 277
Potato Border, Creamed Fish, etc., 85
Potato Cakes, Mashed, 160
  Patty Cases, 126
Potatoes, American Style, 163
  Anna, 161
  Au Gratin, 162
  Baked, 160
  Boiled, 159
  Hashed, in Ramequins, 161
  Lyonnaise, 163
  Mashed, 160
  Melting, 159
  in Milk, 162
  Physical Properties, 7
  Preparation for Boiling, 159
  Saratoga, 164
  Sautéd, 162
  Sweet, Boiled, etc., 167
  Sweet, Broiled, 168
Pralines, Pecan, 236
Preserve, Oriental, 263
Pretzels, T. 333
Principles, Food, 5
Proteids, 6
Protein, 9
Prune Jelly, 223
  Parfait, 369
  Pudding, Steamed, 360
  Whip with Custard, 354-355
Prune-and-Nut Salad, 207
Prunes, Stewed, 219
  Stuffed with Cheese, 224
Puffy Omelet, 68
  Cooking on Gas Range, 70
  with Left Overs, 69
Pudding, Blueberry Betty, 359
  Bread, Viennoise, 357
  Cornstarch, 352
  Custard Rice, 356
  Delmonico with Peaches, 357
  Scalloped Rhubarb, 358
  Steamed Chocolate, 360
    Graham, 359
    Orange, 360
    Prune, 360
Pulled Bread, 149
Purée, Banana, 371

Ramequins, Cheese, 50
  Eggs with Cream in, 71
  Hashed Potato in, 161
Raspberries, Canned, 256
Raspberry Jelly with Apples, 260
Rechaufée of Ham, Broiled Apples, 125
  Lamb, Creole Style, 128
Red Pepper Butter, 86
Relish, Philadelphia, 83
Rhubarb, Canned, 255
  Pie, 314, 315
  Scalloped, etc., 358
Rice with Cheese, etc., 53
  Cooked in Double Boiler, 166
  Southern Style, 166
  Dainty, 345
  Molded, 344
  Pudding, Custard, 356
Rizzoletti, 128
Roast Beef Tenderloin, 106
  Chicken, 117
  Duck, Wild, 108
  Hamburg, 107
  Loin, Tip of, 108
  Meats, 104
Roe, Fish, Baked, etc., 90
Rolls, Fruit and Nut, 280
  Lady Finger, 305
  Parker House, 297
Roly Poly, Blackberry, 281
Rye Meal Biscuit, 303
  Muffins, 277

Sabayon Sauce, Orange, 357
Salad, Apple-and-Celery, 208
  Apple Cup, German, 209
  Asparagus, 202
  Astoria, Revised, 210
  Bean, Baked, 203
    Lima, 203
    String, 203
  Beets, Stuffed, 206
  Cabbage, 201
  Chicken, 205
  Dressing, Cooked, 198
  Egg, 205

406 Index

Fleur-de-Lis, 210
Lettuce, 200
Orange-and-Date, 208
Pepper-and-Onion, 201
Plants, Cleansing and Care, 199
Potato, 204
   French Style, 206
Prune-and-Pecan Nut, 207
Rutabaga Turnip, 202
Tomato, 201
Tomato-and-Cheese Ball, 207
Tomato Jelly, 205
Sally Lunn, 278
Salmon, Slice of, Boiled, 79
   Steak, Baked, 86
Sandwiches, 307
   Bacon, 307
   Cheese, Hot, 50
   Cheese-and-Herring, 308
   Noisette, 308
   Olive, 307
   Strawberry, 224
Sauce, Apple, Quick, 219
   Strained, 219
   Brown, 147
   Caper, 146
   Currant Jelly, 356
   Drawn Butter, 145
   Egg, 146
   Frothy, 358
   Giblet, 118
   How to Add Yolks to, 145
   for Ice Cream, 371
   Mock Hollandaise, 146
   Orange, 356
   Orange Sabayon, 357
   Peach, Evaporated, 220
   Prune, Stewed, 219
   Sultana, 225, 361
   Thick for Croquettes, 147
   Thin for Cream Soup, 148
   Tomato, 80
   Wine, 356
Sauces, Proportions of Ingredients, 143
   Regarding, 142
   Theory of Making, 144

Sautéd Fowl, 115
Savory Cheese, 47
Scalloped Rhubarb with Meringue, 358
Scrambled Eggs, Reformed Style, 66
   with Variations, 67
Sermonet, A, 373
Shells, Creamed Fish in, 85
Sherbet, Blood Orange, 368
   Grapefruit, 368
   Peach, 368
Shortcake, Strawberry, 282
Soufflé, Chocolate, 357
Soup, Celery, Delicate, 151
   Chicken-and-Tomato, 137
   Cream of Chicken, 152
   Cream of Corn, 150
   Cream of Oyster, 152
   Cream of Pea, 150
   Cream of Spinach, 152
   Cream of String Bean, 152
   Cream of Tomato, 151
   Emergency, 136
   Lamb-and-Tomato, 138
   Mitounée, 137
Soups, Cream, 148
Soups 1, 2, 3, 4, 5, 133
Sour Cream Pie, 317
Spaghetti Creole, 48
Spanish Veal Balls en Casserole, 113
Spinach, 170
   Chopped, 171
   Cream of, 152
   Left Over, 171
   Purée, Eggs with, 72
Squash, 168
   Baked, 169
   Biscuit, 301
   Pie, 318
   Steamed, 169
St. Honore Cream, 320
Starch, 9
   Molding Centers in, 240
Steak, Broiled Sirloin, 96
   Hamburg Plain, 98
   à la Tartare, 97
   Sirloin, en Casserole, 101

Index

Stock, Chicken Soup, 133
  Soup, from Roasts of Beef or Lamb, 134
  Fowl or Veal, 132
Strawberries, Canned, 256
Strawberries, Sunshine, 264
Strawberry Ice Cream, 367
  Sandwiches, 224
  Shortcake, 282
  Tarts, 320
Strawberry - and Marshmallow Dessert, 345
String Beans, Canned, 267
Stuffing, Bread, 82, 118
Succotash, 180
Sugar, 11, 229
  Boiling of, 229
  Boiling, Degrees in, 230
Supplies Needed in Cooking, List of, 24
Sweetbreads, Broiled, 104
Syrup, Caramel, 230

Table of Comparisons, 19
  Measures, 19
Taffy, Molasses, 246
Tarts, Apple, 321
  Peach, 319
  St. Honore, Strawberry, 320
Tea, Beef, 36
  Beef, Recipe for, 37
  Cake, Blueberry, 283
  Cakes, English, 337
  Composition of, 31
  Pretzels, 333
  Steeping the, 32
Tea Ball and Tea Pot, 31
Tenderloin, Roast Beef, 106
Timbales, Cheese, 48
  Ham and Macaroni, 124
Tip of the Loin Roast, 108
Toast, 306
  Canned Pineapple, 362
  Cheese, 49
  Poached Eggs on, 64
  Tomato Marmalade, 263
  Rice with Cheese and, 53
  Salad, 201
  Sauce, 80

Tomatoes Broiled, 175
  Canned, 268
  Stewed, 175
  Stewed with Corn, 175
Triangles, Hot Apple, 283
Tripe, Broiled, Honeycomb, 104
Turkish Paste, Mint, 238
  Orange, 237
  Raspberry, 238
Turnip Salad, Rutabaga, 202
Turnips, Boiled, 184
  Boiled and Creamed, 185

Utensils for Beating Eggs, 63
  Dining Room, 23
  Kitchen, 20

Veal Balls en Casserole, Spanish, 113
Veal, Blanquette of, 119
  Pot Pie, Baked Dumplings, 121
Vegetables, Canning of, 265, 269
  Compounds in, 155-156, 157
  Cooking of, 154
  Salt and Soda in Cooking, 157
Viscogen, 195

Wafer Jumbles, 333
Wafers with Cheese, Toasted 46
Water, 13, 27
  Boiling and Simmering, 29
  To Heat Quickly, 30
  Safe Drinking, 28
  Temperature for Cooking, 29
  Vegetables, 154
Whip, Banana, 225
  Fig, Date or Prune, 355
  Prune, with Custard, 354
Wine Sauce, 356

Yeast, 288
  Doughnuts, 340
  Plants, 289

Zwieback, 300

CPSIA information can be obtained at www.ICGtesting.com
Printed in the USA
BVOW06s1007211215

430719BV00017B/392/P